21st Century Kaiju

ALSO BY GORDON ARNOLD
AND FROM MCFARLAND

*Flying Saucers Over America: The UFO Craze of 1947* (2022)

*The Rise and Fall of the Future: America's Changing Vision of Tomorrow, 1939–1986* (2020)

*The Afterlife of America's War in Vietnam: Changing Visions in Politics and on Screen* (2006)

# 21st Century Kaiju

## The Resurgence of Giant Monster Movies

GORDON ARNOLD

McFarland & Company, Inc., Publishers
*Jefferson, North Carolina*

LIBRARY OF CONGRESS CATALOGUING-IN-PUBLICATION DATA

Names: Arnold, Gordon B., 1954– author.
Title: 21st century kaiju : the resurgence of giant monster movies / Gordon Arnold.
Description: Jefferson, North Carolina : McFarland & Company, Inc., Publishers, 2024. | Includes bibliographical references and index.
Identifiers: LCCN 2023046316 | ISBN 9781476689623 (paperback : acid free paper) ∞
  ISBN 9781476651774 (ebook)
Subjects: LCSH: Monsters in motion pictures. | Monster films—History and criticism. | BISAC: PERFORMING ARTS / Film / Genres / Science Fiction & Fantasy | LCGFT: Film criticism.
Classification: LCC PN1995.9.M6 A76 2023 | DDC 791.43/67—dc23/eng/20231003
LC record available at https://lccn.loc.gov/2023046316

BRITISH LIBRARY CATALOGUING DATA ARE AVAILABLE

**ISBN (print) 978-1-4766-8962-3**
**ISBN (ebook) 978-1-4766-5177-4**

© 2024 Gordon Arnold. All rights reserved

*No part of this book may be reproduced or transmitted in any form or by any means, electronic or mechanical, including photocopying or recording, or by any information storage and retrieval system, without permission in writing from the publisher.*

Front cover: Kaiju from the 2013 film *Pacific Rim* (Warner Bros./Photofest)

Printed in the United States of America

*McFarland & Company, Inc., Publishers*
  *Box 611, Jefferson, North Carolina 28640*
    *www.mcfarlandpub.com*

# Table of Contents

*Preface*   1

*Introduction*   5

1. Kaiju Rising: *Godzilla, Mothra, and King Ghidorah: Monsters All-Out Attack* (2001)   15
2. Last Gasp: *Godzilla: Final Wars* (2004)   27
3. Return of the King: *King Kong* (2005)   39
4. A Coming-of-Age Story: *Gamera the Brave* (2006)   50
5. A Korean Vision: *The Host* (2006)   61
6. A Return to Horror: *The Mist* (2007)   72
7. Reflecting an Era: *Cloverfield* (2008)   83
8. Improvising with Monsters: *Monsters* (2010)   94
9. For the Love of Kaiju: *Pacific Rim* (2013)   106
10. Hollywood Tries Again: *Godzilla* (2014)   118
11. Reclaiming a Monster's Legacy: *Shin Godzilla* (2016)   130
12. A Monster Within: *Colossal* (2016)   141
13. Reimagining the Beginning: *Kong: Skull Island* (2017)   152
14. To a Battle Royale: *Godzilla: King of the Monsters* (2019) and *Godzilla vs. Kong* (2021)   163

*Conclusion*   174

*Chapter Notes*   181

*Bibliography*   193

*Index*   197

# Preface

Giant monsters have appeared on movie screens for almost a century. The two most famous of these fictional creatures, King Kong and Godzilla, are old, dating from the Great Depression and the early Cold War, respectively. Many motion picture trends have come and gone since those times. But surprisingly, cinema's giant monsters have not gone anywhere. The original eras that spawned Kong and Godzilla have receded into history. Yet, these colossal cinematic stars and numerous other monstrous creations that followed them retain a prominent place in global popular culture.

Half a century ago, probably no one could have known that giant monster movies would still be with us in the 21st century. As early as the 1970s and 1980s, it may have seemed that there was not much more that directors could do with this type of filmmaking. Yet, in the early 2020s, they are still here. Kong and Godzilla remain arguably among the most famous "movie stars" in the world, and they continue to appear regularly in major new productions with global audiences.

They are by no means alone. New giant monsters have joined the scene in a string of films produced in far-flung continents since 2020. Movies of this type have become so common that it would be easy to presume there is nothing unusual about all that. However, the reinvigoration of giant monster cinema in the new millennium is far from a typical story. Indeed, that this type of filmmaking has not only survived but also thrived in recent years is one of filmdom's most intriguing stories.

The durability of giant monster movies is surprising for many reasons, not the least of which is that many critics and much of the public have long derided this strand of movie-making. Indeed, throughout most of the time that studios have produced these films, many have regarded them very dismissively. Many people, especially in the United States, often saw them either as cheaply made "kids' stuff" of no interest to adults or as immature works for a relatively small but enthusiastic fan base whose interests did not reflect those of the general population. Interestingly, these attitudes were similar to how most people regarded superhero movies, which were also treated with near contempt before slowly rising to respectability over several decades.

Somewhat surprisingly, since the early 2000s, the old ideas about giant monster movies have been changing. In the new century's first two decades, a spate of new works hit movie screens worldwide. Some aimed to be spectacular crowd-pleasers, mainly doing what such films had done in the past but adding more stunning effects, big-name actors, and lavish production values. Others took a markedly different approach, essentially reinventing what a giant monster movie could or should be. Not all the new films, though more numerous and varied than in the past, were successful, nor did they win over everyone. However, the sheer level of activity and variety of directions that filmmakers took these new productions represented a notable development. A type of movie-making that in some ways seemed exhausted by the end of the last century somehow found new life in the new one.

This book is a brief history of sorts. It explores a collection of giant monster motion pictures in an effort to contribute to the larger, multi-faceted story about movies and the movie-making business of which they are parts. Adopting the perspective that 21st-century giant monster movies are an intrinsically interesting phenomenon, the book looks at some of the movies in terms of how they came to be made, what they may be trying to say, how people reacted to them, and how they fared in the highly competitive cinematic marketplace.

The book is an attempt to examine a subject that, for multiple reasons, is often not taken seriously. However, a central premise here is that topics that may seem ephemeral and esoteric to some people are worthy of a closer examination than they often get. Giant monster movies have never lacked a devoted fan base, and that alone makes them an intriguing subject. Perhaps just as interestingly, studios have spent vast amounts to make some of the recent films in this category, generating combined ticket sales amounting to well over a billion dollars.

This volume is written for general readers interested in giant monster movies. It also aims to offer a helpful overview to those interested in popular culture and the film industry more generally. For those wanting to get a picture of the phenomenon overall, it can be read straight through. However, since some readers may be interested in some movies more than others, the book is written so that readers can also read chapters individually or in any order the reader chooses.

For as long as there are humans, there are likely to be monsters—if not real, then imagined. We may not literally *need* monsters in our lives, but we seem to keep them close to us, in the back of our minds, nonetheless.

As scholar Jenny Hamilton writes, "Monsters show us something of what it means to be human, playing a complex role in the process of survival and adaptation, in the struggle to come to terms with existential threats and overwhelming events."[1] No wonder, perhaps, that in today's world of huge problems, some of our most high-profile monsters are giant-sized, too.

∼

A note about name conventions: Several of the works discussed in this book were created in Japan. For many decades, it has been common practice in the West to render Japanese names in Western format with the given name listed first and the family name listed last. However, name conventions in Japan (as in most of East Asia) traditionally are ordered with the family name first, followed by the given name. The Japanese government recently promoted restoring the traditional order (family name first) when Japanese names are used in Western publications. Accordingly, I have tried to follow that practice when referencing persons primarily residing and working in Japan. Hence, most Japanese names list the family name followed by the given name. The main exception is for people of Japanese ancestry who live or are active mainly in the West and have themselves adopted Western name conventions. In those cases, I render their names according to that name-order preference.

Korean names also frequently appear in one of the following chapters and appear here in family-name-first order. Unlike Japanese names, the practice of placing the given name first was never widely adopted in Western publications.

# Introduction

Movies featuring giant monsters (sometimes called *kaiju*, the Japanese word meaning "strange beast") have appeared on screen for decades. Studios in the United States, Japan, and other nations have created many such works. These films have thrilled, amused, frightened, and intrigued audiences worldwide. They have earned a devoted fan base among movie-goers, many of whom eagerly await the arrival of each new kaiju movie. And beyond their ranks, some of the cinema's greatest giant monsters—notably Godzilla and King Kong—have crossed over into popular culture writ large. Many years after their debuts, they remain among the most recognizable fictional characters in the world.

Given their formidable renown and loyal fandom, it may have seemed that these movies were here to stay. As the 20th century drew to a close, new entries in the genre[1] still appeared somewhat regularly. Then Hollywood got into the act with TriStar Pictures' officially licensed *Godzilla* (1998), a big-budget affair with blockbuster aspirations. The film initially generated excitement and did respectable business at the global box office. However, it soon lost its luster, which, among other signs, seemed to herald a possible shift in attitudes about the genre overall.

Indeed, by the early 2000s, the genre's heyday seemed to be in the rearview mirror, and many people may have thought it was well past its prime. Evolving audience tastes, competition from other blockbusters, and radically changing cultural and political conditions seemed to have finally taken a toll. Giant monster movies increasingly seemed like quaint nostalgia—something remembered fondly but increasingly irrelevant. After the violent terror attacks in the United States on September 2001 disrupted the status quo, it appeared likely that a seismic shift might disrupt popular culture in that nation and possibly beyond. In the United States, which was deeply traumatized by the crisis, it was not clear kaiju movies had anything more to offer. The genre looked increasingly anachronistic, like a relic of a world swept away by current crises. In that context, it was reasonable to ask, why make any more giant monster movies?

Is there anything left for filmmakers to say or for audiences to see in them?

Considering the circumstances, it would not have been wholly unexpected if the giant monster genre had faded away. After all, it was generations old by then and still often reflected the values and sensibilities of a bygone era. But improbably, that did not happen. On the contrary, it was not long before the genre found new life and new purposes. Without any significant interruption, studios from the United States, Japan, and elsewhere soon brought a string of new productions to theater screens. Some featured familiar kaiju characters, and some had brand-new beastly creations. More importantly, the new films showed various approaches as filmmakers reconsidered where these works would fit into the contemporary film world.

The new giant monster movies demonstrated not only the genre's durability but also its adaptability. Indeed, among the many post-2000 giant monster movies, viewers can find a variety of works, ranging from blockbuster-style films focusing on pure entertainment to serious and thought-provoking movies that address real-world issues.

It may surprise some people the genre has benefited from contributions made by several of the most acclaimed filmmakers in recent years, some not usually associated with kaiju movies. Among them are Academy Award winners Peter Jackson, Guillermo del Toro, and Bong Joon-ho, each of whom has brought unique insight and rich experience to the genre. In the first years of the new millennium, films by these directors and a few others have shown the type of breadth and ambitiousness that seems to confirm the genre's inherent promise.

One result is that some kaiju movies of the 2000s are markedly different than those of a generation or more ago. As directors have pushed the genre into new territory and expanded the range of its storytelling, many of the old assumptions about what kaiju movies are or what they can be no longer seem sure.

Still, audiences and critics differ about whether, on balance, this is a good thing. Some welcome the new directions, but others sometimes express disappointment. So, when a director veers from the traditional approach to making giant monster movies, it is difficult to predict the reactions. Indeed, some of kaiju movies' biggest supporters express discomfort when directors take liberties with the type of movie they love.

Years ago, the genre tended to hang together more neatly than today. Partly, this was because most of the earlier giant monster movies operated within a relatively well-defined and somewhat limited set of ideas about what these films should entail. The stories were mostly about humans fighting monsters or humans watching monsters fight other monsters.

*Introduction* 7

Much of that outlook stems from the 1950s when so-called "creature features" like *Them!* (1954) and *Tarantula!* (1955) became popular in the U.S. youth market. (That was the context in which the first Godzilla movie was imported into the United States from Japan in 1956.) In that era, movies with giant monsters tended to be seen as a subcategory of science fiction movies, a larger family of films that mainly had low prestige and poor reputations at the time.

In an influential 1965 essay, Susan Sontag summarized the basic recipe in many mid-century science fiction movies. Most of what she says in "The Imagination of Disaster" aptly applies to the kaiju movies of that era, too. Sontag held that fantasy and science fiction movies of those years helped people cope with the "age of extremity," in which people lived "under continual threat of two equally fearful, but seemingly opposed destinies: unremitting banality and inconceivable terror."[2] (In kaiju movies, this dichotomy is expressed by contrasting ordinary life and terrifying giant monster attacks.) In her view, science fiction films served to "reflect worldwide anxieties, and ... to allay them."[3]

Sontag observes a predictable, five-step formula in many science fiction movies. In an abbreviated form, the five steps are (1) "The arrival of the thing," which typically goes unnoticed except for one or a few characters; (2) "confirmation [of the menace] ... by a host of witnesses to a great act of destruction"; (3) emergency "conferences between scientists and the military" and the declaration of a "national emergency"; (4) "further atrocities" and "massive counterattacks"; and finally, (5) discovery of the enemy's weakness, a final counterattack that destroys the enemy, and then "mutual congratulations" to all who helped defeat the enemy.[4]

Although Sontag did not have kaiju movies specifically in mind in her essay, the formula she describes coincides with the overall narrative shape of many giant monster movies of that era. As time has passed, however, many (though not all) kaiju films strayed from that simple template. In some post–2000 productions, in which directors sometimes took the genre in decidedly new directions, that formula was significantly altered or discarded.

As giant monster movies diversified in terms of aims and purposes, the genre's parameters became less clear. And although many people retained definite (often traditional) ideas about what constitutes a kaiju movie, the reality became increasingly more complex over time. Of course, some superficial similarities remained. Almost always, at least some parts of a new kaiju film continued to "look" like something that would be in a giant monster movie. Beyond that, however, what common characteristics held this category of works together was far less apparent. When filmmakers sometimes used a giant-monster angle to explore themes not usually associated with the genre, confusion—and sometimes controversy—often followed.

Today, the kaiju genre label functions as a broad canopy under which are varying types of films with divergent aims and purposes. Of course, they all include one or more strange and colossal beast(s). But beyond that, what can audiences expect to see? What are the filmmakers trying to do? Those simple questions can have multiple answers.

Although the aims and purposes of contemporary giant monster films are highly varied, individual movies tend to fall into two broad categories. Some, usually regarded as traditional, emphasize spectacle and special effects. Others, which are more exploratory, use giant monsters almost entirely for metaphorical or symbolic purposes.

Cinematic spectacle has always played a part in the motion picture industry, and a ready and willing audience has always been there for it. Although high-brow critics have often dismissed that type of production over the years, nothing about them is necessarily less valid than works that aspire to loftier reputations. Thrilling, surprising, or larger-than-life scenes can provide film-goers with a visceral and very satisfying experience. With the escapism they provide, movies with that focus offer a respite from the monotonous routines of daily life and its troubles.

For those who like that type of experience, it is easy to understand the lure of many traditional kaiju movies—the works that do not propose to make a big statement about humanity or the world but instead simply offer some enjoyment. Such viewers are not necessarily looking for a movie with a profound message when they watch a kaiju film. They merely want to be entertained for a while by something exciting that does not interfere with their lives.

In some ways, watching giant monsters doing battle on a movie screen is analogous to watching organized train wrecks, dozens of which were staged in the United States between the early 1890s and the 1930s for entertainment purposes. Joseph S. Connolly, who organized many of these events, once told a newspaper reporter, "Somewhere in the makeup of every normal person, there lurks the suppressed desire to smash things up."[5] Those words also could be used to describe the allure of many kaiju movies and other contemporary blockbusters.

Wanting something more than that from a film, some movie-goers (and more than a few critics) would likely not be impressed by this reasoning. However, sometimes a movie that features much spectacle is all some people want. Indeed, in those cases, the excessive destruction that permeates some kaiju movies is not perceived as a drawback. On the contrary, it is the main reason they choose to see that type of film in the first place.

From that perspective, the whole point of seeing such a film is to witness spectacular sights outside of everyday experience and thereby experience vicarious thrills from the safety of a movie theater.

The exploratory category of kaiju film has very different aims. While these movies have some degree of monster mayhem and violence, directors use spectacle not for its own sake but for some other purpose that usually involves illuminating one or more human-centered themes. This type of film can disappoint some ardent fans of classic kaiju movies because it typically does not offer the same visceral, action-oriented experience. And in some of the exploratory work, the monsters hardly appear at all, to the point where some viewers may feel those productions do not fully qualify as giant monster movies. However, one can counter that the exploratory productions are simply a different take on the genre. When taken on their own terms, films adopting that approach include some of the most satisfying and intriguing kaiju films of the new century.

It is not that the more experimental kaiju films lack powerful gargantuan beasts with destructive tendencies. On the contrary, those films also include such creatures. But here, the monsters' actions are connected to complex, symbolic, or mythological stories and overarching themes about the human experience. The human side of the stories in these works is more crucial than the destructive actions of the monsters. In other words, the monsters provide a backdrop against which filmmakers can explore themes about many things, including loss, relationships, and the meaning of life.

Of course, the dividing line between the two types of giant monster movies is porous. Although most films emphasize one approach or the other, nearly all have at least some elements of both. The difference is mainly one of emphasis.

This book aims to provide a multi-faceted, global overview of early 21st-century giant monster movies of both types. It explores some of the issues and motivations involved in creating these works, the overall shapes of the stories they try to tell, how they have been interpreted, and various reactions to them. The book also considers changes in the international film business and shifting audience tastes and preferences amid rapidly changing contexts.

As the following chapters demonstrate, studios and directors from around the world have experimented with ways to refresh the genre throughout the early 21st century. Some have chosen the traditional route. Primarily sticking with already-established giant monster characters and conventions, they focused on updating, perhaps jumpstarting that approach to make works that could compete in the brutal film marketplace. These movies tended to employ the latest special effects technologies at considerable cost, meaning they needed to aim for a mass audience to recover production expenses.

Other filmmakers retained only a few recognizable elements from past kaiju works. Instead of trying to make movies that were more spectacular and filled with more sensory overload than ever, they focused on creating something far less familiar. The results were often works that are more personal than is common among kaiju movies.

This book does not try to cover every kaiju movie of the period. Instead, it focuses on a group of examples, each functioning as a case study. The selections are not, nor are they intended to be a scientific sample. Indeed, some people might have chosen a different slate of works for this undertaking.[6] However, these movies show the genre's considerable variety and the wide range of themes and issues involved. As such, each contributes to an overall story that is bigger than the sum of its parts.

Although there is minor variation, the individual chapters of this book share a similar format. Each covers the background of the given film and the circumstances and decisions that went into making it. Next, because many readers may not have seen all the works covered here, a brief synopsis is provided to give readers enough understanding of the film's narrative content to make sense of the larger discussion. Each chapter also covers some of the film's key aspects and an overview of critical and box-office reactions.

A few words about money. Although many books of this type pay little attention to it, the economic aspects of filmmaking and the movie business are integral to the genre's story in the 21st century. Almost universally, giant monster movies are commercial undertakings. They are made because someone is willing to commit financial resources to create them. The people funding these productions aim, at minimum, to recoup their initial investment and hopefully turn a profit.

That may seem too obvious to mention. However, that is not the case. The history of kaiju movies in the 21st century is a story of haves and have-nots that sometimes involves enormous financial risk. Some of the films discussed here were made with shoestring budgets. But others required astronomical sums—some well over $125 million.

Spending vast amounts can help a director gain access to top-flight special effects, household-name actors, and everything else that goes with A-list productions. However, expenditures at those levels come with colossal risks. The pressure to get an acceptable financial return on investment for theatrical films means filmmakers must hit a proverbial home run. They must make a movie that attracts a large, ticket-paying customer base because anything less than massive success at the box office could spell a financial disaster.

A problem here is that for every large-budget movie released, multiple competitors also seek to attract movie-goers. So, it is not merely that a film must appeal to potential viewers on its own terms; it must carve out a space in a film market crowded with much competition. Again, these concerns may seem far removed from the movies considered in this volume. However, these financial pressures undoubtedly influence what appears on screen—from the type of story to the quality of the special effects and many other things. For that reason, the chapters include some discussion of this subject.

It is also worth noting that since money plays some role in all commercial filmmaking, it may seem directors working with small budgets are necessarily at a decided disadvantage. In some ways, this is true. First-rate, cutting-edge special effects, for example, are expensive. So, too, are the costs associated with hiring A-list actors, seasoned crew members, building detailed sets, and such. Yet, as a few of the films discussed here demonstrate, a small, even tiny, budget does not automatically doom a movie. Some of this century's most original and intriguing kaiju movies have been made at a meager cost compared to industry averages. In some ways, when they are freed from the pressures of conforming to the many expectations that accompany making a blockbuster movie, directors sometimes come up with some of their best work.

It should be noted that this book is not primarily about the Godzilla and Kong franchises, but those franchises appear prominently. The reasons are straightforward. These characters remain the two most recognizable characters in giant monster filmdom, and studios have continued to pour hundreds of millions of dollars into keeping them relevant in the new century.

Several chapters in this book discuss films that feature one or both of these creatures. Movies such as *Godzilla, Mothra, and King Ghidorah: Monsters All-Out Attack* (2001), *Godzilla: Final Wars* (2004), and *King Kong* (2005) are part of the discussion in the first half of the book. These are traditional works in which directors tried hard to update the genre in the early 2000s.

In the book's latter portion are Godzilla and Kong films with two different twists. One is Legendary Pictures' effort, which required considerable legal wrangling, to create a Monsterverse franchise that included Godzilla and Kong. The result was a string of big-budget spectacles: *Godzilla* (2014), *Kong: Skull Island* (2017), *Godzilla: King of the Monsters* (2019), and *Godzilla vs. Kong* (2021). As that series was ongoing, Japan's Toho Studio released *Shin Godzilla*, a far different type of Godzilla movie entirely unrelated to the American-produced Monsterverse and a film that is nearly everything that the Legendary productions featuring the character are not.

The other movies discussed in these pages are examples chosen to illustrate the astonishingly wide range of motion pictures the genre has produced since 2020. *Gamera the Brave* (2006) reimagines the beloved giant tortoise kaiju character, which first appeared in a 1965 film from Japan's Daiei Film Company, in a charming modern coming-of-age story.

A trio of other very different movies released between 2006 and 2008 shows an unusual—and to some, welcome—willingness to seek out territory that has seldom been seen within the genre. Bong Joon-ho's *The Host* (2006), the most satirical of the works discussed here, shows how adaptable kaiju movies can be and how they can usefully do much more than tell stories about humans fighting monsters. Meanwhile, *The Mist* (2007), adapted from a Stephen King horror novella, offers a stark reminder that giant monster movies, so often trivialized, can still deliver stark and profound commentary about what living under a reign of terror can do to ordinary people. *Cloverfield* (2008) is perhaps the kaiju movie most reflective of how the 9/11 attacks affected ordinary people.

In the 2010s, other films continued to mine the genre's possibilities. Guillermo del Toro's *Pacific Rim* (2013), somewhat traditionalist in nature, attempts to reinvent kaiju movies. It is also an homage to the director's memories of the giant monster movies of his youth that bring audiences a new sensibility. *Colossal* (2017), arguably one of the most adventurous and creative giant monster movies ever produced, treats serious issues such as abuse in a groundbreaking way within the genre.

The book examines various aspects of these works while observing how they are embedded within their local societies' cultural assumptions. Though sometimes neglected, that dimension of films in the genre is essential. Film is a cross-national, cross-cultural medium. Yet, individual movies tend to reflect, sometimes strongly, the cultural assumptions of the society in which they are produced. Home audiences may not notice this since many cultural presumptions are so taken for granted that people within a society often fail to see them. However, the situation becomes more complicated when a movie produced in one society is viewed by people in another where the cultural assumptions may be quite different. Indeed, people can easily misunderstand culture-specific content in a film (which can include many more facets of a film than are often realized) when that movie is produced elsewhere.

This book starts with a basic premise. It presumes the giant monster movie genre is, on its face, just as valid as any other genre. Millions of people have felt drawn to these films enough to buy tickets to see them, and many enjoy them immensely. Moreover, it seems reasonable to conclude that any movie genre surviving over a long period is worth examining.

That said, approaching the kaiju movie genre from that perspective may seem unusual to some. That is because, historically, some people have treated giant monster movies with nearly automatic disdain. It is one of several genres in popular culture that has been dismissed outright or viewed with hostility, as though the films pose a danger to society or weaken minds and morals.

Bosley Crowther, the venerable *New York Times* film critic, wrote about *Godzilla, King of the Monsters* (the highly edited and Americanized cut of 1954's *Gorjira*) soon after its U.S. release in 1956. His review set a tone that would plague the giant monster movie genre for many years. *Godzilla, King of the Monsters* is an "an incredibly awful film," he said. "The whole thing is in the category of cheap cinematic horror stuff, and it is too bad that a respectable theatre has to lure children and gullible grown-ups with such fare."[7]

Today, there are still differing points of view on the subject. On one extreme, some see almost the entirety of the genre dismissively and think it is of little value or interest. On the other extreme are those who revel in kaiju movies and have little doubt about their merit. Neither viewport is adopted here. Instead, this book aims to look at recent giant monster movies with fresh eyes. It tries to look at the genre's output of recent years straightforwardly as a popular culture phenomenon.

In some ways, this is the story of a beloved and long-running genre in search of an audience amid rapidly changing circumstances. As the following chapters reveal, studios and directors explored multiple avenues to maintain and refresh the genre in the early 21st century.

# 1

# Kaiju Rising

*Godzilla, Mothra, and King Ghidorah:*
*Monsters All-Out Attack (2001)*

Dozens of grim-faced military officials have assembled to confront an imminent danger. After nearly five decades of relative calm, a terrifying monster has reawakened, and its intentions seem clear. The monster aims to wreak havoc on Japan, destroying everything and everyone in its path.

As the officers plan their response to the dire situation, a three-star general asks a simple question. Why does Godzilla want to destroy Japan? The officials look baffled. Finally, a field officer says what no one else would admit. No one knows why.

This scene appears roughly a quarter-hour into *Godzilla, Mothra, and King Ghidorah: Monsters All-Out Attack*. The 2001 production was the 25th entry in Toho studio's storied Godzilla franchise. Yet, despite the monster's numerous appearances on screen over more than four decades, the question of what drives the colossal creature's frequent apocalyptic rampages had seldom received more than superficial attention. This movie, however, is different. Godzilla's motivations are front and center. Director Kaneko Shusuke's decision to delve into that question yielded an unexpectedly rich narrative potential, though not necessarily one the series' traditional fans thoroughly embraced.

Spectacular action scenes and over-the-top special effects are the main draws of a giant monster film for many viewers. And usually, directors are happy to comply. By design, kaiju movies almost always emphasize the spectacular. Convincing and fully fleshed-out stories are often left on the sidelines.

It was not always that way. Although there was much extravagant action in the first Godzilla movie, it was also a thoughtful, message-oriented production. Arriving during the early Atomic Age in 1954, *Gojira* was well attuned to the fearful psychological mindset of that era. (That message was somewhat garbled and largely lost in the highly edited and revised 1956 cut of the film that was released in the United States as *Godzilla, King of the Monsters!*) The story in the original Japanese version of the film is profound and filled with thoughtful and fearful symbolism of atomic warfare. Famed director Honda Ishiro uses the giant monster to push the mood and theme forward.

But that original conception changed over the years. Within a decade, Godzilla movies morphed into escapist fantasy works aimed at pure entertainment. In those films, the kaiju action mattered most. The reasons why the giant monsters were causing devastation on-screen were much less critical. That point was obvious by the time of classic Godzilla movies of the 1960s. In those days, if the reasons that Godzilla—or any other giant monster—fought and wreaked havoc were hazy, that was not necessarily a problem for the filmmakers or their audiences.

A basic kaiju movie formula was entrenched by that time: Monsters arrive at the scene; they attack, battle, and flatten cities. If the creatures have a convincing appearance and the special effects are good, that would be enough to satisfy many fans. There was little pressure to explain why the monsters wreaked havoc. Indeed, leaving an element of mystery to a frightening creature's motivations can sometimes heighten excitement, as Steven Spielberg convincingly demonstrated in his blockbuster 1975 hit in a different genre, *Jaws*.

For a long time, the Godzilla franchise showed little urgency about delving too deeply into the motivations behind Godzilla's mayhem. Almost any pretext would suffice. Audiences took for granted that a path of destruction leading to Tokyo or some other Japanese city would come next whenever Godzilla appeared. The reasons were unimportant as long as they provided an excuse for directors to give viewers what they wanted—electrifying and special-effects-laden kaiju battles.

That approach left much untapped narrative potential for many years. As the Godzilla series—and indeed, the entire giant monster genre—entered the 21st century, it was perhaps time to put more effort into telling stories that explored such possibilities. If makers of giant-monster films wanted to attract viewers beyond the ranks of hardcore fans and young children, something had to be done. Perhaps a new emphasis on the genre's often-unrealized narrative potential would help make giant monster movies relevant to the contemporary world and give them a fighting chance amid numerous other spectacle-oriented film genres.

Yet, at first glance, audiences in 2001 may have thought that *Godzilla, Mothra, and King Ghidorah: Monsters All-Out Attack* would be a throwback to the beloved classic kaiju movies of the 1960s and 1970s. The title may have given some people the idea that the new film would be like a 1968 favorite, *Destroy All Monsters*. However, director Kaneko Shusuke had something different in mind. He ignored the many sequels of the original Godzilla movie. Instead, he looked back to Honda's classic *Gojira*, the 1954 film in which the famous monster debuted as a terrorizing threat to humanity.

That dark, horror-infused tone that permeates *Gojira* did not last long. By the 1960s, Godzilla sequels depicted the monster with a different personality. The creature eventually was portrayed as mostly benign and entertaining. The once-terrifying beast often seemed to be a force for good. Despite flattening cities and inflicting widespread destruction, the colossal juggernaut became a cranky antihero—not humanity's outright enemy. That version of Godzilla essentially survived until 1975, when Toho paused the Godzilla series.

When the studio resumed the franchise a decade later, the new movies partially portrayed the monster as a definite menace. However, even when the franchise was revived in the mid–1980s, the vestiges of Godzilla's more sympathetic 1960s and 1970s incarnations were not erased completely. Indeed, the famous kaiju was sometimes shown with some positive traits, as, for example, in a 1995 entry, *Godzilla vs. Destoroyah*.

By the 1990s, Godzilla was long-established as a global brand. Yet, it increasingly became clear that simple renown did not always equal box office success. Indeed, despite the international fame of the star character in Toho's storied stable of kaiju characters, the Godzilla franchise experienced many ups and downs over the years. At the century's end, it was no longer a completely reliable money-maker.

In their dominant market of Japan and the United States, Toho's Godzilla films had settled into a familiar but somewhat limited niche. The movies tended to attract audiences mainly of younger spectators and kaiju enthusiasts of various ages. The studio's kaiju films were usually well-received in these narrow market segments, but very few everyday people considered them part of the mainstream movie world.

That was especially true in the U.S., where most kaiju films were only minor attractions. Many giant monster films given a theatrical release in Japan were relegated to secondary outlets in the United States. In the U.S. market, they primarily surfaced in broadcast television syndication, cable, or home video formats rather than theaters. So, although these movies often fared moderately well in Japanese theaters, they had garnered a reputation as little more than specialty items and second-tier films in the United States.

By the 1990s, few could have doubted that the Godzilla franchise was getting old, literally and metaphorically. As pop culture everywhere quickly evolved, consumer tastes changed. In that context, it was unclear that Godzilla, conceived a half-century earlier, would continue to draw widespread public interest. At the time, Toho also faced another growing reality. Along with the rest of the Japanese film industry, it had to contend with Hollywood's increasingly strong ambitions to dominate the worldwide film and media markets. Even in Japanese theaters, Toho constantly faced fierce competition from Hollywood's global blockbusters.

Multiple factors indicated that the ground beneath Toho was shifting dramatically. Given these pressures, simply churning out one more kaiju movie that was more of the same was not a promising option. So, to keep its most iconic franchise both relevant and profitable, Toho executives concluded that they should take a different path. And indeed, in late 1992, Toho made a momentous decision. Facing challenges and uncertainty on multiple fronts, the company decided to license Godzilla to a studio based in Hollywood. It was a move designed to generate income and reinvigorate the Godzilla brand.

In December of that year, news of the impending licensing deal circulated in the U.S. press. According to media accounts, Toho would grant the Columbia studio (which the Sony Corporation had acquired in 1987) permission to make a big-budget Hollywood-style Godzilla movie under the auspices of Columbia's TriStar Pictures subunit. Under the terms of the deal, Toho reportedly would receive a substantial cash payment and a percentage of the profits. TriStar would control casting, story and production, but it evidently agreed to consult with Toho about the script and Godzilla's character design.[1]

Originally, TriStar planned to release its Godzilla movie in time for the 1994 Christmas season. That was an ambitious goal since it only gave them two years to complete and market the film. In the end, TriStar came nowhere close to meeting that self-imposed deadline. Instead, squabbling between a potential director and TriStar executives and other matters led to delays.

That might have spelled doom for the movie, but TriStar was not ready to give up. Feeling the project could be salvaged, executives pressed on. The search for a new director eventually resulted in a deal with Roland Emmerich, who helmed the hugely profitable *Independence Day*.

The production finally got underway with a big-name director signed to the project. By 1998, four years after TriStar had hoped to debut the film, *Godzilla* was ready for its international theatrical release. TriStar had high expectations.

As expected, Emmerich delivered a big, bold Hollywood spectacle that did relatively brisk business at the U.S. box office. The film took in more than double its production costs—a respectable but unspectacular result. Interestingly, it also performed reasonably well in Japan, where audiences were curious to see what the Americans had done with the beloved franchise.

To some extent, Emmerich wowed audiences with high-end, computer-generated visual effects. The production was meant to impress, and on some levels, it did. It benefited from a high-profile cast headlined by stars Matthew Broderick of *Ferris Bueller's Day Off* fame and international favorite Jean Reno. Many other well-respected actors, including Hank Azaria, Harry Shearer, Maria Pitillo, and Michael Lerner, appeared, too.

In the end, however, initial enthusiasm for TriStar's *Godzilla* did not last. Fans hoped Hollywood would give them a big-budget version of the character they knew and loved. However, Emmerich's movie failed to capture the hearts of many hardcore Godzilla fans, especially in the United States. Indeed, within a short time, many kaiju devotees began referring to the film dismissively, famously referring to it as *GINO*—meaning "Godzilla in name only." Even Toho executives, who had signed off on the project, seemed disappointed with what TriStar had done with the company's most globally visible property.

But from Toho's perspective, there was a silver lining. A clause in the 1992 contract with TriStar stipulated that the deal was non-exclusive. That meant Toho retained the right to continue making its own Godzilla films if it chose to do so. With no legal impediments to relaunching the Godzilla series on its own, Toho took matters into its own hands and set out to relaunch its franchise.

The result was Toho's "Millennium" reboot. As had been true years earlier, the studio started issuing new Godzilla movies more or less annually. The latest movies, though slightly updated, returned to the types of stories and special effects that were the hallmarks of those classic films. The first of these, Toho's *Godzilla 2000*, was released in Japan in late 1999 and in the United States and several other countries shortly after that. The following year, Toho released *Godzilla vs. Megaguirus*, which debuted in Japanese theaters in December 2000.

Unfortunately, these first two Millennium films did not meet the studio's expectations. Faced with disappointing financial returns and lackluster public interest, the studio questioned whether moving forward with the franchise was advisable.

Still, Toho was not quite ready to give up. Hoping to salvage the franchise, the studio turned to Kaneko, a move that was no doubt influenced by the director's recent success in resurrecting the well-known Gamera kaiju series for another studio. It helped that Kaneko was also a lifelong fan of Godzilla and had long been interested in working on the franchise.

Undoubtedly, all involved expected Kaneko to bring a fresh

perspective to the series. The director initially planned to use Varan and Anguirus, two of Toho's relatively obscure kaiju characters, as Godzilla's primary opponents in the new movie. However, the studio wanted to be sure Kaneko's movie would be a big hit with fans, and some executives wondered if Varan and Anguirus would give the film enough box-office appeal to deliver the desired results.

Around the same time, it appeared that the studio might be having second thoughts about the whole project. Seeking a clear indication of the movie's production status, Kaneko visited the studio's front office to discuss the situation.

Toho executives informed the director he could continue making his Godzilla movie, but there was a catch. They asked Kaneko to substitute Mothra and King Ghidorah for the two lesser-known kaiju he planned to use. The reason was simple: Mothra and King Ghidorah were two of Toho's most famous kaiju characters, and they were clear audience favorites. As a business proposition, the studio reckoned that these monsters had more box-office potential than Varan and Anguirus, the obscure kaiju Kaneko had wanted to use. At that point, realizing he had limited options if he wanted to continue, Kaneko agreed to make the switch.[2]

First and foremost, *Godzilla, Mothra, and King Ghidorah* is a kaiju movie, and for fans, the true stars are Godzilla and the other kaiju. As important as the human characters might be, there was little doubt that the monsters would be the main attractions. That meant that the movie had to get the monsters "right" for the film to be a success. The production team was obviously under much pressure since they needed the movie to make a strong statement that the franchise was alive and well.

The goal was to broaden the series' appeal to mainstream audiences. First, however, the filmmakers needed to shore up the series in the eyes of hardcore fans. And to do that, they needed to pay close attention to the visual design of their giant-monster centerpieces and bring convincing kaiju action to the screen.

Still mostly avoiding Hollywood's CGI-laden approach that TriStar had adopted for its 1998 *Godzilla*, Kaneko stayed true to the Toho tradition of "suitmation," the actors-in-rubber-costume method that was the studio's usual practice. Some adjustments were made to Godzilla's appearance. Advanced mechanics were employed to provide the monsters with more expressive capabilities, especially for conveying facial expressions. However, the change that caught many viewers' attention was relatively small. The new Godzilla's dark eyes are eerily without pupils, giving the creature a more menacing and supernatural look. Though a tiny detail in most respects, it was significant to telegraphing the monster's remorseless intentions.

When it came time to make casting decisions, the leading roles were given to Niiyama Chiharu, a young and relative newcomer who plays a young reporter, and Uzaki Ryudo, a well-known musician and actor, who plays the reporter's military-official father. Supporting roles went to veteran Japanese actors. One small but essential part was given to Amamoto Hideyo, an actor with many years of experience. He played a leading role in Toho's *King Kong Escapes* (1967) a generation earlier. Overall, the large cast possessed steady professionalism more than star power.

With a clear vision but a somewhat limited budget, Kaneko went about his work and completed the film. In the end, he delivered much of what kaiju fans loved. *Godzilla, Mothra, and King Ghidorah* is relatively simple and familiar, at least superficially. There are many battle sequences and much urban destruction. Yet, despite these standard elements, the film differed from most previous Godzilla movies in some respects. In a significant departure from most previous outings, Kaneko infuses the movie with prominent spiritual and folk-tradition elements. These define much of the film and provide the motivating forces in its narrative.

The story is simple. Godzilla mysteriously returns to life and goes on a rampage, leaving a trail of death and destruction as it proceeds.

A young reporter named Yuri (played by Niiyama Chiharu) meets with a mysterious older man (played by Hideyo Amamoto). The authorities think he is a crank, but she is unsure. The man warns her that Godzilla is not simply a giant monster. He says the creature embodies the spirits of those who perished in the Pacific region during World War II. He also says Godzilla is endowed with a spiritual purpose, and it has returned to Japan to avenge those who died in the conflict decades ago.

The old man explains that Japanese society has turned away from time-honored beliefs and customs, making it susceptible to avenging spirits. But there is hope, he says. Long-forgotten guardian spirits have the power to defeat Godzilla. If the people of Japan can correct their moral path, the guardian spirits might reawaken and save the country. To make his point, the man shows the reporter an ancient book in which the spiritual guardians are identified as Mothra, King Ghidorah, and Baragon.

These three kaiju had appeared in previous Toho productions, but they are significantly repurposed here. Early in the film, Kaneko telegraphs to ardent fans of the franchise that he intends to depart considerably from previous movies in the series. As he does with Godzilla, the director adds a new spiritual layer to their backstories. Most strikingly, Kaneko presents King Ghidorah as a potential savior of humankind, a noticeable change from earlier movies in which Ghidorah is portrayed as a clear-cut villain.

As the story unfolds, the director explores several other themes, including responses to kaiju devastation and questions about the appropriate use and the limitations of military power. There is also the secondary story of the idealistic young reporter, Yuri, and her estranged father, a top officer in charge of the military's efforts to end Godzilla's rampage.

Eventually, the guardian spirits rise and sacrifice themselves in failed attempts to defeat Godzilla. Meanwhile, Yuri, the intrepid reporter, successfully escapes several dangerous situations.

Near the end of the film, Yuri's military officer father (Uzaki Ryudo) leads the defense forces' fight against Godzilla. He rams a submarine directly into the monster, leaving Godzilla defeated but not entirely destroyed.

In the film's final epilogue, Yuri and her father resolve their differences and reconcile. As the film ends, audience members who choose to do so are left to ponder the film's central themes, which encompass moral traditions, human suffering, and atonement. These are all somewhat heavy topics for a Toho kaiju movie.

From his vantage point in the early 2000s, Kaneko set out to re-envision his movie's kaiju stars. As part of his attempt to do that, he returned the franchise to its roots nearly a half-century earlier. The director depicts Godzilla as a dangerous and seemingly malicious monster, similar to the creature's original portrayal in 1954's *Gojira*. Like that first film in the franchise, Kaneko's Godzilla exhibits is not a sympathetic monster and decidedly is not humanity's ally or savior. Instead, Kaneko's Godzilla is a destructive, emotionless force that kills and destroys. That, at least, is how it appears on the surface.

However, that interpretation, though popular, may be too simplistic, especially if a spectator looks beneath the film's surface. Indeed, for viewers looking for something more than simple entertainment, Kaneko offers a surprisingly intriguing film. Beyond its mayhem and spectacle, *Godzilla, Mothra, and King Ghidorah* is a thoughtful movie introducing several serious philosophical themes.

Intriguingly, Kaneko probes various moral questions while injecting significant spiritualism throughout the film. Many sequences resonate with references to Japanese belief systems and cultural traditions. The elements are woven organically into the story, giving the production a thought-provoking subtext.

Much of that emerges as the narrative explores why kaiju have appeared and why they are fighting. Kaneko answers these questions by turning to Japan's cultural traditions. For some viewers, these parts of the film may distract from the action on screen. However, from another perspective, Kaneko's additions provide intriguing layers to the production.

That said, the director's overall approach to the philosophical subtexts of the film is not at all heavy-handed. The film alludes to authentic belief systems and folk wisdom, but it does not interpret this source material literally, nor does the director belabor it. In other words, the end product is inspired by tradition but not a literal illustration of it. Still, the film has obvious references to Japanese culture. For example, Shinto ideas can be found in the portrayal of Godzilla as a vengeful monster embodying wronged war victims and in the presentation of Mothra, King Ghidorah, and Baragon as protector spirits.

Throughout the movie, there are hints, though not literal invocations, of traditional Japanese cultural concepts such as *kami*, *yokai*, and *oni*. At the most basic level, Kaneko touches on the idea of *kami*, a Japanese concept that deals with "all divine beings of heaven and earth," especially "spirits that abide in and are worshipped in shrines" and "extend throughout the natural world and its creatures."[3]

Additionally, the movie's kaiju also invite some association with *yokai*, a concept that refers to spirits that are particularly "mysterious, strange, or bizarre" and elicit a "sense of foreboding."[4] Indeed, traditional descriptions of a *yokai* refer to "monster, spirit, goblin, demon, phantom, specter, fantastic being, lower-order deity, or unexplainable occurrence."[5]

Professor Michael Dylan Foster notes that Western academics have sometimes mentioned *yokai* in reference to Godzilla.[6] Although Foster believes the relationship between *yokai* and kaiju concepts is "murky,"[7] it seems possible to see Kaneko's version of Godzilla at least partially in that light. The great beast is more than simply a monster in Kaneko's conception. It is a spiritual being, something more meaningful than an evolutionary accident or the byproduct of humankind's foolish use of nuclear weapons.

Professor Yuki Tanaka writes that Godzilla could also be interpreted as *oni*, adding yet another layer from Japanese tradition. Those mythical creatures are generally regarded as huge, powerful, and threatening demons with frightening appearances. Moreover, they are frequently associated with specific geographical places and various natural phenomena.[8] In Kaneko's film, Mothra, King Ghidorah, and Baragon, which are explicitly identified as spiritual defenders of particular areas, can be seen in this way.

It seems evident that these types of traditional Japanese spiritual concepts—notions that are not well known or understood in the United States and other Western societies—inform the narrative of Kaneko's film at some level. The story's internal logic presumes a connection between specific places and the spiritual realm and the idea that the spirits of the deceased can manifest in monstrous forms. The guardian kaiju represent the former; Godzilla represents the latter.

Such ideas fit comfortably within a more or less traditional Shinto worldview, in which supernatural entities are not necessarily entirely positive or entirely negative. In other words, the world is such that good and bad aspects can coexist in an unfixed state. That notion can seem unfamiliar and perhaps even unsettling to those immersed in the dichotomous absolutism of the Judeo-Christian moral outlook, which starkly divides the world into discrete categories of good and evil. However, the Japanese tradition explains much in *Godzilla, Mothra, and King Ghidorah*. There is no need for Godzilla (or any kaiju) to be entirely good or entirely evil. Instead, the monster can embody aspects of both. (In some ways, that type of portrayal superficially resembles the antiheroes of American cinema.)

Kaneko does not need to explicitly or literally attribute concepts such as *kami*, *yokai*, or *oni* to the giant monsters in his movie. Still, the film's monsters seem straightforwardly influenced by traditional ideas of those kinds to some degree. That is not to say it is an entirely new connection for a kaiju film. But although some earlier movies in the franchise suggest a relationship between giant monsters and traditional beliefs, Kaneko makes the link more explicit than in the past.

Interestingly, Kaneko's film also implicitly raises awareness of another Japanese concept, the *hibakusha*—a term used for the Japanese people who were directly affected by the atomic bombing of Japan at the end of World War II. Uncomfortably, the *hibakusha* are reminders of terrible events from that conflict that some may want to forget. Yet, by making his Godzilla the embodiment of the spirits of those who died in the conflict, evidently due to Japan's wrongful behavior, Kaneko places such remembering as a driving force in his film. So, when Godzilla leaves a path of destruction in Japan, the devastation is not because Godzilla is inherently evil. According to the story, Godzilla's vengeance is aimed at correcting wrongs committed by the Japanese government decades earlier. Godzilla's rampages, in other words, are about restoring balance to reharmonize the world.

Similarly, the protective spirits of Mothra, King Ghidorah, and Baragon are not just giant monsters randomly looking for a good fight. Their motivations are not that they necessarily hate Godzilla. Instead, they are spirits simply returning to their sacred roles as defenders of specific places—that is, of the locations in nature to which they are bound.

The idea that Japanese society's harmony has been ruptured is also apparent in other parts of the story. According to the narrative, many Japanese, especially the younger generation, had drifted from the correct path and had neglected the traditional ways. They create chaos and even disrespect sacred shrines. These ideas appear blatantly in the film.

One sequence in *Godzilla, Mothra, and King Ghidorah* shows young hooligans riding motorcycles and disturbing the peace of a small town, harassing a truck driver in the process. (The scene is mildly evocative of the 1953 American film, *The Wild One,* which helped propel Marlon Brando to stardom.) Later, the film shows other teenagers trying to drown a dog and defacing a shrine. In the context of the movie, the shrine is just a place in the eyes of the young troublemakers. They do not believe in the old traditions, so they do not realize they have defiled a kami home, disturbing the universe's harmony.

Such scenes seem intended to show a Japan that has lost respect for the traditional social order. According to the film's plot, that separation led people to forget about the spiritual forces—embodied as the guardian kaiju in the movie—that had protected Japan in earlier times.

In this way, Kaneko presents a story in which the kaiju are more than garden-variety creatures destroying the countryside and doing battle for no reason other than being monsters. But they are not moral agents representing good and evil in the Western sense. Instead, Kaneko's kaiju are part of a greater whole, fulfilling their roles to restore the world's harmony and balance. In these and other respects, *Godzilla, Mothra, and King Ghidorah* is a film best understood within Japan's cultural milieu and that nation's ongoing conversation with its complicated past.

Domestic Japanese audiences were equipped to know and understand the film's many references to historical and cultural elements relating to Japan. Whether audiences elsewhere paid much attention or even recognized Kaneko's cultural allusions and intentions is hard to say. However, it seems reasonable to surmise that most spectators in the United States may have overlooked those aspects of the film. That would not be unexpected since most Americans have a minimal understanding of even basic Japanese cultural traditions and history—or, indeed, those of any Asian society. For that reason, it seems likely that most viewers in the United States, a large and traditionally important market for Toho kaiju movies, may not have fully appreciated the spiritual aspects of Kaneko's presentation.[9]

Of course, philosophical and cultural elements are typically not the primary draw for a kaiju movie, even from the genre's most ardent supporters. But Kaneko, who was coming off success with several Gamera films at the time, understood that and his audience very well. So, while the ideas appear throughout the movie, he treats spiritual and philosophical issues matter-of-factly. He uses those elements mainly to provide an understandable rationale for the monsters' behavior. The supernatural and spiritual dimensions add an intriguing dimension to the film for those open to it, but the director does not aggressively push it. Viewers could— and many probably did—ignore those dimensions of the movie and the questions and issues they may have raised.

Regardless, *Godzilla, Mothra, and King Ghidorah* addressed a glaring issue for the giant-monster film tradition overall. It signaled that at least some filmmakers in the genre were willing to do new things and look for ways to make these movies relevant in the contemporary world.

Although hardly a blockbuster, the film did respectable business and generated positive feedback from many fans and even some film critics. In many ways, it was the most successful of the half-dozen "Millennium" Godzilla movies. It earned $18 million at the box office and ranked eighth in the list of top theatrical movies in Japanese theaters that year.[10] All of that was reasonably good news.

Yet, a closer look at the performance of movies in Japanese theaters shows a troubling reality for the kaiju genre at that time. The top film on that list in 2001 was another Japanese production, the animated *Spirited Away*. It was a wildly popular film that year, grossing over $230 million. That figure was more than twelve times what *Godzilla, Mothra, and King Ghidorah* could muster.[11]

In addition, even though the Millennium Godzilla was partially a product of Toho's dissatisfaction with TriStar's *Godzilla*, none of the Millennium films did exceptionally well at the box office. The most traditional Godzilla fans may have preferred Toho's new entries to Roland Emmerich's perceived misfire. However, beyond core fans, the new Toho films seemingly did not appeal to a broader audience. Given that reality, the future of the Godzilla series and that of giant monster movies, in general, appeared to be in jeopardy.

In any case, *Godzilla, Mothra, and King Ghidorah* reflected a Japanese perspective on the unsettled state of the world early in the 21st century. And in late 2001, when the film premiered, there was much to cause worry—indeed, much to invoke the anxious psychological state reflected in the movie. Although spectators lacking a basic appreciation of Japanese history and traditions probably missed or misunderstood some parts of the film, the kaiju movie formula, which Kaneko mostly follows, provided plenty of action, conflict, and entertainment. Moreover, 2001 provided a new and frightening backdrop against which international viewers, especially in the United States, could interpret the death and destruction that appeared on screen. September 11 had plunged America and some of its allies into a new regime of fear. Even when audiences in those societies indulged in the escapism that Toho kaiju movies could provide, anxieties stemming from that context lurked in the background.

# 2

# Last Gasp

## *Godzilla: Final Wars* (2004)

In the early 2000s, the Godzilla franchise continued to languish despite Toho's efforts to breathe new life into it. The studio's 2001 film was a qualified success by some measures, but its director, Kaneko Shusuke, did not continue with the series. With his departure, the spiritualism and other new qualities he had introduced in *Godzilla, Mothra, and King Ghidorah* were mostly left behind, too.

The continued viability of kaiju movies was not assured, but Toho pressed ahead. The subsequent two films in the franchise, *Godzilla Against Mechagodzilla*[1] (2002) and *Godzilla: Tokyo S.O.S.* (2003), appealed to some fans. Overall, however, these works generated little enthusiasm at the box office.

Meanwhile, executives at TriStar studio, and its parent, Sony Corporation, remained disappointed with the reception and box-office business that its Hollywood-style *Godzilla* had generated in 1998. TriStar's deal with Toho was still in place, but there was no eagerness to sink additional money into it by making a second Godzilla movie. With little fanfare, TriStar let its licensing contract with Toho quietly expire in 2003.

In some ways, Godzilla and the rest of Toho's kaiju cinematic world may have seemed like anachronisms in the 21st century. Times had changed, and the film business and audience tastes had changed, too. As the 50th anniversary of *Gojira* approached, the franchise's best days seemed to be in the rearview mirror.

For years, kaiju movies had faced stiff competition at the box office. Even in Japan, Hollywood films often outpaced domestic releases. Consider, for example, the top-grossing films in Japanese theaters in 2002. Of the five top-performing films in Japan that year, all were huge Hollywood spectacles. In first place was *Star Wars: Episode II—Attack of the Clones,* followed by *Monsters, Inc., The Lord of the Rings: The Fellowship of the Ring, Harry Potter and the Chamber of Secrets,* and *Spider-Man.* Even in Japan, *Godzilla, Mothra, and King Ghidorah: Giant Monsters All-Out Attack* (admittedly released late in the year) could manage no better than a distant 49th place.²

In 2003, the year before the fiftieth anniversary of Godzilla films, Japanese box office numbers were no more encouraging for kaiju fans. A Japanese movie did reign over that nation's box office that year. *Bayside Shakedown 2*, a Toho-distributed action comedy based on a popular television series, took the top honors at the box office, generating over $155 million. However, the rest of the top five were Hollywood blockbusters: *The Matrix Reloaded, Terminator 3: Rise of the Machines, Lord of the Rings: The Two Towers*, and *Pirates of the Caribbean: The Curse of the Black Pearl*. The lone Godzilla film released that year, *Tokyo S.O.S.*, came in at a dismal 69th.³

Such statistics suggest the unabated globalization of film markets, in which Hollywood continued to play the leading role. The U.S. movie industry continued to show it could attract massive audiences internationally, sometimes crowding local productions out of their own markets. With production and marketing budgets that studios outside Hollywood often found difficult to match, the American film industry frequently steamrolled over local competition.

The Godzilla franchise also faced a challenge far closer to home. That came in the form of the immensely popular Pokémon, the star attractions in the handheld video game revolution heralded by Nintendo's hugely popular Game Boy system. First introduced in 1996, Pokémon games featured tiny "pocket monsters," including Pikachu, Bulbasaur, Charmander, and Squirtle. The games quickly developed a worldwide following, especially among children. Based on this success, Pokémon soon spread across popular culture and, not surprisingly, to the big screen.

In 2000, Toho's *Godzilla 2000* managed to do about $10 million in business at the box office. It was the second-highest-grossing Japanese-made film that year. Yet *Pokémon 2000*, the top-ranking Japanese-made production in 2000, brought in more than ten times that amount, amassing more than $130 million at the box office.⁴

Although Toho was again making a Godzilla movie annually at the time, it could not place any Godzilla film among the top-ten box office successes the following year, either. *Spirited Away*, acclaimed director Miyazaki Hayao's animated fantasy, easily took the top spot among Japanese-made motion pictures in 2001. *Pokémon* handily came in at number two.⁵

In 2002, the pocket monsters returned as the highest-grossing Japanese-made film with *Pokémon Forever*. A Godzilla movie was again missing from the top ten. In 2003, *Pokémon Heroes* slipped back to the number two position, but Godzilla again remained absent from the top ten.[6]

Given the success of Pokémon movies in Japan and internationally, it seems that monster subject matter was not the problem facing the Toho kaiju movies. The Pokémon series, based solely on monsters, was going strong. However, part of Pokémon's appeal probably was related to the smallness, even the cuteness of the tiny fictional creatures, which kaiju cinematic creatures could not match. Indeed, the popularity of the pocket monsters seems to have been at least partially built on the *kawaii* tradition in Japanese popular culture, which dates from the early 20th century.[7]

According to scholar Jason Bainbridge, Pokémon not only reflected *kawaii* culture's embrace of cuteness. It also rewrote "some of the elements of *yokai* culture as *kawaii* culture, the 'loveable,' 'adorable' or 'cute' culture that ... [had] become a recurrent feature of Japanese popular culture since the 1970s."[8] Of course, the Pokémon phenomenon spread far beyond Japan. Given that very few Americans had even heard of *kawaii*, this suggests the appeal was based on something more than that. More likely, the growing popularity of its video games had much to do with Pokémon's box-office success.

The Pokémon case offered a sobering lesson for the makers of kaiju movies. Pokémon had acquired a solid fan base in only a few years, especially among the young. It was succeeding at the box office while Toho Godzilla films were struggling. Arguably, Godzilla and the other Toho kaiju were about as well known as the pocket-monster newcomers, but the aging kaiju franchise was having trouble attracting an audience. Something had to give.

Toho was well aware of the franchise's difficulties. After assessing the situation, the studio took drastic action. In a story circulated by the Associated Press, reporter Kenji Hall summed up the situation: "Hit by slumping box office sales," he wrote, "Toho Co. is planning to shelve its [Godzilla] series after this year's finale."[9]

The reporter wrote candidly about the franchise's problems. "Stale storylines and outdated special effects have eroded Godzilla's appeal," he wrote. The earliest films in the series had attracted many movie-goers, but over time, those days were long gone. Average movie-goers did not take Godzilla films seriously, and the franchise's core audience had been reduced to "fanatics or children."[10]

Studio executives knew that such a limited audience was insufficient to sustain the franchise but did not see an immediate solution. "We have done all we can do to showcase Godzilla, including using computer-graphics technology," Toho executive producer Shogo Tomiyama said, "and yet, we haven't attracted new fans."[11]

Considering the reality of the situation, it seemed that the giant green monster might need a rest. Toho had done that before when it made no new Godzilla films between 1975 and 1984. And now, nearly two decades later, the situation was again untenable, and it seemed to be time to take a break.

Without knowing whether the franchise would slumber permanently or simply take a long rest, Toho executives decided to pause the series. However, Godzilla was a storied franchise, and the studio wanted the series to go out with a bang and not a whimper. With that in mind, Toho authorized one last Godzilla feature, which would coincide with the franchise's fiftieth anniversary in 2004. It was to be a statement film before the series was put into limbo.

Toho needed a fresh attitude and a new perspective to produce a film that was more than a retread of the past. The studio selected Kitamura Ryuhei to helm the production with that in mind. The filmmaker was then in his mid-thirties and mostly known for independent genre films in the horror and fantasy categories.

Kitamura grew up in Japan and then studied visual arts in Australia. While abroad, he began making films, a developing passion that continued when he returned to his home country. He gained attention with *Versus* in 2000, a sword-and-zombie movie that earned a cult following.

Not long after that, Toho became interested in the young director and hired him to direct *Azumi* (2003), a manga-based movie about a young female assassin in the Edo period. The film drew mixed reviews, especially outside Japan. (A somewhat scathing *New York Times* article concluded that the director brought "nothing new to the samurai-swordsman game."[12]) However, *Azumi* generated ticket sales that exceeded its production budget, which seems to have impressed at least some Toho executives.

With a resume of films that included much blood and horror, Kitamura may have seemed like an unusual choice to direct a high-profile Godzilla movie. However, he had one critical quality in his favor. The director was a huge fan of the franchise and especially of entries in the series from the 1970s. He was especially fond of 1974's *Godzilla vs. Mechagodzilla*, a movie that many kaiju fans considered fun and entertaining.

From the outset, it was clear that Toho's new film would attempt to recapture some of the magic—or at least, what devotees of the franchise considered magic—from the previous generation of Godzilla movies. Yet, even if the fiftieth-anniversary film succeeded in satisfying its hardcore fan base, it remained to be seen if the venture could attract average movie-goers internationally.

With the director on board, attention turned to script development and casting. As to the story, it was a foregone conclusion that in addition

## 2. Last Gasp

to Godzilla, the cast of kaiju creatures would also include other prominent monsters in Toho's kaiju pantheon. But what about the human characters? It would not be enough to have two hours of battling monsters. The film would need to have some sort of solid human cast and a story to go with them. These, at least, were the presumptions. From the beginning, then, Kitamura faced a tricky balancing act. The movie would need spectacular thrills and spills from its kaiju stars, but it also required a human-centered narrative to give the film a sense of heart and emotion.

Ultimately, the final script called for Godzilla to face off against a dizzying array of other giant monsters. Toho's sizable inventory of kaiju properties meant that Kitamura had many options when he searched for supporting members of the kaiju cast. The lengthy list of final selections includes Mothra, Rodan, Gigan, Anguirus, Hedorah, Manda, Kumonga, Kamacuras, Ebirah, and King Caesar. All, especially Mothra and Rodan, were well-known to the franchise's fans. The film also includes the re-appearance of a cute mini-kaiju. Minilla (sometimes called Minya), Godzilla's young and still human-sized offspring, is a creature known to be friendly with humans, especially children.

In a surprise addition to those familiar Toho monsters, the script also called for Godzilla to fight a creature called Zilla, which would be rendered entirely using CGI techniques on screen. The name may not have been familiar, but Zilla was not new. Instead, Zilla is none other than the renamed version of Godzilla from Roland Emmerich's controversial TriStar film.

*Godzilla: Final Wars* adds a new foe to these previously known kaiju. Monster X is a new creature resembling a gigantic version of the extraterrestrial hunter in 20th Century–Fox's popular *Predator* franchise.

The roster of kaiju that would appear in the film was impressive. But what was Kitamura to do with such a lengthy list of giant creatures? From the outset, one challenge would be constructing the film in a way that would be more than simply a series of mindless kaiju battles. To this end, he needed a story to tie everything together.

The result included a human-centered plot involving an extraterrestrial invasion of earth mounted by human-like aliens called Xiliens. The aliens present an existential threat to humanity. According to the story, they create and manipulate events that cause the kaiju to battle each other. With the cast of kaiju creatures mainly set, designers needed to finalize the details of the costumes that the actors portraying the monsters would wear. Fortunately, the essential look of each monster character was well understood.

The next task was to find the right actors to fill the roles of human and Xilien characters. One possibility for a leading role would be to choose a well-known international star. That option would signal that Toho was serious about its ambitions for the film. It also could help with marketing, especially in markets outside Japan. The widely admired Moroccan-born French actor Jean Reno was one possibility officials considered. In addition to his international renown, Reno co-starred in TriStar's *Godzilla* movie in 1998, which could have been an advantage for publicity purposes. That idea, however, did not work out.[13]

According to Kitamura, Christopher Lambert was then considered. The director had admired Lambert in *Highlander*, but that idea, too, eventually proved to be a nonstarter.[14] Another thought was Don Johnson, who had risen to global stardom in the wake of his 1980s *Miami Vice* television series. Because of that, he was also very famous in Japan, which was a plus. However, the projected cost for his services would be very steep, so that idea also went nowhere.[15]

At some point, Kitamura and the studio changed course. Instead of seeking a famous movie star, they turned to a burly American-born pro-wrestler, Don Frye. In Kitamura's words, Frye "was a big star in Japan."[16] And although Frye was inexperienced as an actor, Kitamura was a fan. Ultimately, Frye was selected to play Captain Douglas Gordon, the main human character in the film.

As for the rest of the cast, Kitamura and Toho primarily looked to Japanese actors and celebrities. For the mutant soldier Shinichi Ozaki, they chose Matsuoka Masahiro. He was then a member of the musical supergroup TOKIO and recently had added acting to his list of accomplishments. For a United Nations biologist, they chose Kikukawa Rei, a model and television host. The remainder of the large cast, many of whom are on screen for only a few moments, is mainly filled with veteran Japanese actors, including some who had appeared in previous Godzilla films.

The final script is a blend of classic Godzilla movie fare mixed with elements that borrow liberally from U.S. blockbusters such as *The Matrix*, *Star Wars*, and *Independence Day*, according to *Boston Globe* reviewer Ty Burr. For American viewers familiar with the iconic 1960s U.S. television series *The Twilight Zone*, some plot elements involving the Xiliens' disturbing but hidden motives are reminiscent of a classic episode entitled "To Serve Man."

The leading American character, Captain Gordon, also adds a subtle nod to the rising video game world. Movie critic Ty Burr wrote that the character "looks like Joseph Stalin and talks like [comic book character] Sergeant Rock." But many viewers may have been reminded of someone else: the Mario character in the Nintendo *Super Mario Bros.* video game, whom the character strongly resembles right down to the signature mustache and hat.

## 2. Last Gasp

The movie's plot is somewhat complicated. In the not too distant future, an international group called the Earth Defense Force (E.D.F.), made up of both human and mutant members, has successfully kept kaiju at bay for many years. They even have managed to subdue Godzilla, imprisoning it in ice. That relative calm is disrupted when many kaiju suddenly appear and launch a global rampage. Rodan, Zilla, and King Caesar overwhelm humanity's defenses. Places like New York, Paris, Okinawa, Phoenix, Sydney, and other vital areas suffer horrible devastation.

As quickly as this mayhem started, however, the attacks stop. This unexpected development coincides with the arrival of a spaceship carrying extraterrestrials called Xiliens, who claim they have come to help humanity. It soon becomes clear that a Xilien leader, Controller X, has far more evil plans. The Xiliens have come to crush human civilization, and they had orchestrated the abrupt kaiju attacks that preceded their arrival for that purpose. But the Xiliens' ultimate goal is even more chilling. They regard earth's humans as little more than cattle—a convenient food source.

Most of humanity is oblivious to the danger posed by the Xiliens. Still, some people in and around the E.D.F. are suspicious, especially Ozaki, a mutant E.D.F. soldier, Miyuki Otonashi, a biologist, and Captain Douglas Gordon, the commander of the E.D.F.'s most powerful flying submarine, the Gotengo. This core group soon discerns the Xiliens' real goals, and as earth's defenders, they decide to take action. Captain Gordon devises the unlikely plan: to free Godzilla, which they have discovered is immune to Xiliens' control. Then they will try to orchestrate events so that Godzilla disposes of the other kaiju, thus eliminating the Xiliens' most powerful weapons.

The E.D.F. group quickly puts the plan into action. In a lengthy series of battles, Godzilla defeats each adversary. Then, it all boils down to a showdown between Godzilla and the powerful Monster X. The two kaiju seem evenly matched until the Xilien commander suddenly transmits supercharged energy to Monster X, transforming the menace into the seemingly all-powerful Keizer Ghidorah. Just in time, however, Ozaki, the mutant E.D.F. soldier, then transfers his energy to Godzilla, giving the king of the monsters more than enough power to defeat his foe.

In the end, the Xiliens and the kaiju they controlled are beaten. The Gotengo, which was shadowing Godzilla, is destroyed in the process. With his other enemies defeated, Godzilla is ready to kill Captain Gordon and the other Gotengo survivors. At the last moment, however, Minilla, Godzilla's young son, convinces the mighty kaiju to leave the humans alone. As the story ends, Minilla and Godzilla return to the ocean, and equilibrium between humanity and the king of the monsters is restored.

In many ways, that final scene is a fitting conclusion. Minilla provides a critical link between the ferocious kaiju, creatures that in this movie largely ignore the human world even as they destroy it, and the humans who feel nearly helpless as kaiju battles inflict death and mayhem all around them. Ultimately, Minilla fulfills the role of an intermediary connecting the kaiju and human worlds to restore balance.

Since Toho already had announced that *Godzilla: Final Wars* would be the last movie in the franchise for the foreseeable future, the main things at stake were return on investment and leaving audiences with warm memories. There was no pressure to make something that would spark a direct sequel because there would be no sequel. Still, the film's budget was nearly $20 million. It was a fraction of what Hollywood spent on its blockbusters at the time, but it was substantially more than Toho had ever spent on any of its previous Godzilla movies.[17] If the studio were to make a profit, the film would need to be reasonably popular.

Money was not the only factor in play, though. The film was intended to make a statement. According to the executive producer, the studio's goal was nothing less than "to make the best Godzilla movie ever."[18] With so many previous entries in the franchise, that goal would be difficult to achieve. Director Kitamura later said the finished product was "more like a Hollywood movie" than previous Godzilla films.[19] That, he suggested, was the reason for the story's evolution from "basically Godzilla versus everybody" to one that also included many other elements, not the least of which was the humanity-versus-extraterrestrials storyline. However, for some viewers, the results were not wholly satisfying. *Boston Globe* film critic Ty Burr wrote that the film is "engaging for a while, but at two hours-plus you may come out feeling captivated dead."[20] It is "too much of a good thing," he says, "since it calls on seemingly every monster in Toho's basement."

Kitamura put much effort into trying to make something new and fresh. However, the project was saddled with many, perhaps too many, expectations. From one perspective, the movie may have seemed overloaded and excessively episodic to many viewers. By trying to include something for everyone—and especially in trying to satisfy hardcore Godzilla fans—it may have made its task more complicated than it might have been otherwise. For example, the long series of battles in which Godzilla vanquishes one foe after another does not necessarily convey the sense that the proceedings are building to a crescendo. Instead, viewers might easily see that part of the movie as a string of curtain calls, with one kaiju after another trotting out before the camera to make a final bow.

Yet, in other ways, the film primarily met the expectations of at least some critics and other viewers. Writing for *Film Inquiry*, Kevin L. Lee notes that the director "approached the material with the sole intention of creating the mother of all monster rumbles. Don't expect anything more than action, and you'll do fine."[21] However, although he enjoyed the movie, he also concludes that the action sequences sometimes go "overboard ... to the detriment of its tone and narrative coherence."

Like many previous films in the franchise, *Godzilla: Final Wars* is not short on ambition. However, the goal of delivering an attention-getting movie that would serve as a triumphant send-off for the franchise was largely unfulfilled. Initial reviews were mixed, and the film failed to impress at the box office, even in Japan. It opened in Japan on December 4, 2004. Unfortunately for Toho, that was the same day as the premiere of Pixar's animated *The Incredibles*, which proved to be a major hit.

Published sources indicate that the Pixar film earned over $7 million in Japan that weekend, crushing the Toho kaiju feature, which brought in less than $2 million.[22] A few weeks later, *Godzilla: Final Wars* had managed only to reach a distant fifth place in Japanese box-office receipts for the month. Its $9.1 million monthly total in Japan was surpassed by *The Incredibles* ($49.9 million in Japan), *The Terminal* ($39.6 million), *Windstruck* ($17.7 million), and *Alien vs. Predator* ($16.2 million).[23]

Including foreign markets, the *Godzilla: Final Wars* box-office tally at the end of its initial theatrical run was less than its production expenses. It generated additional revenue in later years but never became the spectacular franchise send-off the studio had so publicly desired.

Meanwhile, the movie's reception in the United States was equally disappointing. It was not because Toho had not tried to market it. On the contrary, before the movie's release, the studio attempted to drum up enthusiasm for it. As part of advance publicity efforts, a star for Godzilla was arranged along Hollywood's famous Walk of Fame, which generated some press and may have raised awareness of the forthcoming film.[24] And a few months later, *Final Wars* was booked for a high-profile premiere in Los Angeles.[25] That, too, attracted some attention. However, none of these efforts translated into much interest from the American public in the new film.

Kitamura set out to make a "fun movie,"[26] and in a certain way, he may have succeeded. But *Godzilla: Final Wars* may have tried to do too many things as a film. The attempt to make an updated throwback to the kaiju movies from the late 1960s and 1970s may have presented many pitfalls that were hard to avoid. In aiming for an aesthetic that Kitamura and many Godzilla fans revered, the "rubber suit" aesthetic is front and center in the film. Hardcore and younger fans may have been delighted with that retro look. However, mass-market movie audiences had grown accustomed to more contemporary and high-tech special effects by that time.

Hollywood blockbusters of the era, which aimed for bigger and better special effects in nearly every major outing, had trained global viewers to expect a specific look. Kitamura's choices, which undoubtedly were conditioned by a limiting budget, were inconsistent with those audience preferences. In some ways, it was similar to changing tastes in animated films during this period, in which movies created with the older so-called 2-D animation techniques were increasingly unable to compete with modern 3-D computer-generated productions. It is hard to envision a scenario in which the visual choices in *Final Wars* would have appealed to mass international audiences who expected to see spectacular hyper-realistic computer-generated special effects.

Another issue may have been the overloaded script. In aiming to check off many boxes and please fans looking for various things, the film may contain too many plot elements, characters, and story arcs. The large number of characters, including Earth Defense Forces, mutants, extraterrestrials, and many kaiju, leaves little room to develop a cohesive story. Arguably, this complexity diluted whatever focus Kitamura envisioned at the outset.

Beyond these issues, though, there is a more overarching question. How were movies featuring giant monsters—creatures most people might find more preposterous than frightening—going to attract modern 21st-century audiences? Unfortunately, *Godzilla: Final Wars* did not appear to have an answer to that question. The film may have worked as fan service and the end of a chapter in the Godzilla story. But it offered little to entice anyone beyond the cadre of faithful fans.

There is nothing wrong with making movies explicitly designed for a particular market segment, but the people overseeing the Godzilla franchise had bigger ambitions. Yet, the franchise seemed headed for irrelevancy internationally and even in Japan. Although many children and a community of committed kaiju fans still eagerly awaited each new Godzilla film, the series' appeal had become limited for everyone else.

Toho's options may have been few. Many hardcore fans resisted the idea of thoroughly modernizing either the character or its production values in a way that would veer substantially from the old-school approach they cherished. In any case, *Godzilla: Final Wars* was the least-attended recent film in the series. That outcome was no doubt disheartening to Toho executives and the people who had invested so much time in effort in making the movie. However, it hardly can have been a total surprise. After all, Toho already had many qualms about continuing the series. *Godzilla: Final Wars,* in some ways, just proved what the studio had concluded months earlier.

Despite disappointing returns from this most recent film, not much had changed in some ways. Godzilla movies had never dominated the U.S. box office even though Toho's giant monster had become one of the most famous fictional movie characters globally. As the Millennium series ended, Godzilla, and probably all kaiju films, remained in a niche category, especially in the United States, just as they were before. To say that U.S. film audiences did not take *Godzilla: Final Wars* seriously as a movie would miss the point. More accurately, general U.S. audiences hardly even noticed it existed.

American movie-goers had been immersed in blockbuster cinema culture for decades. The main problem with Godzilla films and potentially other giant-monster movies was not that they were seen as too outlandish or silly, though some may have seen them that way. Being outlandish, even absurd, has seldom been a problem at the box office when a film delivers on expectations and strikes the right notes to resonate with the public. Rather than that, *Final Wars* was likely a case of an intended blockbuster not living up to studio hype, at least in the United States. There was not enough 21st-century style or technique in terms of special effects.

The perception of "foreignness" also may have dampened enthusiasm for the movie with U.S. audiences, which are notoriously resistant to films they deem insufficiently American-centric. The film's star, Don Frye, was American, but interestingly, he was mostly unknown in the United States. And from the perspective of many mainstream American movie-goers, the whole production may have seemed to have too much of the look and feel of much earlier Japanese films—productions still labeled in the U.S. as "foreign." Unfair as it may have been, in the post–9/11 and early 2000s context—when U.S. society remained self-centered, if not outright xenophobic—that most likely did not bode well for box office success.

Americans also had many other things on their minds then. The U.S. military campaign in Iraq, which seemed to be going well only a year earlier, suddenly appeared to be in trouble. In the summer of 2004, disturbing allegations of torture and possible human rights violations by U.S. soldiers at the Abu Ghraib military prison in Iraq shocked and revulsed many. Soon after that, a bitter presidential campaign battle between sitting president George W. Bush and Democratic challenger John Kerry weighed heavily on the national psyche. That mindset may have created an environment in the United States that was far from ideal for marketing a Godzilla film.

*Final Wars* never got a wide release in the United States. But even if it had, it is difficult to imagine that it would have fared well against the movies Americans chose to see in the last weeks of 2004. In the United States, people still went to movie theaters and embraced escapism, just as they often had done in the past. With much on their minds and looking for relief, they turned to movies like *The Incredibles, National Treasure,* and *Meet the Fockers.*

Godzilla was as famous as he had been for decades in the United States, Japan, and many other places. But the creature was increasingly like yesterday's movie star—a nostalgic name from the past that no longer drew much interest. Sony-TriStar had tried to push the king of the monsters into global superstardom and came up short. Now Toho had tried and failed, too. Was it time to put aside the idea that giant monsters had a place in the cinematic world of the 21st century? As it turned out, such a conclusion would have been premature. Toho's star monster was somewhere at the bottom of the ocean, but other contenders were waiting in the wings.

# 3

# Return of the King
## *King Kong* (2005)

Long before Godzilla, there was Kong. The colossal primate launched the giant-monster movie genre in RKO studio's 1933 sensation, *King Kong*, and *New York Times* critic Mordaunt Hall was impressed. "The narrative is worked out in a decidedly compelling fashion," he wrote, adding that the film had "enough thrills for any devotee of such tales."[1]

The original movie was wildly popular, and a sequel was soon in the works. RKO rushed *The Son of Kong* (1933) to the screen only months after the first Kong movie. It did nowhere near as much business as the original, which dampened the studio's enthusiasm for further outings. So, after that movie finished its initial run, there was a considerable lull before another Kong feature.

After World War II, filmmaker-adventurer Merian C. Cooper, the man behind *King Kong*, decided to try again. He produced a vaguely similar film, RKO's *Mighty Joe Young* in 1949. Some people liked it, and it seemed enough to satisfy demand. But after that, movies with any connection to Kong (or a similar character) mostly disappeared for a long time.

In the meantime, other cinematic giant monsters became popular. Toho's Godzilla is perhaps the most remembered of them, but in the 1950s, there were numerous other giant creature movies, too. For a time, Hollywood churned out many low-budget "creature features" for the youth market in that era. One favorite was 1954's *Them!* But interestingly, the Kong character remained dormant. The colossal primate did not reappear until 1962, when the Toho studio, then ramping up its Godzilla franchise, licensed the character. The oversized ape finally reemerged in Toho's *King Kong vs. Godzilla* (1962) and *King Kong Escapes* (1967).

In the following decade, famed impresario Dino De Laurentiis produced a popular update of the original movie. His production of *King Kong*, directed by John Guillermin, premiered in 1976. It did well and eventually led to a sequel, *King Kong Lives*, a decade later. After that, interest waned again, and a lull lasting many years followed. By the time the 21st century arrived, it had been many years since the last major King Kong film.[2]

Interest in the character had not entirely evaporated, however. Universal Pictures had considered making a new King Kong movie off and on for some time. By the early 2000s, Universal executives finally decided the time was ripe to bring the cinema's colossal primate back to the big screen.

That decision may have been related to evolving audience tastes and preferences. In the troubling early years of the War on Terror, American movie-goers often indulged in their appetite for fantasy and the fantastic. For example, debuting just weeks after the shocking events of September 11, 2001, spectacle-filled blockbusters based on the famous *Harry Potter* and *Lord of the Rings* novels furthered that trend. The first film in the former series, *Harry Potter and the Philosopher's Stone*, debuted in late 2001. New entries in that franchise appeared regularly over the rest of the decade, each generating substantial ticket sales and a legion of fans.

Concurrently, Peter Jackson's well-regarded trilogy based on J.R.R. Tolkien's *The Lord of the Rings* fantasy books was a success story of its own. The three movies—*The Lord of the Rings: The Fellowship of the Ring* (2001), *The Lord of the Rings: The Two Towers* (2002), and *The Lord of the Rings: The Return of the King* (2003)—were hugely popular. They were great financial successes as well. Indeed, the trio of films generated close to $3 billion in box-office receipts.

By coincidence, Jackson had been a lifelong fan of the original *King Kong*. When he was a boy, he first saw the black-and-white classic on television, which made an indelible impression. The film sparked the New Zealander's interest in a movie career. "I'd never heard of *King Kong*," he told a reporter. "But I sat there, and I watched this film, and it just had such a profound effect on me. It was the defining moment in my life as a filmmaker."[3]

Before being hired to helm *The Lord of the Rings*, Jackson had landed an unrelated directing deal with Universal for a different movie. The film, *The Frighteners* (1996), is a mixture of horror and comedy. Since it starred box-office favorite Michael J. Fox, Universal had high expectations as the film neared release. Executives believed in the movie and had faith in Jackson. More than that, the studio still owned rights to *King Kong*. So, before even seeing how *The Frighteners* would perform at the box office, the studio offered Jackson what seemed to be a dream project: the opportunity to develop a new movie featuring the great ape.

Despite his affection for the original, Jackson was reluctant at first. The 1933 film was dear to him, and perhaps he thought it might be "tempting fate by messing with a classic," as one writer later said.[4] However, after some thought, Jackson eventually accepted the assignment. If someone was going to make a new Kong movie for Universal, he seems to have thought, why leave it to someone who might have less respect for the original?

At that point, it looked as though the project was on track. Universal even approved an initial script and planned to start production in 1997.[5] But then, other circumstances intervened. For one thing, *The Frighteners* had premiered by then, and it soon became apparent it would underwhelm at the box office. Indeed, the movie generated tepid ticket sales and mixed reviews. When it became apparent that Jackson's movie would fail to meet the studio's expectations, that was probably enough to give executives a reason to reexamine the *King Kong* project. But there was more. It turned out that other giant-monster films were being developed at rival studios. Disney was working on a remake of *Mighty Joe Young*, later released in 1998. At the same time, Sony's Tri-Star studio was pushing ahead with its lavish *Godzilla* remake, also scheduled to hit U.S. theaters in 1998.

At that point, Universal executives realized that if they pursued the *King Kong* project, three major giant-monster movies would arrive in U.S. theaters simultaneously. Universal dropped the project, saying that such a development would dilute the potential audience for its film. *King Kong's* return to the big screen would have to wait until another day.

Canceled projects are far from unusual in the film business, but Jackson was undoubtedly disappointed. However, he had other options and quickly moved to Disney's Miramax division. There, he undertook what would be a defining project of his career: a significant new screen adaptation of J.R.R.'s immensely popular trilogy of *Lord of the Rings* books.

Jackson's *Lord of the Rings series* became blockbusters, catapulting him to the lofty ranks of the industry's most widely known and sought-after directors. Meanwhile, although Universal had parted ways with him after halting the *King Kong* project, the studio had never lost interest in working with the director in the future. Thus, as the *Lord of the Rings* trilogy ended, Universal approached him and floated the idea of reviving that project.[6]

By this time, Jackson had proven that if he had the right ingredients and circumstances, he could deliver visually stunning and financially successful films. It was, therefore, not surprising that Universal was eager to secure his services again. To close the deal, the studio offered him an alluring contract to bring the director back into the fold. In return for helming a new *King Kong* movie, Jackson would earn $20 million in cash and 20 percent of the profits.[7]

Arrangements were soon finalized, and work on the new *King Kong* project began in earnest. However, Jackson did not simply pick up from where he left off when the project was canceled. In the years since then, he had come up with new ideas, heightened his skills, and developed self-confidence. So, the Kong story he had planned in the 1990s, which would have been a modern adventure tale, was scrapped. Instead, Jackson now envisioned a period piece, placing the action in the 1930s. The direction was going back to the beginning to make a new version of the classic movie he loved.

The giant ape obviously would be the star attraction for the new film. Therefore, it was essential for Kong to be rendered on screen in a way that would be realistic and compelling. The 1933 original used stop-motion animated models and oversized props to portray the creature. At the time, these were state-of-the-art techniques that wowed audiences. But by the early 2000s, special effects technology zoomed far beyond that approach. Since filmmakers now had a variety of digital technologies at their disposal, Jackson planned to take advantage of the new opportunities they provided. It would be a necessity. Numerous Hollywood blockbusters had conditioned audiences to expect the contemporary visual experience that only those modern, computer-generated effects could provide, especially in films with fantasy or science-fiction elements.

Fortunately, Jackson was well-experienced in weaving the latest special effects techniques into his productions. His *Lord of the Rings* trilogy relied on state-of-the-art effects to produce stunning visuals, which many people knew. But his experience with advanced techniques predated that. Indeed, in 1993, Jackson and two partners founded Weta, a company specializing in digital effects, to work on his film *Heavenly Bodies*. By the middle of the next decade, the firm had grown substantially, especially during the many months when Jackson was making the lavish *Lord of the Rings* movies.

As the central character in the film, King Kong needed to express a wide range of reactions and emotions. Jackson was mindful that a realistic portrayal of Kong's eyes would be essential to convey the creature's feelings in many scenes.[8] Accordingly, much work focused on the effects used for that. That attention to detail was typical of Jackson's thorough and demanding methods, evident throughout the film.

Actor Andy Serkis was selected to perform many of Kong's scenes using motion-capture technology, which Weta used as the basis for its computer-generated animated version of the character. Serkis had worked with Jackson before. He did motion-capture performances and voice work in the *Lord of the Rings* films. The director and actor had a good working relationship and understood how to use the process to achieve Jackson's vision.[9]

Jackson's recent success seemingly opened up many casting

possibilities for the human characters. Jackson decided on Naomi Watts for the starring role of Ann Darrow, the aspiring entertainer (played by the legendary Fay Wray in the 1933 film) who develops an emotional relationship with Kong. Watts gained much attention for her performance in David Lynch's *Mulholland Drive* (2001). She may have seemed an unlikely choice to be in a film about a giant ape, but she was drawn to Jackson's project due to her great admiration for his recent trilogy. "The director plays a big part in my choices," she said in one published report. "I don't know if I'd do *King Kong* if Peter Jackson wasn't attached."[10]

For other roles, numerous actors were considered. According to author Ray Horton, performers such as Robert De Niro, George Clooney, and Ian McKellen were all considered.[11] Ultimately, Jack Black and Adrian Brody were cast in two leading roles. Brody was already a seasoned film veteran at the time. Black was a less obvious choice in some ways. He was known for comedy and his starring role in the *School of Rock* (2003). His part in *King Kong* would have some amusing aspects, but the film was a drama, somewhat outside Black's usual work. Still, Jackson appears to have been confident that Black had the necessary skill to bring the part to life.

The new *King Kong* was to be a complex and expensive undertaking. Jackson worked out of his home base in New Zealand, following his usual procedures. His cast and crew assembled there to begin production.

Jackson's very detail-oriented approach to filmmaking was expensive. According to published reports, the film soared $32 million beyond its already sizeable budget during production. The total cost is thought to have skyrocketed to $207 million by the time Jackson was done,[12] but the visual results were impressive. Jackson's reputation for perfectionism yielded a visual spectacle. The state-of-the-art computer graphics throughout most of the film were very costly. But the director's exacting approach also led to other expenses, such as when he ordered the construction of detailed physical sets. His high standards demanded time and care to bring out actors' performances that lived up to his vision, as well. Perhaps that was all to be expected since this was a project Jackson had dreamt about since childhood. No one who knew him would have expected anything other than the type of intensity he brought to the production.

News reports said Universal executives were happy with Jackson's work even though the film went far over budget. Even before its official release, the vice-chairperson of Universal Pictures boasted that the new *King Kong* would be a "three-hour feast of an event."[13] And in the end, Jackson delivered an immersive movie luxuriating in the look and feel of the 1930s as it tells its story.

The finished movie is, in many respects, a loving and respectful homage to the 1933 classic. The film is presented in three acts and stays close to the story and spirit of the original. Yet, there are some significant changes. Some are simply updates and differences in narrative focus. But other alterations attempt to make the story more palatable for contemporary sensibilities.

For example, some of the more problematic aspects of the Depression-era classic have been removed or toned down, especially with regard to sexist and racist elements. For example, the bizarre sexual implications between Kong and the Ann Darrow character are significantly reduced. In addition, the overt racism of the 1933 film, which was evident in the portrayal of the indigenous people of Kong's mysterious home, Skull Island (and even, in some respects, in the Kong character), is also minimized, though arguably not completely erased. Indeed, some problematic attitudes about race that are thoroughly woven into the original King Kong narrative seem to linger regardless of Jackson's intentions. At least in part, that may be due to the nature of the source material. As Professor Kwame McKenzie wrote shortly after the premiere of Jackson's film, "The story feeds into all the colonial hysteria about black hyper-sexuality. This imagery has a long history and is difficult to shift."[14]

Such alterations and the noticeable technological differences aside, Jackson's film mostly remains remarkably close to the original. More than that, many specific shots in Jackson's film either outright replicate or closely resemble shots in the earlier film. Indeed, when watching the 2005 movie, it is evident just how closely Jackson had studied the film he loved so much as a boy.

For such reasons, most of the plot is familiar. The film's first section takes place in New York City and sets up what will come. Down-on-his-luck filmmaker Carl Denham (Jack Black) is determined to make a name for himself by creating a new kind of nature-inspired film. Denham hoodwinks downtrodden vaudeville performer Ann Darrow (Naomi Watts) and writer Jack Driscoll (Adrian Brody) and talks them into accompanying him on a hired ship. Their destination is an uncharted island that rumors say is the home to a mysterious creature.

In the second act, the director and his party arrive on Skull Island, where almost immediately, they are met with an indigenous population unaccustomed to the modern industrial world. The first encounter is marred by violence, and before long, Ann Darrow is captured and offered up as an apparent sacrifice to an unknown creature.

Before long, King Kong arrives to seize the human offering. Surprisingly, Ann and Kong slowly develop an unusual and unlikely appreciation for one another after her capture. (In the original film, Kong seemed to harbor a romantic interest in the Ann Darrow character. However, in

Jackson's version, Kong is presented as a protector.[15]) Despite having affection for the woman, however, the beast is not ready to turn his captive free.

Much of the second act involves the crew chasing Kong in an effort to rescue Darrow. Along the way, they encounter giant beasts (including dinosaurs), and various types of mayhem ensue. Some crew members die during the commotion, and Kong fights dinosaurs and other beasts. The situation looks dire for Ann Darrow and the people trying to save her. Eventually, however, Darrow is rescued, after which the other survivors emerge from the jungle and wind up on the ocean shore. Kong is close behind them, but he is weakened and soon subdued.

The third act finds the giant ape in captivity after being transported to New York City. There, Kong is tied up and presented on stage as entertainment for a live theater audience. But his captors have underestimated his strength and resolve. Almost immediately, Kong bursts out of his bonds and tries to escape. But Manhattan is an unfamiliar and unfriendly concrete jungle.

As he is pursued by forces trying to kill him, Kong comes across the distraught Ann Darrow, who still emotionally connects with the colossal beast. The creature grabs Darrow and brings her with him as he is chased. Darrow hopes for a good outcome, but things are clearly out of hand. Eventually, Kong climbs the Empire State Building, desperately trying to escape, taking Darrow with him.

With nowhere to run, Kong sets Darrow down on a high ledge to preserve her safety. At that moment, airplanes armed with mounted machine guns swoop down. Although Darrow remains safe, Kong is shot and falls to his death. In the aftermath of this tragic turn of events, Denham observes, "It was beauty killed the beast," the same line uttered in the conclusion of the 1933 original.

There has always been something slightly ambiguous about labeling the cinema's giant creatures as "monsters," especially with King Kong. From one point of view, monster is a relatively straightforward and benign word. The authoritative *Merriam-Webster Dictionary* lists the primary definition of the word as "an animal of strange or terrifying shape" or "one unusually large for its kind."[16] That simple description does not necessarily imply any moral assessment. However, the word is often used differently. It is frequently associated with cruelty and evil intent, a definition that does not necessarily fit well when applied to the screen's colossal beasts.

Many devotees of giant monster films know that these cinematic creatures often do not function as traditional screen villains. Typically, the behemoths are beyond such categorization and are no more villainous than an earthquake or an animal in the wild. They may do troublesome or even deadly things to humans, but it does not make sense to presume they have malicious intent in many instances. If by a screen "monster" one wishes to talk about an overtly evil character, the example of serial killer Hannibal Lecter in *Silence of the Lambs* may be far more suitable than a kaiju character like King Kong.

Still, as evident as this may be to those familiar with kaiju films, it may be far less apparent to the general population. Superficially, filmdom's giant monsters usually function at least partially as antagonists. That can suggest superficial readings emphasizing something malicious, even though that interpretation does not seem warranted in many of the genre's films. Jackson was evidently aware of these issues while making his version of *King Kong*. "People call Kong 'a monster,'" he said. "He's not. There's nothing evil about Kong. He's just another creature who has opened up a little bit of his heart to Ann [Darrow], which proves his undoing."[17]

Throughout various screen incarnations, Kong's human qualities, especially emotion, often have been as central as his incredible size and destructive power. That implied connection to humanity, somewhat rare in giant monster films, suggests an essential question. Who, exactly, are the monsters in these films? On the surface, the quick answer might be Kong or any other kaiju. Yet, even a preliminary analysis suggests that the real monsters are often found among human characters.

The last section of Jackson's *King Kong*, which, like the 1933 original, takes place high atop the Empire State Building, makes that point. Here is a cornered creature simply trying to survive. The giant ape ended up in that no-win situation through no fault of his own. He was merely trying to free himself from bondage. What else would a creature do in those circumstances? In other words, describing Kong's actions as villainous seems problematic.

Indeed, in Jackson's movie, as in the original, Kong is portrayed as a victim. A crucial scene in the New York theater, which closely mirrors the original, invokes troubling associations from U.S. history to reinforce that point. Kong appears on stage as if "manacled on an auction block," supporting the idea that the captive primate is a "symbol of American slavery," as scholar Alan Rice points out.[18]

Jackson's tableau is generally similar to the corresponding scene in the 1933 production, but there are notable differences. In the earlier movie, Kong is positioned on a large pedestal, standing with his arms outstretched and chained to a T-shaped frame. The visual references to a slave market auction block and a crucifix are so blatant that they could scarcely be missed. By contrast, Jackson somewhat tones down this visual reference. In his version of the scene, Kong's outstretched arms are secured to two imposing columns that are part of a stage set that resembles the sacrificial scene on Skull Island. These subtle differences from the original make the slave market and crucifix associations more nuanced than the original.

In other ways, however, Jackson pushes into terrain that the 1933 movie avoided. In the 1933 version, Ann Darrow is brought on stage as a guest, dressed in an elegant white dress suitable for a rising show business star. Jackson, however, uses the Ann Darrow character in another way. The 2005 film shows Ann portraying a captive. She is posed on a sacrificial altar in front of the imposing Kong, shackled directly behind her. And like Kong, she is shown facing the audience, standing with her arms outstretched and bound to two poles. Indeed, as composed by Jackson, the scene invites a reading in which Ann and Kong are both presented as objects held in captivity for the crowd's amusement.

Jackson includes yet another element to complete his staging of this scene. Along with Kong and Ann, the stage is filled with people dressed as indigenous Skull Islanders. They act somewhat as window dressing for the tableau. Still, their stereotyped appearance and movements are also a reminder that Kong comes from a land of the Other, a place that New Yorkers (and presumably all Westerners in the film) look down upon.

The 2005 version of this scene possesses more visual complexity and arguably has more layers of meaning than the Depression-era classic. Yet, both share one thing. Ultimately, each evokes profoundly ugly and even repulsive associations. The *King Kong* story may focus mainly on the colossal primate and, to a lesser extent, on the world from which Kong was stolen. As it appears on screen, the narrative may also say something about women in society at the time each film was made. However, the 1993 and 2005 versions of *King Kong* (and, to a lesser extent, the remake made in 1976) seem to confirm Jackson's observation about the giant ape. Kong is hardly a monster in the moral sense. Instead, the supposedly civilized people of so-called Western civilization seem better suited to that label. That is especially evident in Jackson's film. His *King Kong* updates the technical and special effects aspects of the film. But it also presents the story, dressed up as a period piece, as a parable about modern Western society's shortcomings in dealing fairly and equitably with human differences.

On another level, Jackson's film differs in its overall emotional tone. According to scholar Cynthia Erb, Jackson's *King Kong* centers on "the concept of melancholy," which was not the case in the 1933 film.[19] Erb sees "Kong's status as a grieving, melancholy hero, and an overall atmosphere that plays upon a confusion of the terms 'Depression' [that is, the economic period known as the Great Depression] and 'depression' [as a psychological condition]."

Indeed, an unmistakable sense of sadness pervades Jackson's *King Kong*. As Erb notes, "Kong's association with the dispossessed," combined with the negative psychological portrayal of New York City, especially in the latter third of the film, emphasizes this mood.[20] At another moment in history, this dimension of the film might have passed relatively unnoticed. However, in the wake of the devastation of the terror attack on the city just a few years earlier, Jackson seems to have evoked—intentionally or not—a sense of poignancy specific to the early 2000s.[21]

By 2005, the painful memories of 9/11 were still not close to subsiding. In addition, the United States also remained immersed in wars in Afghanistan and Iraq. Given these circumstances, a climate of uncertainty and anxiety could be felt across much of U.S. culture. Whether Jackson, who was ensconced in his New Zealand homeland during the movie's production, actively sought to link his film with post–9/11 melancholia is uncertain. Very possibly, that was not his specific intent. However, given the context of that time, it seems reasonable to conclude that American viewers (the film's primary audience) likely brought some of the nation's troubled mood to the theaters.

Jackson's *King Kong* fared better than many films featuring giant monsters of the era. However, it was tremendously long—well over three hours from start to finish—which may have put some potential viewers off seeing it in a theater. Still, the movie dominated the U.S. box office when it opened. It continued to do well throughout the early weeks of its domestic run. It also performed reasonably well in other markets, indicating that a movie starring a giant beast could draw across international borders and cultural lines under certain circumstances.

Probably few people saw the film without some preconceptions. King Kong, after all, was a well-established cultural icon making a comeback in a crowded movie environment. As *New York Times* critic A.O. Scott observed, Jackson's film was "burdened with impossible expectations and harassed by competition from all sides."[22] Still, its box office performance in the United States was very respectable, totaling $218 million. Receipts from markets outside the U.S. increased the domestic total by well over $100 million. Eventually, the film reportedly earned $550 million at the box office.[23] And after its theatrical release, brisk sales of the film's release in DVD and Blu-Ray formats are thought to have raised another $146 million.[24]

*King Kong* did well, but it was not the biggest box-office winner of its time. That was probably not surprising since it was released in the era of megahits like *Harry Potter and the Goblet of Fire* (2005), *Star Wars, Episode III: Revenge of the Sith (2005)*, and *Pirates of the Caribbean: Dead Man's Chest* (2006). However, even considering Hollywood's sometimes byzantine accounting practices, Jackson's film appears to have been very profitable.

The film's box office performance suggests that Jackson successfully attracted a broad audience for his updated version of the classic movie. Many, though not all critics, generally agreed. A.O. Scott was among those who were impressed, concluding that Jackson "succeeds through a combination of modesty and reckless glee, topping himself at every turn and reveling in his own showmanship."[25]

With *King Kong*—the cinema's prototypical giant monster in most respects—Peter Jackson seemingly provides evidence that 21st century audiences could still respond to kaiju films in the right circumstances. Yet, in public perception, *King Kong* seems to exist somewhat apart from the giant monster universe overall. With human-like emotions and a complex storyline that touches on all-too-human themes, many movie-goers may not have thought Jackson's movie had much to do with the kaiju genre. In many ways, it may have been taken as a simple fantasy or allegory, more like *Beauty and the Beast* than *Godzilla: Final Wars*. In other words, *King Kong* was more than simply a giant monster movie. It was the latest Peter Jackson film. Many may have chosen to see it because of the director's reputation or because they had enjoyed his *Lord of the Rings* series. The giant monster angle, though apparent, may not have played much of a role in the choice to see. In any case, it remained to be seen if *King Kong's* success could be matched by other filmmakers interested in telling different kaiju stories for global audiences.

# 4

# A Coming-of-Age Story
*Gamera the Brave* (2006)

Although Peter Jackson's *King Kong* (2005) made oblique references to the terrorist attacks of 2001 in the United States, *Gamera the Brave's* director Tasaki Ryuta was far more direct. A scene late in *Gamera the Brave* connects fiction and fact. It shows a 200-foot-tall, super-powered tortoise crashing into the side of a skyscraper. As the camera pulls away, the similarity of that image to familiar shots of the smoldering Twin Towers in New York City on September 11, 2001, is too blatant to miss. For a movie that viewers probably expected would deal mainly with the fantastic, *Gamera the Brave* is surprisingly blunt in alluding to the uncomfortable global realities of its era.

References to terrorism might seem unusual in a film primarily geared toward the children's market. But this film ventures far beyond typical kaiju movies in many ways. Indeed, it is a layered, textured film with plenty of content for adults to ponder. However, Tasaki also offers a work that younger audiences could enjoy as something more straightforward than that. Indeed, on one level, *Gamera the Brave* is a Spielberg-like coming-of-age fable, on par, in some respects, with his 1982 classic, *E.T.: The Extra-Terrestrial*.

In part, *Gamera the Brave* is an ambitious continuation of a franchise that began in the 1960s. However, in the context of the early years of the new millennium, the film is another example of a giant monster movie that had difficulty finding an audience. It would have been unrealistic to expect a global blockbuster that could compete with Hollywood spectacles. Still, it was reasonable to aim for a film that would at least win the approval of the genre's core audience for such movies while broadening its appeal to some extent.

Those goals may have seemed achievable, but they were not necessarily easy to achieve. At the time, the Gamera franchise's outlook seemed promising. Going into the 2000s, some of the most ardent Gamera fans

## 4. A Coming-of-Age Story

basked in the glow of Kaneko Shusuke's reboot of the series in the 1990s. His trilogy of Gamera movies appealed to kaiju audiences and brought a modern edge to the franchise. The success of those movies, which Kaneko made for the Daiei studio, was a big part of the reason Toho subsequently hired him to direct *Godzilla, Mothra, and King Ghidorah*.

However, when the time came to make *Gamera the Brave*, circumstances were different. A shake-up at the Daiei studio brought changing ideas about going forward, resulting in a clean break from the recent past. The revamped studio brought in Tasaki, who had a distinctly different vision.

Given these conditions, it was perhaps inevitable that some of the biggest fans of the recent Gamera movies would be hard to please. That soon turned out to be the case. Although some kaiju movie devotees grudgingly saw positives in the new work, the film never caught on with a broader viewership. The movie achieved neither great commercial nor much critical notice upon release. It always had some supporters, but it disappointed many faithful advocates of the franchise. Some saw it as evidence that the Gamera series was headed in the wrong direction.

There is no denying that, in some ways, *Gamera the Brave* drifts far from what many kaiju movie fans expected. But considering the performance of then-recent Japanese kaiju movies, it is easy to understand why the studios wanted to shake up the kaiju movie world. Indeed, if things continued down the path they were on and kaiju films did not evolve, the genre's future looked grim.

Such background factors suggest that the effort was worth the attempt even though it yielded underwhelming returns. Of course, things did not start that way. When the movie headed into production some months earlier, the studio had reasons for optimism.

The storied franchise had a deep history and traditionally aimed at a particular market. Somewhat unusually, Gamera had long been promoted as a child-friendly character, something that was somewhat lost in the 1990s iterations of the character. That angle gives the creature a unique identity in the kaiju movie universe, setting it apart from most other cinematic giant monsters. Although less famous than Toho's Godzilla, the sometimes-campy Gamera character generally possesses an endearing charm and is a perpetual fan favorite in Japan and the United States, the most important secondary market for these movies.

Gamera starred in eight Japanese movies between 1965 and 1980, providing a string of entertaining outings for youthful Japanese audiences. In addition, the steady stream of films offered ample, relatively low-cost material for the U.S. television market, where Gamera movies often aired on Saturday afternoon and late-night broadcasts over the years, which helped build a strong secondary viewership. When the cable era arrived, the giant tortoise was there, too. Many Americans became aware of the franchise via the comedy cable series *Mystery Science Theater 3000*. Overall, the movies appeared frequently enough on television in various countries to attain reasonably widespread brand recognition.

The first Gamera movie premiered in 1965 under the banner of the Daiei Film Company. At one time, the studio was one of the brightest lights in Japanese cinema. It was responsible for several international hits since its creation in the mid-century and was highly regarded. Indeed, among its legendary productions are Akira Kurosawa's *Rashomon* (1950) and Kenji Mizoguchi's *Ugetsu* (1953).

By the early 1960s, Daiei had become one of Japan's top studios. However, that decade brought many changes and challenges to the film industry in Japan and internationally. With the rise of solid competition from television, the aging movie business was increasingly precarious globally, and Japan was no exception. And as the 1960s wore on, business prospects looked increasingly uncertain. It turned out that Japan's film industry was headed into a period of "long decline."[1]

Those conditions provided a backdrop to the production of the first Gamera movie, which came as Daiei executives looked for new types of films to jumpstart its stalling business. Trying a kaiju movie seemed feasible. Rival Toho had developed its initially standalone Godzilla movie into a reliable franchise. Perhaps there would be demand for a new kind of kaiju content, too. Against this backdrop, Daiei moved forward with the production of one of the earliest and best competitors to Toho's Godzilla films. Director Yuasa Noriaki's *Gamera, the Monster,* was ready for release in 1965. It set the tone for what was to come.

The movie did well in Japan, and it spawned a series of annual sequels for the next several years. These movies predictably featured the giant monster battling a rotating cast of enemy kaiju. When people saw *Gamera vs. Barugon* (1966), *Gamera vs. Gyaos* (1967), *Gamera vs. Viras* (1968), *Gamera vs. Guiron* (1969), *Gamera vs. Jiger* (1970), and *Gamera vs. Zigra* (1971), they knew what they were getting. Youthful Japanese audiences enjoyed them.

The initial run of Gamera movies came to an end in 1971 when Daiei's business fortunes looked increasingly bleak.[2] Faced with daunting challenges, the studio succumbed and filed for bankruptcy that same year. A media firm called Tokuma Shoten revived the company three years later. However, times had changed, and the new parent corporation's interests shifted to other areas.

That essentially erased any realistic hope for a new kaiju movie anytime soon. Indeed, several years passed before the studio showed a change of heart. Eventually, in 1980, the company's Daei unit revived the creature for a movie called *Gamera, Super Monster*. But the film, which was primarily pieced together and included some previous material, made little impact. It appeared to mark the end of the giant turtle's screen career for the moment.

Few films were issued under the Daei name over the following years. Instead, Tokuma Shoten, Daei's parent company, focused its attention elsewhere. In a stroke of good fortune, the company backed director Miyazaki Hayao's animated film, *Nausicaä of the Valley of the Wind*, in 1984. Based on that relationship, Tokuma Shoten established Studio Ghibli as a subsidiary the following year. (Studio Ghibli remained part of the Tokuma business until 2005 when it became independent.)

By the 1990s, the string of successful animated features from Studio Ghibli had yielded significant acclaim and income. Against the backdrop of these successes, Tokuma executives decided it was finally time to reboot the Gamera series once again under the auspices of its Daei division.

With director Kaneko Shusuke at the helm, the new Gamera movies brought new life and energy to the old franchise. In short order, three new films were added to the series: *Gamera: Guardian of the Universe* (1995), *Gamera 2: Attack of Legion* (1996), and *Gamera 3: Revenge of Iris* (1999). Kaiju movie fans responded enthusiastically to them. Kaneko's trilogy took the Gamera franchise into a more adult-oriented realm than before. The films were literally and metaphorically darker than previous entries and attracted viewers beyond the ranks of children and veteran kaiju fans. The movies performed well at the box office in Japan.

In the United States, the series received unusual critical notice. The first film in the trilogy, *Gamera: Guardian of the Universe*, was even favorably reviewed by the influential critic Roger Ebert, a writer not known for admiring kaiju fare. Ebert wrote that Kaneko had delivered "precisely the kind of movie that I enjoy, despite all rational reasoning."[3] The film was "fun," he said, even despite "laughable acting, a ludicrous plot, second-rate special effects." It was faint praise, but it was a positive reaction, nonetheless. Although the series seemed to be in good shape after Kaneko's three entries, that momentum quickly came to an end. The studio again shelved the franchise after *Gamera 3's* release amid many changes at the company.

Tokuma Shoten corporation's founder, Yasuyoshi Tokuma, died in 2000, resulting in a shake-up at Daei's corporate parent. Within two years, Tokuma Shoten sold Daei's production facilities and its library of films to Kadokawa, a much larger firm. The Daei name persisted in a new incarnation, Kadokawa Daei Motion Picture Company. By 2004, however, even that vestige of the old studio had disappeared. The division's name was shortened to Kadokawa Pictures, erasing the once venerable Daei name.[4]

When the dust settled, Kadawaka Pictures decided to make another Gamera movie. For something new, studio leaders chose to look beyond the kaiju world for its core creative team. Attuned to the immense popularity of television and youth-oriented action genres, they chose director Tasaki Ryuta to helm the production. The director was an experienced contemporary storyteller and had directed numerous episodes of the long-running Japanese television series, *Kamen Rider* (sometimes translated as *Masked Rider*). In the early 2000s, he made three feature-length *Kamen Rider* adaptations, as well.

Tasaki's successful experience with the Kamen Rider franchise was more critical to his subsequent work with the Gamera character than it may appear. Although less well-known in the USA than some other fictional creations from Japan, Kamen Rider has been a regular part of the Japanese pop-cultural landscape since its creation in the early 1970s, regularly appearing in many iterations across film, television, books, and manga. Tasaki's success with that enormously popular franchise gave him the kind of experience the studio sought. Even a brief look at the series gives a sense of why Tasaki's work on the Kamen Rider franchise would have appealed to Kadawaka Pictures.

*Kamen Rider* first appeared on screen in a 1971 Japanese television series. The show proved to be popular, spawning many sequels over the years. The character has appeared in many different incarnations across many productions. These works mostly follow a basic formula: the super-powered "motorbike-riding, insect-faced cyborg hero"[5] battles villains also endowed with superpowers. Interestingly, throughout these adventures, the "grotesque human-machine-animal hybrids [the various Kamen Riders] … differ from their opponents only in the kindness of their hearts and the strength of their spirits."[6]

In some ways, the franchise follows a template that is not tremendously different from most kaiju movies. The Kamen Riders do not share kaiju's colossal size, and they have human qualities. But like many kaiju productions, the emphasis in their screen adventures is more on the action, fight scenes, and quirky costume heroics than on plot or character development.

However, Kamen Rider is sometimes about much more than that. For example, scholar Sophia Staite writes that in the "2002 television season [with which Tasaki was deeply involved], *Kamen Rider Ryuki*, tackles difficult questions about what justice, heroism, and monstrosity mean, through the medium of a children's martial arts and live-action special effects hero television program." She adds that season's episodes reveal the "blurred boundaries between monster and hero in Kamen Rider, in the context of social attitudes toward children."[7]

## 4. A Coming-of-Age Story

What can be gleaned from this would be significant for Tasaki's Gamera movie. Someone unfamiliar with the subtleties of that era's Kamen Rider series may have thought the director's accomplishments were limited to putting together entertaining storytelling. However, as his work with *Kamen Rider* showed, he was already interested in narratives that dealt with more than straight action. Thus, although they were different from kaiju-oriented productions, Tasaki's experience with *Kamen Rider* offered some clues about the direction he would take for the new Gamera film.

The selection of *Gamera the Brave*'s screenwriter was also noteworthy and further indicated an aspiration to achieve something new. To find a suitable writer, the studio looked outside the cinematic kaiju world and beyond the horror or action genres. The final choice, Tatsui Yukari, indeed signaled a very different direction. The selection of a woman in a traditionally male-dominated genre was noteworthy.

Tatsui was new to the kaiju movie scene. Selecting her for the job within a genre dominated by men was somewhat surprising, but it undoubtedly added a fresh perspective to the production. Although she had little experience with giant monster movies, she was impressed by some parts of *Gamera 3*, the last in the 1990s trilogy. Perhaps unsurprisingly, it was not the film's apocalyptic aspects—especially the mayhem-filled kaiju battle scenes that appealed to the film's movie's core fans—that intrigued her. Quite to the contrary, Tatsui was drawn to the Ayana Hirasaka (played by Maeda Ai). That character, a girl who holds a grudge against Gamera and is haunted by the memory of her parents' unintentional deaths, resonated with some of Tatsui's work in writing family dramas.[8]

Indeed, at that point in her career, Tatsui was a seasoned writer known for several made-for-television movies and a steady stream of multi-episode television dramas. Her work involved serious adult themes often woven into complex, multi-layered stories. The 1995 drama *Heaven's Coin* (*Hoshi no Kinka*), one of her earlier scripts, tells about a woman suffering hearing loss who becomes engaged to a man who then loses his memory. The 2002 script for *Forget Love* (*Ai nante irane yo, natsu*) is about an ex-convict, a blind woman, and a plot to steal an inheritance. *On the Single Bed Tonight* (*Konya hitori no bed de*), from 2005, is a complicated story of marriage, adult love, cheating, and betrayal. The writer cultivated a reputation for dealing with serious themes set in the real world in these and other works.

It was apparent from the start that the new Gamera movie was likely to push back against the series' past trajectory to some extent. But how it would do so was not entirely clear. The old style of kaiju movies, though beloved by enthusiasts, had become too outdated for many contemporary film audiences. Adding to that problem, their stories often seemed mired in cultural presumptions and political concerns of the past. However, then-recent efforts to update the genre by remaking kaiju cinema to appeal to wider audiences had been disappointing. Toho had closed down its Godzilla franchise only two years earlier, and that did not bode well for the genre.

The 1990s Gamera trilogy had performed reasonably well in its time, but a half-decade had passed, and audience tastes continued to evolve. The new millennium seemed to call for something fresher and more original than merely retracing the path of earlier Gamera movies. Accordingly, continuity with the 1990s trilogy was ditched in favor of something wholly new. As Tasaki's vision for the franchise went into production, the question was whether he would be able to deliver something original and engaging without alienating the franchise's fans.

Although the nature of franchise movies means that some elements must remain intact, Tasaki and his collaborators did craft a new angle for the film. One change was in the design for the giant tortoise, a tricky topic since character alterations that veered too much from the core fandom's expectations could trigger angry responses.

Gamera's appearance in the 1990s trilogy was threatening and foreboding. As designed for those movies, the creature gives off an angry, powerful aura. However, the version of the monster in *Gamera the Brave* elicits a nearly opposite feeling. Here, Gamera seems very much the overgrown pet tortoise that the film's story makes it out to be. The creature's shell and body are rounded; its coloration is bright; its eyes are big and inviting. Indeed, the monster's overall look seems consciously designed to reinforce the traditional "friend of children" associations that the 1990s movies mostly abandoned.

The character redesign projected a new and arguably softer image for the creature. It was a sign that Tasaki planned to refocus Gamera's overarching story back to its relationship with children. Tasaki planned to make a movie in which children would again be the focus, which in some ways would bring the franchise back to its roots in the 1960s. Indeed, *Gamera the Brave* seems mainly a story about young people and the whole process of growing up, making it a movie for and about children. However, even if children were to be front-and-center, Tasaki aimed to make a movie that would have something to say to older audiences, too. The final script delivers just that, weaving a narrative about the maturation process into a film that, in other ways, remains faithful to many kaiju film conventions.

Placing children at the center of the story meant casting choices for those roles would be critical. The main human character is a 12-year-old boy named Toru. Filling that role was a similarly aged young actor named Tomioka Ryo. New to the industry, Tomioka had little prior experience. Still, he projected a natural presence on screen and worked diligently with the director and production crew to convincingly bring the character to life. Mai, the other central young character, is portrayed by the Japanese actor Kaho. She was 15 years old and projected an innocent and genuine persona on screen. Although this was the accomplished actor's first film role, she had already appeared in several television dramas.

The primary adult parts went to seasoned actors. Tsuda Kanji, a veteran of numerous productions, including *Kamen Rider Ryuki* (2002), was cast as Toru's father. Mai's father was played by another actor with a long list of credentials, Terajima Susumu. Other roles were given to actors with a similarly wide range of experience. That extended even the actors cast in cameo roles, such as Taguchi Tomorowo, a busy actor who appeared in *Gamera 2* and *Gamera 3* a few years earlier.

The film's story is relatively simple but rich in thematic content. It begins with a flashback to 1973. As a village under attack burns in the background, the original Gamera makes the ultimate sacrifice by self-destructing in a fiery explosion. After this brief prologue, the next 40 minutes follow the story of Toru, a young boy who recently lost his mother and has a strained relationship with his father. Early on, Toru discovers a mysterious egg from which an adorable tortoise hatches. Toru adopts the tiny tortoise as a pet but does not tell his father. Only two other boys and Toru's friend Mai, a slightly older girl with a medical condition, know the secret.

The entire film weaves the tale of the tortoise's amazing growth and acquisition of superpowers with multiple coming-of-age storylines. Toru's pet evolves from a tiny, cute pet to a powerful flying kaiju. Concurrently, Toru works through the grief process and has issues with his father. Mai successfully faces her illness and surgery. Along the way, the film raises themes of friendship, maturation, and dealing with life's challenges squarely.

As the story progresses, it turns out that Toru's pet is none other than Gamera's offspring. Although audiences may have suspected this all along, Mai and Toru only realize this halfway through the film, by which time Toto has gone missing.

All of this sets up the movie's second half when finally, *Gamera the Brave* turns to familiar kaiju movie territory. At this point, an evil new kaiju, Zedus, appears and attacks the city. A much larger Toto appears immediately, too, leading to several giant monster battles. For most of the film's second half, the giant tortoise is still not big or strong enough to defeat its enemy. Meanwhile, with pandemonium all around them, Toru worries about his former pet's fate and argues with his father, who wants the boy to keep his distance.

As the kaiju battles unfold, Mai is recuperating from surgery across town. When she sees the kaiju battling far in the distance, she suddenly realizes that a red stone Toru had given her for good luck is somehow connected to Toto's powers. She becomes determined to bring the rock to Toto, but unfortunately, she is in no condition to do that.

A remarkable sequence follows. Seemingly out of nowhere, a younger girl offers to deliver the stone instead. She runs toward the monster through the crowded city streets. As most of the population runs away from the creature, the little girl runs toward it, dodging the steady tide of fleeing citizens as she races forward.[9] Eventually, she can go no further, and it seems the stone will not reach Toto in time. Just then, however, another child takes the stone for the next leg of its journey.

In the following scenes, the stone is passed from child to child as if they are passing the baton in a relay race. Finally, after being carried by several boys and girls, the stone reaches Toru, who has independently been running to find his once-small pet. Toru's father has caught up with him by this time, and he does not want his son to go any further. Toru is insistent, however, and rushes the stone to Toto. With the stone's energy, Toto quickly gains full power. The now-colossal creature rises and handily vanquishes Zedus. When the dust finally settles, Toru has reconciled with his father and is ready to let Toto go. The mighty kaiju blasts off into the sky, and Toru, who has always addressed his pet as Toto, watches and poignantly whispers, "Goodbye, Gamera." The change in language signals the boy's emotional growth throughout the events depicted on screen.[10]

Although Tasaki ends the film in familiar kaiju-movie terrain, he has not arrived there in the usual way. Indeed, *Gamera the Brave* may seem only tangentially a kaiju film in some ways. The giant tortoise is indeed integral to the narrative, but ultimately, the story is more about growing up and facing life's challenges. Gamera's transition to adulthood and the responsibilities that go along with that parallels and illuminates Toru's similar life journey.

Interestingly, the literal translation of the film's Japanese title is *Little Heroes: Gamera* and not *Gamera the Brave*, the title developed for the overseas market. It is a significant difference. By relegating Gamera to the subtitle, the original version overtly suggests that children are the focus. That contrasts sharply with the title used in the English-speaking world, in which only Gamera is even mentioned. Presumedly, the *Gamera the Brave* title was chosen for marketing reasons in secondary markets, including the United States. It seems safe to conclude that the filmmakers' true intentions were to make an untraditional kaiju movie in which the giant monster would be used to tell a story about the film's human characters and not vice versa. It is a movie about growth and the trials that come with maturing, both for Gamera and the boy with whom the giant creature forms a bond.[11] And although there are kaiju battles, much of the conflict arises not from the kaiju battling on-screen but instead emerges in scenes between the father and young son, who are struggling to cope with the death of the boy's mother a year earlier.

Despite ambitions to relaunch the Gamera franchise with something new, the viewing public met *Gamera the Brave* with lackluster interest. That was largely true even among fans of the series. Some resistance to the new movie was rooted in the apparent abandonment of the edgy and dark tone Kaneko Shusuke had made the centerpiece of his 1990s Gamera trilogy. What *Gamera the Brave* delivered instead was something different— an innocent story with a somewhat cuddly and lovable version of the giant tortoise. It may have seemed like little more than kids' stuff to many fans who had embraced the solemn and sinister 1990s Gamera outings.

Many viewers, especially kaiju fans in the United States, also lamented the relative lack of dramatic giant monster fights in the new movie. Indeed, *Gamera the Brave* places little emphasis on such battles. In large sections of the film—including most of the first 40 minutes— giant monsters are seldom anywhere in sight. For some, that was an almost unforgivable mistake.

That response was somewhat predictable. For many of the genre's enthusiasts, the giant-monster fight scenes are nearly the *raison d'être* for kaiju films in the first place. Many (though certainly not all) fan discussions delve into a detailed analysis of the battle sequences. The scenes sometimes influence how a given kaiju film is judged overall. When the fights in a particular movie are deemed lacking, that alone can significantly weigh down a kaiju film's reputation among its core fandom. That is particularly true of the Japanese kaiju movies, where many fans take for granted that much of a film's run time will be devoted to monsters battling other monsters.

Of course, there are some battle sequences in the film. While a few of those are presented in the usual manner of Japanese kaiju cinema, many of the scenes resemble actual human conflict. Indeed, in a break with tradition, the movie presents the kaiju in scenes that resemble real war scenarios much more than in the highly stylized version in most giant monster movies. And more than that, *Gamera the Brave* sometimes portrays a type of warfare—urban and inflicting much collateral damage— that was prominent in the global war on terrorism.[12] Even the prologue to the film, which shows Gamera self-destructing, could be read as an allusion to a suicide bombing. Some battle scenes recall those in earlier films that are stylized fun, but some also remind viewers that real-world war is not entertainment—far from it.

Overall, *Gamera the Brave* was probably never going to win over those audience members who demanded such a strong focus on kaiju battles. Indeed, the movie's thematic emphases and narrative purposes do not require extensive screen time for kaiju fights. Although Tasaki's film fits within the kaiju universe, he was pushing the boundaries of the genre in ways that may have been beyond what some in the audience were willing to accept.

More than that, some elements openly defy the preferences of hardcore kaiju enthusiasts. A viewer looking for a spectacle in this film would find it only in small amounts and on a limited scale since the film's giant monsters—including its supposed star, Gamera—are also not on-screen very often or for very long. With the monsters frequently off-screen, *Gamera the Brave* ultimately could be regarded as a hybrid kaiju film. As mentioned above, it is just as much or more a human-centered story about family, loss, personal growth, and even war as it is about any of the strange beasts that appear on the screen. Significantly, while the colossal beast saves the day for humanity, that is only because of the help Gamera receives from Toru and the other children. Without the young, there is no salvation.

In Japan, the movie resulted in underwhelming box-office receipts. That year, the top four films in Japan were *Pirates of the Caribbean: Dead Man's Chest* and *The Da Vinci Code,* each of which earned over $70 million in Japanese ticket sales, and two Japanese movies, *Tales of Earthsea* and *Limit of Love: Umizaru,* both of which earned more than $60. Meanwhile, *Gamera the Brave* placed a dismal 90th on the list, bringing in only about $2.6 million.[13] The film was later released in the United States as a home video product with little fanfare.

Arguably one of the most intriguing kaiju movies to appear in a long time, this was not enough to keep the franchise afloat. Although some critics and viewers at the time did have kind words for the film, and some people recognized its unique vision, there was little business reason to continue. So in the end, there was disappointment, and like Toho's Godzilla franchise two years earlier, the Gamera series was sent into hibernation.

# 5

# A Korean Vision
## *The Host* (2006)

A few weeks after *Gamera the Brave* opened to lackluster interest in Tokyo, a different type of giant-monster movie was garnering attention half a world away. The Cannes international film festival season had arrived, and Korean filmmaker Bong Joon-ho's new production, *The Host* (*Gwoemul*, meaning "monster" in Korean), was making waves. When it screened as part of the festival's prestigious Director's Fortnight in May 2006, the crowd realized the rising filmmaker had delivered an engaging, genre-busting giant-monster movie that ventured far beyond the usual fare.

The response to the movie was quick. Within a day of its Cannes debut, *Variety*, Hollywood's widely read industry newspaper, published a glowing review. "On almost every level, there's never quite been a monster movie like *The Host*," wrote Derek Elly.[1] It is "egregiously subverting its own genre while still delivering at a pure genre level," he said. Noting the movie's "straight-faced character humor," he described it as both a "social parable" and a "character-driven, offbeat drama."[2]

Bong was still early in his career and was clearly not a kaiju movie insider. Indeed, there was little in his background that suggested he would be interested in delving into that type of movie. On the contrary, he had established a rising reputation as a director to watch by making different kinds of movies. Notably, he directed *Barking Dogs Never Bite* (2000), a dark, satirical film about a man who preys on dogs, and *Memories of Murder* (2003), a thriller about a serial murderer that earned widespread critical praise.

Given his resume, the new film surprised those who knew him and were familiar with his work. Bong was aware that he was moving into unexpected territory. As he later said, the pivot to a monster movie "shocked and dismayed" his peers.[3] According to reporter Park Chan-kyong, Bong's colleagues feared the choice to direct that kind of film meant he would be "selling out his art-house roots."[4] But whether or not it actually meant that, many people probably thought making a film of that type could be a blemish on a rising career.

In retrospect, such fears proved to be unfounded. Bong had selected the type of subject matter that could have resulted in a routine, perhaps even schlocky film. However, he retained the independent-minded outlook that informed his previous films. "I don't care whether my film should be an art-house movie or a commercial movie," he told the reporter. "I just make a film because I want to see it myself as a viewer and because others don't make it for me to see."[5]

Despite initial appearances, careful viewers of Bong's earlier films may not have been completely surprised by Bong's turn to a monster movie. Ultimately, *The Host* brought some of the same themes and sensibilities he had explored before to the screen. To viewers who know his work, there is little doubt that it is, first and foremost, a Bong Joon-ho film, and his imprint is discernible throughout.

Although some in the international film community may not have been aware of it, Bong's choice of genres was not entirely entering uncharted territory in Korean filmmaking. In some ways, *The Host*, like many movies elsewhere, was partially inspired by the fame of Japanese kaiju movies, most notably the Godzilla series. However, a few filmmakers on the Korean peninsula had ventured into the genre before.

A South Korean production entitled *Bulgasari*, loosely inspired by both *King Kong* and *Godzilla*, appeared in 1962. That movie, now considered lost, had not made a good impression. Indeed, an article in *Chosun Ilbo*, a major Korean newspaper, was disarmingly blunt in its assessment. The publication described it as a dull and outdated children's movie with bad acting.[6]

A slightly more successful Korean giant monster movie, *Great Monster Yongary* (retitled *Yongary, Monster from the Deep* for the U.S. market), was released in 1967. It did some business in South Korean theaters and often appeared on American broadcast television. (Many years later, in 1999, there was a mildly received sequel, *Yonggary*; it was later revised and retitled *Reptillian* for distribution in the English-speaking world.) The year 1967 also saw the release of *Space Monster Wangmagwi*, but it, too, drew meager interest.

For more political than cinematic reasons, a more intriguing and unlikely kaiju movie appeared on the Korean peninsula in 1985. That film was *Pulgasari*, which was produced in communist-controlled North Korea under very unusual circumstances. The film itself seems to have been unremarkable, but there are very few films that could top its bizarre backstory. (Its director, the acclaimed South Korean filmmaker Shin Sang-ok, had been kidnapped and forcibly brought to North Korea, where he was coerced into making several movies—including *Pulgasari*—as a part of that government's filmmaking aspirations.) The film was never officially released in South Korea, partially due to legal restrictions on North Korean content. However, some years later, a home-video format version of the film was released in the United States, where it unexpectedly developed a reputation as a campy cult classic.[7]

By the time of Shin Sang-ok's death in April 2006, he had returned to South Korea, and *Pulgasari* was a distant memory—a coerced production that was only a minor footnote in an otherwise illustrious career. There is no direct connection between Shin Sang-ok's kaiju movie and Bong's *The Host*, but it is worth noting that Shin's is involvement with the film does not seem to have damaged his reputation.

In an interesting coincidence, it was only a month after Shin's passing that Bong Joon-ho, one of the most promising Korean filmmakers of the new generation, brought *The Host* to Cannes for its debut. As audiences soon could see, it possesses some recognizable elements from previous giant monster movies. However, it also pushed the boundaries of the genre's conventions to something innately reflective of Korean culture.

The inspiration for *The Host* came in the form of a "real-life case involving a U.S. military employee who illegally dumped formaldehyde into the South Korean sewer system."[8] That incident was enough to spark Bong's imagination. The result was an idea for a monster movie that was far from ordinary. Indeed, as Bong developed his script, it stretched out to be about much more than a monstrous creature that was created by toxic chemical contamination in the Han River. More than that, *The Host* is also a biting, closely observed, and oddly poignant satire that takes aim at many South Korean institutions.

Working with producer Choi Yong-bae and his Chungeorahm Film company, Bong rounded up financing from multiple sources for the project. About half of the approximately $11 million budget came from Japan, which figured to be an important secondary market for the film.[9] That budget was small compared to major or even mid-budget Hollywood films. The budget for TriStar's *Godzilla*, released six years earlier, was well over $125 million. Peter Jackson's *King Kong*, released in 2005 (financed by Hollywood but made in New Zealand), reportedly clocked in at over $200 million. These numbers towered over the funds available for Bong's giant-monster production.

Yet, the vast sums Hollywood spends can skew perceptions. Compared to the relatively modest amounts typically spent in making movies in East Asia, rather than to American budgets, *The Host's* funding looks far more workable than it may appear. Outside of Hollywood and its immediate orbit, films seldom are budgeted at the enormous amounts often available for American movie productions. For example, although Toho spent just under $20 million to make its lavish would-be spectacle *Godzilla: Final Wars* in 2004, that was the most it had ever spent on a kaiju movie to that point. Most then-recent Japanese giant-monster movies had much smaller budgets, generally more in line with Bong's. Indeed, his financing looks reasonable considering that the Korean market, which presumedly would be the film's primary market, was not large. (Since South Korea's population at the time, around 40 million people, was only about 40 percent of Japan's 125 million, the potential for ticket sales was presumably much lower.)

Bong Joon-ho had one significant advantage as he was planning. His excellent reputation meant that he could attract highly skilled actors. And indeed, he assembled an exceptional cast, each of whom turned in first-rate performances. Several key roles were filled by actors Bong knew well and had cast in his earlier films.

Bong turned to Song Kang-ho to play the main character, Park Gang-du. Song had received stellar notices for his performance in the director's *Memories of Murder* a few years earlier. The two had an excellent working relationship, and indeed, they would join forces again in future projects, such as *Snowpiercer* (2013) and the Oscar-winning *Parasite* (2019). Similarly, Park Gang-du's sister, a major character, is played by another accomplished actor Bong already knew, Bae Doona. Early in her career at the time, Bae appeared in Bong's *Barking Dogs Never Bite* (2000).

Another essential character in the story is Park Gang-du's young daughter. That role went to a Go Ah-sung, who was only 14. She was new to film roles, but her work in *The Host* was well-regarded. Indeed, she won the prestigious Blue Dragon Film Award for it in 2006 and would work with Bong again in *Snowpiercer* a few years later. Other parts were also filled by experienced actors, giving Bong a capable cast to bring his vision to life despite the budgetary constraints.

Another aspect of the film was somewhat trickier to pull off with available funding, namely, the special effects that would be used to render the monster. The "rubber suit" approach, which was still endearing to many fans of Godzilla movies and other Japanese kaiju productions, would hardly be suitable. Although the film was to feature some fantasy and science-fiction elements, Bong was interested in telling a story with parallels to the real world. Therefore, for the movie to work best, the monster needed to look like it would fit into a real-world environment and have as natural an appearance as possible. Bong wanted "a creature that you could actually find somewhere."[10] This concern also dictated that the monster, while frightening and large, should not be portrayed as too colossal.

Bong's attitude was that "the bigger the creature is, the less realistic he becomes."[11]

Given those aims, digital techniques were the best option to produce those effects. That approach would satisfy the filmmaker's expectations and, just as importantly, those of audiences who had come to expect sophisticated visual effects by then. Extensive use of digital special effects is costly and labor-intensive. Perhaps that would not present too much of an issue for a big-budget Hollywood blockbuster. However, it was a challenge considering Bong's budget realities. There would be no way to bypass dealing with this matter for *The Host*. It would be essential to figure out how to add realistic special effects without shipwrecking the budget.

As a first step, Bong worked with Jang Hee-chul, who had previously served as a game designer, to develop the creature's visual appearance. Working back and forth to arrive at a look that would fit the script, hundreds of potential versions of the monster were created and tossed out before reaching the final design.[12] With a detailed vision of what the creature should look like in hand, the next step was finding an effect studio to implement it. Bong looked for a firm with solid experience and a good track record for achieving quality results. To that end, he first contracted with Weta Digital in New Zealand. That was the company co-founded by director Peter Jackson, who frequently used its services in his films, including 2005's *King Kong*.

Weta began work and developed a detailed maquette of the creature. However, hiring Weta to do the rest of the work did not pan out. Eventually, the project was transferred to the United States. There, a Los Angeles firm called Gentle Giant Studios scanned the maquette. The scans were then sent to The Orphanage, a small company in San Francisco, which produced the 125 needed special-effects shots.[13]

Despite the attention to detail about creating the monster and the obvious connections between *The Host* and monster movies generally (and giant-monster movies, specifically), Bong's main concerns were not about the creature. Indeed, this is a monster movie that involves several overlapping storylines. The beast is more a glue holding the different narrative strands together than the film's sole, or even necessarily primary, focus.

The movie opens with a fictionalized reenactment of the "McFarland incident," a real-life event from February 2000 that caused an uproar in South Korea and inspired the film. The scene takes place in a dimly lit morgue of a U.S. Army base in South Korea. An older American mortician orders his assistant to pour hundreds of bottles of contaminated formaldehyde down the drain. When his Korean assistant hesitates to dump the toxin down drains that flow into the Han River, the American, who doesn't seem to care, says, "That's an order."

Twenty-four months later, two men fishing at the river's edge see something odd: a small, mutant amphibian creature. But before they get a good look at it, the creature gets away. An abrupt cut to the next scene pushes the action forward to 2006. On a bridge spanning the Han River, a man in a business suit is about to jump to his death. Despite the pouring rain, he sees something huge in the water below. The man jumps anyway, bringing the film's brief prologue to a close.

When the main body of the film begins, the central characters are introduced. At the center is a man named Park Gang-du. He is a simple, dimwitted man who helps his father run a small snack shed in a park beside the river. Gang-du has a daughter named Park Hyun-seo, a sharp and worldly teenager whose mother is not around. The girl is devoted to her father, grandfather, aunt (a famous archer), and uncle (a college graduate and former student activist).

Before going much further with the Park family's story, Bong defies genre conventions and introduces the monster in broad daylight. This occurs less than twenty minutes into the film, much earlier than is typical. Audiences meet the creature when it abruptly jumps from the Han River on a sunny day when many people are blissfully enjoying the riverside park. The monster, a 40-foot-long, four-legged amphibious creature, generates instant panic when it comes ashore. It chases people gathered along the walkway, apparently intent on attacking as many humans as possible in its path.

As the monster runs amok, the crowd panics. Gang-du and his daughter try to run to safety, but they get separated. The monster snatches the girl, Hun-seo, and takes her to a concrete pit in the city's drainage system. The creature holds her and the other victims as a future food source. However, neither the girl's father nor the relatives of other victims know that some of the people taken are still alive. Believing all the victims have died, authorities hold a mass memorial service where families lament their losses.

Next is a scene of the emotional mass memorial for the monster's victims. That transitions to the focus of the remainder of the film: the Park family's struggles with bureaucratic government officials, most of whom are cold and inept. The officials want to hide the incident from public scrutiny as much as possible, so they create a cover story. They concoct a tale about a virus and then look for ways to make sure any witnesses to the monster's attack do not make waves. Gang-du is forced to undergo unnecessary brain surgery as part of that effort.

Meanwhile, Hyun-seo hides in a corner of the sewer pit that is beyond the monster's reach. Understandably terrified, she manages to place a mobile phone call to her father. Elated to discover his daughter is still alive, Gang-du tries to convince authorities to go to the girl's rescue, but they refuse to believe him. From this point, if Hyun-seo is to be saved, it seems her family will have to do it. To that end, Gang-du escapes from the hospital where he had been taken. With the authorities in pursuit, he embarks on a quest to locate and rescue Hyun-seo, eventually getting help from the rest of the family.

Red tape, bureaucratic incompetence, and government misconduct continually hamper the family's search for Hyun-seo. In the meantime, the monster dumps a boy, who is a few years younger than Hyun-seo, into the sewer. He is quickly befriended by Hyun-seo, who tries to keep him alive. The culmination of the desperate quest to save Hyun-seo is a tragicomedy of errors, which at times is accompanied by circus-like music. In a series of mishaps, many things go wrong, and Gang-du's father ends up dead.

As the film nears the end, however, it looks like things may all work out after all. Gang-du and his siblings locate the girl and devise a plan to kill the monster. However, those efforts are complicated by the government's cover-up scheme, which involves a U.S. military plan to fumigate an area along the Han River with Agent Yellow. Then, just as it seems that the girl and young boy will be rescued, the situation takes a tragic turn. Gang-du kills the monster, but Hyun-seo does not survive.

Later, the scene returns to the snack shed. It is winter, and Gang-du looks warily at the frozen Han River, holding a rifle as though waiting for something foreboding. The scene pivots to Gang-du sharing a meal with the young boy, who lives with Gang-du as his adopted son. In the background, a television news story reveals that the United States and South Korea have successfully covered up the entire incident. The monster is dead, but no one could reasonably conclude that life is any better. The things Bong was satirizing are all left intact at the end of the film.

Despite early critical accolades, some giant-monster movie enthusiasts were tentative about the experience that Boon Joon-ho provided them. The story was obviously about a huge, menacing creature, even if its size was smaller than the skyscraper-tall monsters in some kaiju films. Yet, in many ways, *The Host* was so different from the genre's classic movies that it proved challenging for some viewers. Indeed, the film ventures into thematic territory that is unusual for the genre. Interestingly, although Bong was well aware that the film has a solid connection to the monster movie genre, that is not how he mainly sees it. "If you really want to be picky about it," he told a reporter, "I don't think you can say *The Host* is a monster movie. It's more of a kidnapping movie. The kidnapper just happens to be a creature."[14]

Bong's focus on the plight of the Park family, especially Gong-du, whom Bong has characterized as a "lovable loser,"[15] is critical. Many giant monster movies also contain some emotional human story, of course. Usually, however, such storylines are secondary to the monster-focused action and destruction, not the centerpiece of the whole production. However, while Bong was interested in connecting *The Host* to the giant monster tradition, that was not necessarily his primary concern. Indeed, if a person accepts his characterization of *The Host* as a kidnapping story, it is not hard to see that some version of the film could have been made without any imaginary monster at all.

The director does not keep the audience waiting before he signals the kind of film they can expect to see. Indeed, within the first few minutes, Bong shows that he aims to deliver a story about something more than humans versus a terrible creature. It starts with a fictionalized version of the true story that inspired the film, a scene in which personnel at a U.S. Army base dump toxins in the Han River. Although it may have seemed like pure fiction to international viewers, Korean audiences would have instantly recognized that scenario was based on fact.

In a subsequent scene, Bong shows a well-attired business executive committing suicide by jumping from a bridge that also spans the Han River. That scene, too, may have struck international audiences as generic fiction. Yet, most Korean audiences, especially in 2006, would likely have recognized that it referenced the South Korean economic crisis of the late 1990s and the subsequent response of the International Monetary Fund (IMF).[16] A *Los Angeles Times* headline from 1998 gives a sense of how poorly that response went: "IMF Blunders Through Asia, Leaving Disaster in Its Wake."[17] Indeed, the IMF's plan to put Asia economies on stable footing backfired and "actually worsened"[18] the economies it was designed to help. South Korea was especially hard-hit, triggering more economic woes and rising suicide rates.[19]

With these two brief introductory scenes, Bong lays out backstory elements that have some universal qualities. After all, bad human behavior and despair are familiar across time and cultures. But at the same time, the director also makes far more specific references to real-world events. Those connections may not have resonated with people unfamiliar with the cultural context, but they would have been evident to most of his Korean audience at the time. That same type of parallelism, of universal and culturally specific storytelling, runs throughout the film.

As the central part of the film gets underway, the film's emphasis switches more squarely to the Park family, especially on Park Gang-du and his daughter, Hyun-seo. Although the Parks are portrayed lovingly, they have dysfunctional relationships with one another. That sets them up for difficult times when crises arise.

The family faces many challenges. In some respects, their problems are also recognizable across cultures. But again, despite a universality in certain aspects of the film, other elements refer more specifically to South Korean culture and politics of the era. Indeed, much of the movie explores—and sometimes satirizes—the nation's complicated institutional bureaucracies and the legacies of South Korea's then-recent political past, a period that was at times contentious and violent.

The Park family's struggles shine a spotlight on what Professor Nam Lee identifies as Bong's "central theme": the South Korean government's "incompetence or inadequacy."[20] Bong's focus on the hardships faced by a low-status family's attempts to deal with tragic circumstances provides an effective platform for directing attention to lingering issues that arose during South Korea's long and arduous evolution to a full, functioning democracy.

Indeed, the Republic of Korea faced a tumultuous, uphill battle to achieve that status. The ambiguous cessation of overt hostilities in the Korean War—a conflict that, as of this writing, has not officially ended—was followed by decades of challenges, not the least of which was long periods of military rule and dictatorship. During the Cold War, the United States often looked the other way at the excesses of South Korea's government since the country remained an essential and staunchly anti-communist ally and the site of major U.S. military bases. However, for ordinary Korean people during these years, life was often difficult. Many South Koreans lost faith that their government was on their side.

One result of this frustration was the Gwangju Uprising of 1980, a time in which nearly a million demonstrators challenged the government. In an infamous incident that occurred in May 1987, about 20,000 protestors faced off against armed and highly-trained paratroopers. The exact figures are difficult to ascertain, but the violent confrontation, which Bong references in *The Host*, when he shows Gang-du's brother hurling Molotov cocktails at the monster, led to more than a hundred—and perhaps more than a thousand—deaths. Some reforms followed the Gwangju Uprising, but much still remained unsettled as late as 1987 when the June Democratic Struggle eventually led to the first democratically elected president in many years.

Even as South Korea slowly became more democratic, the disconnect between average citizens and the government bureaucracy lingered. In Nam Lee's view, this is the picture of South Korean society that Bong presents: the persisting "inability of Korean government authorities to protect ordinary citizens."[21]

Most giant-monster movies take the form of a hero-versus-monster saga. Even when the hero is untraditional or unlikely—as, for instance, in the case of the boy Toru in *Gamera the Brave*—the films usually show a character rising to heroism—becoming a hero by virtue of a brave struggle against the monster. In *The Host*, however, that does not fully happen.

That is not to say that heroics are entirely absent. Gang-du and his siblings face the monster in a climactic battle that requires significant bravery. And in a scene reminiscent of many different dragon slayer images, Gang-du finally defeats the creature by thrusting an iron rod down its throat. To that extent, the Park siblings become heroes. What is more, in the film's coda, Bong shows that the struggles against the monster and the government have somehow transformed Gang-du. (Bong subtly telegraphs this visually by showing that Gang-du has abandoned his badly dyed and unkempt hair for a more groomed appearance in the film's coda.) And in narrative terms, the last appearance of Gang-du shows him acting maturely by managing his late father's food shed and taking care of the boy he has evidently adopted. These elements also follow the well-worn "hero's journey" narrative form.

Yet, in some respects, Gang-du's apparent transformation is incomplete. He may be more responsible than before in a traditional sense. However, he is still marginalized, still a victim, and, as evident from the film's closing moments, still very much feeling powerless and alone against the threats he fears are on the horizon. Indeed, the film's last moments suggest that not much has changed. But maybe the point was never to show that Gang-du had become truly heroic in that way. It is enough, perhaps, that he survived despite getting no help from the government. After all, the film hints that official forces could have killed the creature right away if the government felt it was a priority to do so. That they did not do that and instead left the potential problem unsolved illustrates one of the film's key themes.

Commentators often mention a perception that a strand of anti-Americanism runs through *The Host*. Indeed, some aspects of the narrative raise that question. Most obviously, the very first scene, which recalls the real-life McFarland incident, portrays an American official's uncaring and dismissive attitude toward Koreans. And later in the story, the U.S. officials orchestrate a cover-up and come up with a plan to release a deadly toxin, "Agent Yellow" (a name clearly chosen to evoke memories of the chemical Agent Orange, which the U.S. used extensively in the Vietnam War), along the Han River even though it will harm Koreans living in the area.

Although Americans were hardly Bong's intended core audience, he was aware that these aspects of the movie could prove problematic when and if *The Host* was picked up for U.S. distribution. In an interview, Bong recalled that one Korean critic said this was "Korea's first legitimate anti–American film."[22] Yet, he maintained that anti–Americanism is not the movie's "focus" and "if you compare *The Host* to a Michael Moore film, its social commentary is very soft."[23]

For those wishing to find them, these allusions to American hubris and its sometimes poor, even immoral judgment are not difficult to discern. Yet, Bong's belief that these are not the film's center is well taken. Indeed, most of the negative attention is focused not on the United States but on the South Korean government. On the notion that *The Host* is too cynical in this respect, he notes that "Korean audiences don't receive it cynically or serious, but as comedy."[24] Partly a legacy of the country's long march to functional democracy, corruption and ineptness are, for better or worse, recognized by Koreans as part of the society, in other words.

Still, as much as Bong devotes considerable attention to socio-political satire and the lovable but essentially powerless Park family, *The Host* remains securely aligned with giant monster movies. Numerous aspects of it are reminiscent of elements found in popular kaiju movies. But as reviewer Jim Emerson notes, it also conjures up mid-20th-century "creature features," such as *Them!* (1954) and *Tarantula!* (1955).[25]

It turned out that the positive advance word the film earned at the Cannes Film Festival was indeed a harbinger of what would come. *The Host* was a huge commercial and critical success, especially in Korea, where it was the highest-grossing Korean movie in history at the time.[26] Ultimately, the film brought in about $89 million at the box office, a number that is eight times its production costs.[27] In the United States, Magnolia Pictures picked it up for distribution. Although it only ever played in about 120 theaters in the U.S., it received serious attention. That was enough for it to find a fan base when it moved to home video and other outlets. It gained further attention when Bong Joon-ho's *Parasite* (2019) won the Academy Award for Best Picture more than a decade later. American audiences began to look seriously at his impressive output.

If giant-monster movies in the new millennium needed to find relevance and a wider audience, then *The Host* provided evidence that this not only *could* be done; it *had* been done. Yet, it was a unique movie in the *auteur* tradition, and as such, it was inexorably tied to Bong Joon-ho's personal vision. Whether anyone else could come up with such an inventive giant-monster picture—one that would be taken seriously as a film—remained an unanswered question.

# 6

# A Return to Horror
## *The Mist* (2007)

*The Mist* (2007), based on a Stephen King novella, is far from a conventional kaiju movie, and some people might categorize it as outright horror instead. Yet, it features numerous terrifying creatures—including one of immense size—and is worth considering for what it does and does not say about the definition and status of giant monster films in the early 2000s.

Director Frank Darabont undoubtedly had several goals in mind when he embarked on this project. One of the most obvious is the film's use of allegory for overt social and political commentary. Indeed, although *The Mist* differs significantly in tone from Bong Joon-ho's *The Host*, released just a year earlier, Darabont's movie is just as much a work of commentary. However, unlike Bong, who adopted a largely satirical angle for his movie, Darabont chose an almost melodramatic approach. It offers a disturbing portrait of the post–9/11 world as experienced by Americans in the mid-2000s.

That may seem surprising considering that *The Mist* is based on a story by Stephen King that was first published in 1980, two decades before 9/11 and a quarter-century before the premiere of Darabont's movie version. Yet, many horror writers—King included—incorporate relevant social and political themes in their work. That is certainly the case in this King novella, which contains themes of religious fanaticism and the sometimes razor-thin line separating civil behavior and the dangers of a mob mentality.

In some ways, such thematic material could apply to almost any age. However, Darabont's version of the story, arriving in theaters during the heated political environment of the mid-2000s, lends itself to interpretations specific to that context. Indeed, when the film debuted in the post-9/11 climate that featured brutal and agonizing American-led wars in Iraq and Afghanistan, that context invited a reading of the production informed by that fraught environment.

## 6. A Return to Horror

For several years after the terrorist attacks of September 11, 2001, American culture continued to exhibit heightened anxiety, xenophobia, and bitter disagreement about religion in the modern world. At the height of what George W. Bush dubbed the "War on Terror," Americans were on alert, scanning their everyday lives for signs of terrorists, whom they regarded as the true monsters of the early 21st century. Like the fictional monsters in *The Mist*, Americans feared that terrorists would come out of nowhere and wreak death and destruction before receding into a murky background. One unfortunate byproduct of this came in the form of ugly incidents and extreme behaviors that most Americans, in other circumstances, would condemn. Given these parallels between fiction and fact, it would have been unrealistic not to expect that at least some audiences would see *The Mist* as a nightmarish allegory for that era, regardless of intentions.

Darabont had been interested in possibly adapting King's story well before the 9/11 era. But whether by design or coincidence, the new cultural climate was apt for finally making a movie version of it. The era's worries about terrorism provided a context to see the film as a specific reference to that time, though the underlying themes had much broader application than that. At the time, many people knew Darabont from his much-admired directing work on two previous movies also based on Stephen King stories. *The Shawshank Redemption*, released in theaters in 1994, had grown into a popular favorite, especially after many showings on cable television. Darabont's film version of *The Green Mile*, released several years later in 1999, also earned critical praise and a strong following. Based on these two films alone, Darabont possessed a strong reputation as a serious filmmaker. Therefore, his decision to make a horror-monster movie may have seemed like a significant change to some.

But appearances can be deceiving. Before Darabont rose to fame as a director, he was a very successful screenwriter. His interest in horror—and, by extension, monsters—as movie subjects was evident in several early projects. In just a few years, during the late 1980s, for example, he wrote the scripts for *Nightmare on Elm Street 3* (1987), *The Blob* (1988), and *The Fly II* (1989).

Beyond that, Darabont had flirted with the idea of acquiring the rights to *The Mist* shortly after he first read the story in the 1980s.[1] Although he eventually settled on optioning *The Shawshank Redemption* for his directorial debut instead, Darabont never lost interest in *The Mist*. He was still considering it when he made a second Stephen King film, *The Green Mile*, a few years later and another movie, not based on anything written by Stephen King, called *The Majestic* (2004).

Soon after, Darabont and King finally worked out a deal for *The Mist*.

The immediate next steps, however, were not yet settled. Darabont worked under the auspices of his Darkwoods Productions company. With a successful track record as a scriptwriter and director, he felt well-equipped to adapt and direct the story.

There was one potential complication. From the beginning, Darabont believed that King's story's waffly, ambiguous ending would need to change for a successful film adaptation. That much is not unusual since published fiction is often modified during the transition from print to the screen. In this case, however, the change was shocking. Indeed, as he worked up the script for *The Mist*, Darabont arrived at a far darker and more depressing ending than in the original story. King was evidently fine with that decision and later praised Darabont's downbeat conclusion. But selling that kind of an ending to the people who might finance the production was another matter. What Darabont envisioned would be a significant departure from the usual expectations of a Hollywood film.

Darabont received an offer to fund the movie at the $30 million level from a "big producer," according to some sources. However, the potential deal was contingent on Darabont's willingness to write a different, presumably less bleak ending.[2] That condition was a deal-breaker for Darabont. By this time, he was committed to his version of the story and, therefore, declined the offer. Not long after, producer Bob Weinstein of Dimension Films took an interest in the project. Dimension offered to finance the film at $17 million. That amount was considerably lower than the amount Darabont had previously turned down. However, since Weinstein voiced no objections to the director's potentially controversial ending, which was Darabont's top priority, he accepted the proposal. Now, all that remained was to complete the film on a tighter-than-ideal budget.[3]

Around this time, Darabont directed an episode of the hit FX series, *The Shield*. The popular show was known for its free-style cinematography that quickly and efficiently yielded fascinating results using handheld camera techniques. As Darabont worked on the episode and saw these techniques first-hand, he realized he could use the same approach to produce a dynamic visual sense in his upcoming movie.[4] Given the approach's potential cost savings, it would be one way that the director could stave off budget problems.

Holding down costs for casting decisions was another way to keep the budget under control. Fortunately, Darabont's previous works provided an excellent resume, and he was able to attract outstanding actors. The cast may not have included big-name A-listers—the type of actors who regularly commanded salaries far beyond what *The Mist's* $17 million budget would allow—but each of the performers was a capable, seasoned professional. Indeed, the cast turned in excellent and credible performances all around. It is doubtful that adding one or more marquee actors to the roster of actors would have improved it, except possibly for marketing purposes.

Actor Thomas Jane was cast as David Drayton, the movie's main character. He may not have been a household name, but he had previously appeared in numerous television and film productions. Among his prominent roles was a starring part in Lawrence Kasdan's *Dreamcatcher* (2003), another movie based on a Stephen King story. In that film, Jane starred alongside Morgan Freeman and Jason Lee. For another critical role, Drayton's prickly neighbor Brent Norton, Darabont chose Andre Braugher. An actor with decades of experience, Braugher was highly regarded for his portrayal of detective Frank Pembleton in the acclaimed NBC series, *Homicide: Life on the Streets* (1993–1999) at the time, and he had recently appeared in a 2004 cable television adaptation of King's story, *Salem's Lot*.

Laurie Holden was selected to play the schoolteacher character Amanda Dunfrey, another major part. She was known for many television productions (including a ten-episode run in *The X-Files*) and numerous movies. In recent years, she had appeared in Darabont's *The Majestic* (2001) and the horror film, *Silent Hill* (2006), directed by Christophe Gans. Meanwhile, Nathan Gamble, who was only eight years old then, was cast as David Drayton's son. Marcia Gay Harden, who had won an Academy Award in the Best Supporting Actress category for her work in *Pollock* (2000), was chosen to play Mrs. Carmody, the film's central religious fanatic. The versatile British actor Toby Jones (who adopted a convincing American accent for his work in *The Mist*) is Ollie, a supermarket assistant manager. Other seasoned actors (including William Sadler and Jeffrey DeMunn, who had worked with Darabont before) rounded out the cast.

Special effects, which can have significant budget implications, are always a concern for movies featuring monsters. However, specific story elements in *The Mist* made it possible to minimize budget implications. Much of the narrative involves situations that are quite literally cloaked in fog, obscuring what is happening on screen. Other parts of the story, focused on the interactions of the human characters, require few special effects resources.

Still, this is a film with monsters. Many are relatively small, but at least one is truly immense. Given the film's dark overall tone and horror dimensions, Darabont had to ensure that on the relatively few occasions when monsters would appear on screen, audiences would perceive them as seamlessly and believably fitting into the story. Anything less had to potential to ruin the experience. It is the same problem faced by any monster film with a foreboding tone: poorly executed monster design and effects could inadvertently transform what is supposed to be a work of horror into camp.

Darabont successfully negotiated the twin concerns of budget and effectiveness on this front. He consulted with experienced professionals to develop needed visual designs and special effects, the latter of which would be a mix of computer-generated effects and traditional techniques, such as animatronics.[5] Among crucial contributors was Bernie Wrightson, an accomplished artist with many credits as a horror illustrator and comic book artist. Another was Greg Nicotero, an expert in special effects and make-up whose numerous credits included the movies *Day of the Dead* (1985), *Predator* (1987), *Hulk* (2003), and Darabont's *Green Mile*. Production of many effects was left to Café FX, then a busy special effects studio that had contributed to many major films.

The film unfolds much in the manner of a traditional horror movie. It begins by establishing that the action takes place in a small Maine community populated by various colorful and somewhat stereotyped characters.

An introductory scene by a picturesque lake introduces artist David Drayton (played by Thomas Jane), his son, Billy, and their neighbor, Brent Norton (Andre Braugher), a lawyer from the city. After a storm rips through the area overnight, leaving much damage and a widespread power outage, David, Billy, and Brent go into town for supplies. The setting shifts to the local supermarket, where many residents have gathered. Among them are Amanda (Laurie Holden), a schoolteacher, Mrs. Carmody (Marcia Gay Harden), a fanatic, Ollie (Toby Jones), the supermarket manager, several soldiers on leave, and a group of locals.

At first, the situation does not look out of the ordinary, but then military police arrive and tell the soldiers that all leaves are canceled and that they should return to base. Before they can do so, the town's alarm siren blares, and an injured man runs to the store shouting, "Something in the mist took John Lee!" Almost immediately, dense fog rolls in and envelops the store and there is a loud rumble. At first, no one knows what is happening. It seems there is either a natural disaster or the store is under attack.

The people in the crowd quickly turn on each other. Several schools of thought emerge. Brent and his group believe the situation is frightening but explainable as a natural disaster. David thinks there are monstrous, perhaps unearthly forces at work, a belief seemingly supported by vague rumors that the local army base has been working on an ominous, top-secret operation called Project Arrowhead. Others rally around Mrs. Carmody, who believes something supernatural is happening and launches into a long, religiously infused diatribe that acts as background narration of what follows. A few moments later, a store employee briefly opens the door in the back of the stockroom. Suddenly, a huge tentacle grabs the young man and kills him. Most people are in the front of the store and have no idea what just happened, but the few witnesses now realize they are dealing with something terrible.

In the following scenes, many characters make disastrously bad judgments as terrifying creatures break through the plate glass window in the front of the store. This sets off panic and results in some horrific injuries. More questionable judgments and additional deaths follow. Mrs. Carmody rants about God's judgment and the need for a human sacrifice, and the crowd turns on one of the soldiers as a scapegoat, stabbing him before throwing him outside for the waiting monsters. As the supermarket crowd turns into an irrational mob, David's small group decides to attempt an escape. A fight breaks out, however, and only David, Billy, Amanda, and a retired couple make it to the car. From here forward, David and his passengers begin a fearful journey through the mist.

As the thick fog clears in the film's last few minutes, the story dramatically departs from Hollywood movie conventions (and King's original story). An elegiac mood is enhanced by the car's slow, greyed-out journey through the mist. As the film takes an other-worldly tone, the musical soundtrack takes a prominent role. Here, Darabont uses a song called "Host of Seraphim," which had been recorded several years earlier for a 1988 album by the Australian band Dead Can Dance. The song, featuring a lone female voice, is a haunting, slow-moving abstract piece, evoking the distant music of medieval Europe and Middle Eastern laments. The composition's pervasive somberness cues viewers that a traditional happy ending may not be around the corner. The music continues as the car continues through the mist, with one slow shot fading into another. At one point during the journey, the ground begins to shake, and David stops the vehicle. Then, the camera pulls back to reveal a colossal, six-legged monster, hundreds of feet tall, lumbering by without even noticing the car. When David and the others see the immensity of the monster, their remaining optimism evaporates. The car continues for a few moments before the fuel runs out. Only then does the music eventually fade out for a moment.

As the adults listen to ominous sounds in the distance, they make a fateful decision as the boy continues to sleep. With all hope lost, they decide to end their lives. David, the nominal leader, is chosen to shoot the others, his sleeping son included. Although he originally intends to take his own life, too, David learns that with only four bullets and five people, he will need to "figure something out" to end his own life. Billy slowly awakens and realizes something horrible is about to happen.

Cut to an exterior view of the car, which is barely visible in the fog. There is silence and then four gunshots. David screams in horror and steps out of the vehicle, presumably waiting for the monsters to take him. But then a rumble in the mist signals the approach of something unexpected. The ethereal music restarts as U.S. Army tanks and foot soldiers emerge from the fog in slow motion. David watches as truckloads of survivors pass by, escorted by soldiers wielding flamethrowers, a long line of advancing military forces, and helicopters overhead. David drops to his knees and cries out, "They're dead. For what?"

In the final shot, an aerial camera shows a long line of military personnel approaching against clear skies, apparently completing a mop-up operation signaling the monsters' defeat. This grim and gut-wrenching ending is a significant departure from King's novella, and it sets the film apart from almost every other monster movie. The novella stops without telling readers whether the people in the car lived or died. There is no scene in which the car's passengers decide to take their lives, and there is no last-minute arrival of the military to tie things up. Instead, King allows his readers to imagine the fate of the remaining characters for themselves, though he does at least hint at the possibility that they all survived the ordeal. Indeed, the final word in his story is "hope."

The movie version of *The Mist* is rich in allegory related to the post–9/11 world and the wars in Iraq and Afghanistan. But more than that, it casts a critical eye on the entirety of the post–9/11 American mindset. As an allegory for where Americans stood at what was arguably the height of the War on Terror, *The Mist* is a standout film that has few rivals in its presentation of the uncomfortable circumstances in the real world. It embodies an underlying fear that things might not come to a happy ending. That outlook was (and is) very troubling for most Americans. For generations, a mainstay of many U.S. films had been that American know-how, perseverance, and heroism would be enough to save almost every kind of day. However, Darabont's film dispenses with all that.

For the most part, even the nation's unsettling and unceremonious experience with its failed war in Vietnam did little to dampen the triumphalism that held sway in American filmdom. For decades, Hollywood continued to embrace the raw power of its almost always white, almost always male heroes. So, even when popular film such as *Rambo: First Blood, Part II* (1985) did acknowledge U.S. failures, the super-heroics of an alpha male were enough to set things straight. Few movies, especially those aimed at broad audiences, dared—or perhaps, bothered—to imagine any other possibility. So, most films continued to traffic in male fantasies. Cinematic heroes might experience some loss or even make enormous sacrifices, but their efforts are seldom depicted as being in vain.

Such was indeed not the case in *The Mist*. David Drayton, who in many other respects has much in common with traditional film heroes, utterly fails to save anyone—not even his son. On the contrary, his decision-making is flawed, and his ability to grasp the big picture of the townspeople's predicament is no better than anyone else's. The latter point is painfully evident when a woman who insisted on going home to her children early in the film—despite strong opposition from David and others, who thought she surely would die—passes by in a truckload of survivors in the film's final moments. The scene drives home the point that David's attempted heroism had been futile.

David is a rare example of a failed would-be cinematic hero. As noted by scholar Terence McSweeney, this is a film in which there is no "return to patriarchal normalcy."[6] Upending Hollywood conventions in which some heroes make the ultimate sacrifice to save others, David ends up surviving while the people closest to him die by his hand. *The Mist's* presumed hero is thus transformed into a tragic failure. He is well-intentioned but spectacularly unable to achieve a favorable outcome. Indeed, David's defeat is complete; he is denied even a pyrrhic victory. It is a seldom-seen development in the annals of cinematic American heroism.

Some writers have suggested other interpretations. Professor Aviva Briefel, for example, agrees that the film can be seen as a broad critique of the United States in the height of the War on Terror years and notes its reputation as "America's definitive post–9/11 movie."[7] However, she is also mindful of the film's focus on the "coercive effects of American consumerism."[8] Specifically, Briefel considers the film in relation to George W. Bush's notion that one of the best responses to the September 2001 terror attacks would be for Americans to keep consumerism from being interrupted.

Soon after the 9/11 attacks, Bush said Americans should continue participating in the economy as part of an appropriate national response. "Take your families and enjoy life, the way we want it to be enjoyed," he said, even suggesting they should take a trip to Disney World.[9] He was more explicit in 2006 when the nation was fighting twin wars in Afghanistan and Iraq and on the verge of a recession. "As we work with Congress in the coming year to chart a new course in Iraq and strengthen our military to meet the challenges of the 21st century," he said, "we must also work together to achieve important goals for the American people here at home." As part of his agenda to keep the "economy growing" in that precarious era, he suggested, "I encourage you all to go shopping more."[10]

As Briefel notes, the characters in *The Mist* enact a shopping-as-patriotic heroism philosophy when they flock to the local supermarket immediately after the initial storm. Of course, after they have done so, the dire turn of events contradicts that notion. In an apparent inversion of the Bush administration's advice soon after the September 11 attacks, the characters seem not better but worse off because they headed straight to the market that day.[11]

Although political interpretations of this sort make some sense, it is also possible to look at *The Mist* in a much simpler, less context-dependent way. Indeed, apart from its apparent commentary on the cultural mood of the mid-2000s, it is a well-crafted horror movie with a giant monster angle that functions on a general psychological level, even if one chooses to disregard its symbolic dimensions.

*The Mist* is far from a typical giant monster film even though it features colossal, menacing creatures. Like King's novella, Darabont's movie features many monsters of all different sizes and shapes, at least one of which is immense. In the novella, David Drayton, who narrates the story, is often vague about the creatures. Still, he sometimes speaks of a monster "so big that it might have made a blue whale look the size of a trout"[12] "—in other words, something so big that it defied the imagination."

Yet, the monsters in the film are mainly off-screen. That fits with Darabont's goal of making a film that would focus on how a terrifying threat would affect human interactions more than the nature of the threat itself. As with other, more overt giant-monster films, the narrative of *The Mist* requires some sort of existential danger, but that menace arguably could have been something other than monsters, giant or otherwise.

That said, the choice of a colossal, looming monster provides an effective way to introduce the kinds of intense, fearful human responses that interest Darabont. There is no need, for story purposes, to elaborate on the creatures' origins. (The film vaguely implies that the monsters came to Earth because military scientists inadvertently opened a portal to another dimension.) In fact, there is no need to know much about the creatures at all. As long as they are powerful and present a clear and present danger, that is enough to drive the movie's central conflict, in which the human characters are squared off against each other.

In several significant ways, *the Mist* challenges major conventions of giant monster movies. However, it slides into the familiar in at least one important way, especially in the final moments. Although David Drayton's story is one of failed heroism, the film suggests this was an individual shortcoming, not an institutional one. Indeed, for a movie that turns many expected narrative points upside down, it concludes its story in a tried-and-true fashion by explicitly showing that the U.S. military would have been capable of defeating the monsters, after all. Many things may have gone wrong before this last-minute development, but after the ordeal, the U.S. Army, like the stereotypical U.S. Cavalry in Western movies, arrives to save the day. After the tragic, very un–Hollywood deaths of Billy, Amanda, and the two other passengers in the car, Darabont tags on a completely Hollywood ending that is more than slightly reminiscent of the narrative twists in Rod Serling's *Twilight Zone* television series nearly a half-century earlier.

In the end, the distinctive ending is perhaps the film's most original and controversial feature. The downbeat conclusion to the 126-minute viewing experience did little to attract audiences. Add to that was the puzzling decision to release a film with such a tragic ending for the long Thanksgiving Day weekend when audiences often looked to crowd-pleasing films.

Movie critic Roger Ebert voiced one common perspective about the film, calling it a largely predictable story that relies on conventions of "There Is Something Out There" horror movies.[13] In other words, *The Mist* depends on a "formula apparently able to generate any number of horror movies." So, even though Ebert admired Darabont's previous adaptation of works by Stephen King, he said, "I think he picked the wrong story this time."[14] *Variety's* review was only slightly better. Critic Justin Chang was skeptical of Darabont's attempt to inject the film with "dramatic significance."[15] He described the film as a "screw-loose doomsday thriller [that] works better as a gross-out B-movie" and is hampered by inconsistent tone.

Taking a long view, the film performed reasonably well at the box office, eventually bringing over $25 million in the U.S. and nearly $32 million in the international market.[16] In addition, sources estimate *The Mist* did $31 million in home video sales,[17] suggesting it was likely profitable even considering Hollywood's often arcane accounting practices. Ultimately, however, the bleak though original ending probably dampened the film's potential viewership. Darabont's daring conclusion likely veered too far from audience expectations and comfort levels to achieve blockbuster success. Darabont surely realized he was not making a movie for everyone, but to his credit, he stayed true to his vision for what a film version of *The Mist* should be.

Horror movie fans might find that *The Mist* has much they would appreciate, but the film appears to have had little impact among traditional fans of giant monster movies. Many people may regard the film more as a Stephen King horror film than a monster movie, let alone something in the kaiju genre. Thus, while massive, menacing creatures are integral to the narrative, some may see the film as only tangentially a kaiju film. Yet, in terms of conception, narrative purpose, and visual design, the towering colossus striding over David Dayton's vehicle in the film's final section is not much different from traditional kaiju behavior. *The Mist* may not seem like a giant monster movie at first glance, probably because it seems more focused on other things and because the Stephen King connection instantly categorizes it in the marketplace. Yet, despite this perception, it *is* a giant monster movie. Indeed, a version of the same story could have been made with Godzilla or one of Toho Studio's other kaiju characters. After all, huge, a storyline in which terrifying beasts mysteriously arrive on the scene to inflict death and destruction for no apparent reason is a well-worn feature of the genre.

Still, *The Mist* is an outlier among giant monster movies in some respects. It is not the type of film that immediately comes to mind when that category of film is mentioned. Perhaps the monsters are too much in the background for that. And for many classic kaiju enthusiasts, some popular elements in the genre may seem to be missing altogether. For example, there are no dramatic monster battles. The monsters seem remote and very vague. The human story overwhelms any chance of the monsters taking center stage for more than an isolated moment here and there. Perhaps more importantly, *The Mist* is infused with a negative tone from start to finish, something that is atypical in the kaiju movie genre. This is a sober, uncompromising movie, with little room for hope, happy endings, or optimism.

Yet, regardless of how it was or is perceived, *The Mist* convincingly demonstrated that movies featuring giant creatures could still make powerful cinematic statements. It showed that it was still very possible to use elements from the genre to make something viewers had seldom seen before.

# 7

# Reflecting an Era
## *Cloverfield* (2008)

A new and frightening giant monster causes destruction and despair throughout New York City in director Matt Reeves' *Cloverfield*. The 2008 U.S. film, produced by J.J. Abrams and written by Abrams' frequent collaborator Drew Goddard, combines aspects familiar in Japanese kaiju movies with tropes from American B-movie horror features. It also evokes the 9/11 attack on New York City and the confusing and chaotic aftermath.

In some respects, *Cloverfield* covers terrain similar to what *The Mist* had explored a year earlier. Each can be regarded as a classic horror story. Both movies are as concerned with human drama as they are with giant monsters. And to some extent, each uses colossal creatures to evoke the traumatic psychological aftermath of the 9/11 attacks, relying on symbolism—blatant as it is—that acknowledges the ongoing War on Terror in the real world.

Indeed, when *Cloverfield* debuted, the United States was still not finished mentally processing the 2001 terror attacks, even as it was also immersed in global conflict. By then, the great wave of patriotism and national unity that swept over the nation immediately after 9/11 had receded. The wars in Iraq and Afghanistan had become controversial, and the Pentagon found itself in the uncomfortable position of trying to manage two burdensome conflicts. Meanwhile, young Americans were less inclined to sign up for military service that might involve being shipped halfway across the world to fight Islamist extremists. In 2005, the Army failed to meet its enlistment target for the first time since 9/11.[1]

The wars and the methods used to prosecute them had become controversial. For example, reports of abuses at a military prison in Abu Ghraib, Iraq, surfaced as early as 2003. Initially, the story attracted little interest. However, that changed by the spring of 2004 when CBS News and other major outlets circulated shocking photographs documenting torture and human rights abuses at the hands of the CIA and U.S. military personnel. The revelation led to a public uproar and increased questions about both the morality and effectiveness of the U.S. military campaigns that were launched as part of the George W. Bush administration's War on Terror.

Although American voters were not upset enough to deny Bush a second term in the presidential election that year, enthusiasm for the wars appeared to be waning. In some ways, Americans were still reeling from the events of 9/11. Even five years after the terror attacks, the public had yet to come to terms fully with those traumatizing events.

Scholar Thomas Riegler notes that after the 2001 attacks, the U.S. film industry largely "shunned" terrorism as an overt topic and instead turned to "fantastical escapism, science fiction, and family entertainment."[2] That observation is reflected in the top-grossing movies in the United States in those years. In 2002, for example, the most popular films in American theaters included *Spider-Man, Star Wars: Episode II—Attack of the Clones, Harry Potter and the Chamber of Secrets, Signs,* and *My Big Fat Greek Wedding.* Public preference for escapism was not much different in 2003 when the top five films were *Finding Nemo, Pirates of the Caribbean: The Curse of the Black Pearl, The Matrix Reloaded, The Lord of the Rings: The Return of the King,* and *Bruce Almighty.* The situation was mostly unchanged in 2004 when the five-five grossing movies in America were *Shrek 2, Spider-Man 2, The Passion of the Christ, Harry Potter and the Prisoner of Azkaban,* and *The Incredibles*—all of which avoided the 9/11 attacks and the War on Terror.

That said, movies involving the new era of terrorism occasionally surfaced as time passed. Often, however, the subject received indirect treatment, but a few movies adopted a more straightforward approach. One example is Paul Greengrass' 2003 docudrama *United 93*, often considered the first widely released feature film about the terror attacks. Produced on a tight budget of $17 million and featuring a professional, though not widely known, cast, it recreated the story of how passengers on the doomed flight overcame terrorists and thwarted an additional 9/11 attack. Many critics praised the film, and the reaction was mostly positive.

Under a distribution deal with Universal Pictures, *United 93* was widely available for public consumption. Yet, though its box-office numbers more than quadrupled production expenses, the total gross from ticket sales was relatively modest, at a reported figure of only about $76 million. Was it successful? On many measures, the answer would be yes. But the lukewarm ticket sales suggest that audiences may still have been shying away from the subject, which was a raw memory amid the increasingly troublesome wars in Iraq and Afghanistan.

Among other movies to address the topic in those years was Oliver Stone's *World Trade Center*, released in 2006. By that time, Stone—the creator of such movies as *Platoon* (1986), *JFK* (1991), *Natural Born Killers* (1994), and many others—was nearly a household name. Enormously famous and known for controversial takes on hot topics, his involvement almost ensured *World Trade Center* would not lack extensive media attention. Stone's cast was headlined by fan favorites Nicolas Cage, Michael Peña, and Maggie Gyllenhaal, and the film had a respectable $65 million production budget. With Paramount widely distributing the movie, everything seemed in place for a successful run in U.S. theaters. Indeed, the box-office totals were generally good, totaling over $160 million. However, the bulk of that income came from the foreign market. More than $90 million was generated outside North America, which may have indicated that many Americans remained reluctant to spend time in theaters watching a full-length movie on such a raw topic.

On the face of it, films explicitly about 9/11 and the War on Terror may appear to have little to do with the giant-monster genre. However, whereas few U.S. films dealt with that topic directly, the makers of U.S. giant monster movies sometimes eagerly dove into that subject matter without trepidation. Their films may have been fantastical, but the directors included many real-world references to 9/11 and the war on terror. So, while *Cloverfield* may not have been a realistic depiction of the real-world situation, neither was it a refuge from the world then. In that respect, *Cloverfield* cannot entirely be described as an exercise in escapism. Instead, like other kaiju films to one degree or another, it is a work that processes the fraught political and psychological conditions of the era metaphorically.

Although *Cloverfield* can legitimately be placed in the pantheon of productions that somehow addressed the post–9/11 world, its backstory is somewhat atypical for a Hollywood movie. In the early 2000s, producer J.J. Abrams had already experienced a string of successes, especially with television series such as *Felicity* (1998–2002), *Alias* (2001–2006), and *Lost* (2004–2010). Also among his credits was the 2006 spy-action thriller *Mission: Impossible III*, the Tom Cruise global blockbuster that generated $400 million at the box office. Abrams' stature had quickly risen in the industry, and though he was busy making television series, he had many options when choosing additional new projects.

Interestingly, Abrams had been a fan of monster movies from a young age. He was born in 1966, 12 years after *Gojira's* 1954 premiere in Japan, and thus grew up in an era when such films regularly appeared on U.S. television. His early affection for some of those movies remained a positive memory for him into adulthood. Indeed, writer Theresa Shea quotes Abrams saying that his intention behind making *Cloverfield* was "to give people the sort of thrill I had as a kid watching monster movies."[3]

The specific impetus for *Cloverfield* came while Abrams was in Japan for *Mission: Impossible III*'s opening in that market in 2006. Abrams' young son had come along for the trip, and while in Tokyo, Abrams and the boy visited a toy shop. While there, Abrams noticed his son's avid interest in the many Godzilla-related items on display. As the director later explained: "We saw all these Godzilla toys, and I thought, we need our own American monster, and not like King Kong. I love King Kong. King Kong is adorable. And Godzilla is a charming monster. We love Godzilla. But I wanted something that was just insane and intense."[4]

Based on that encounter, Abrams soon decided to pursue a kaiju-oriented project and to serve as its producer. That left open the question of who would direct such a film. However, one possibility seemed obvious. Abrams' longtime friend, Matt Reeves, was an easy choice for that position. The two men met as adolescents and had remained close over the years. Reeves had already directed several films on his own when he started working with Abrams on the hit television series *Felicity*, which he co-created with Abrams in the late 1990s. Given the established friendship and a steady working relationship, Reeves seemed like a natural fit for the new giant-monster movie project.

Given that the film would have a modest budget, it was imperative to keep expenses under control. Rather than choosing big-name actors who would come with hefty price tags, it seemed more reasonable to look for actors with solid abilities but without expensive resumes. The casting process was shrouded in quasi-secrecy. Indeed, the potential cast members did not know anything specific about the project. "None of the cast got a script or had any idea of what kind of film they were auditioning for," Reeves later said.[5] But this was not a typical production, and that approach worked well, yielding a cast of reliable, if somewhat lesser-known, actors.

Eventually, Michael Stahl-David was given the role of Rob Hawkins. He had experience as a stage actor and had recently been in a 2007 episode of the popular television series *Law & Order: Criminal Intent*. Similarly, Odette Annabel (cast as Beth), Mike Vogel (as Jason), Lizzy Caplan (as Beth), and Jessica Lucas (as Lily) also had acting experience, though none had yet to have a breakout role at the time. Meanwhile, T.J. Miller, cast as Hud, had a somewhat different background, mainly having done stand-up comedy. Overall, the team had assembled a group of actors who seemed up to the task before them.

Since the movie's reason for being was a colossal, destructive monster, the creature's design would be crucial. Although inspired by the likes of Godzilla, a knock-off of Toho's classic kaiju was out of the question, as was a cheap, generic stand-in. To bring specificity to Abrams' goal of developing a fresh, original monster design, the team turned to concept artist Neville Page, who defined the creature's pale, sinewy, quasi-lizard look. Tippett Studio, an experienced visual effects outfit that previously had contributed to dozens of high-profile movies, was then engaged to bring Page's designs to the screen.[6]

The filmmakers decided to take a novel visual approach when transferring their story from script to film. Adopting the so-called "found footage" aesthetic, *Cloverfield* is famous for its jittery camera work. This technical choice made sense for a story told as a faux documentary. The technique made sense since he wanted to give the film a sense of immediacy. The handheld look removed the sometimes-leaden feel of cinematography characteristic of more than a few giant monster movies of the past. It was also a style that movie-goers seemed to like. Indeed, several years before *Cloverfield*, the low-budget horror film, *The Blair Witch Project* (1999) achieved great financial success using the "found footage" approach. This method had been used before, but it had never been as impactful as it was in this production. Moreover, given that director was striving to give the appearance that the movie was assembled from pre-existing, real-world video material, this technique provided an inexpensive option. Indeed, when edited together, the resulting feature, though entirely fake, had the look and feel of a real documentary.

It is not difficult to understand why filmmakers in the 2000s were interested in adopting this approach. At the time, the method still seemed fresh. And what is more, *The Blair Witch Project's* jaw-dropping profit margin was undoubtedly alluring. That film's shoot reportedly cost less than $40,000—an astonishing, almost unbelievably low cost for any full-length feature. Even after postproduction costs, the movie's budget was only $500,000.[7] Yet, despite the minimal investment, *The Blair Witch Project* movie generated nearly $250 million in box-office receipts.[8]

It is doubtful that anyone expected *Cloverfield* to reproduce *The Blair Witch Project's* spectacular profits. However, even with tempered expectations, the prospect of making a relatively inexpensive giant-monster horror movie using the found footage technique probably seemed appealing. At about $25 million, *Cloverfield's* production budget was massively more than *The Blair Witch Project*, but that amount was still comparatively modest in terms of typical Hollywood budgets at the time.[9] Its eventual worldwide total sales of over $172 million (not counting post-theatrical home video release) was a good return.

The finished production tells an exciting story in a way that was unorthodox at the time. Beginning with a section that establishes the film's faux-documentary approach, the film's prologue tells audiences that what they are about to see is uncut video material recovered from a camera "found in US-447, [the] area formerly known as Central Park" in New York. "A message on screen indicates the U.S. Defense Department now owns the material and that it has something to do with 'multiple sightings of case designate 'Cloverfield.'"

The following scenes go back to the beginning, a little before the film's main events. The central characters are slowly introduced, starting with Rob Hawkins (played by Michael Stahl-David) and Beth McIntrye (played by Odette Yustman), who spent the night together sometime earlier. Next, the action jumps to Rob's farewell party a few weeks later—an event at which Beth is not present. Those attending include Rob's brother Jason and his fiancée, Rob's friend Hudson "Hud" Platt (T.J. Miller), and Marlena (Lizzy Caplan), another friend. Nothing important seems to be happening. Instead, the attendees are fixated on mostly trivial things.

Suddenly, the situation changes. The lights go out, and reports say an earthquake has struck nearby. A live news report indicates that a disaster is underway when the electricity comes back on. When the panicked partygoers run to the roof, they see a massive explosion in the distance and chaos in the nearby streets. Buildings all around them start collapsing, and the severed head of the Statue of Liberty plummets from the sky. Amid the chaos, Rob thinks he sees a monster in the distance but cannot get a clear view of it.

Now separated from the other partygoers, Rob, Jason, Lily, and Hud realize they are caught in something bizarre and bewildering. Wanting to escape the unknown danger, they head for the Brooklyn Bridge. However, as they make their way there, Rob receives a call from Beth, who reports she is trapped in her father's apartment building in mid-town Manhattan. Hearing that information, Rob and the others decide to attempt a rescue.

Meanwhile, the giant, mysterious monster is on the loose, wreaking havoc and terrorizing the city. And making things worse, the creature is shedding numerous smaller but substantially sized insect-like creatures that attack and kill many people. (Though somewhat different, this part of the story is reminiscent of similar menaces in *The Mist*.) During the trek to rescue Beth, Rob's small group encounters many hazards and is overwhelmed by the circumstances. In a heightened state of anxiety, they make several poor decisions. After one such choice, they are attacked by the human-sized monsters, one of which fatally wounds Marlena.

A chance encounter with military personnel reveals that the authorities have no more idea about what is happening than the rescue party. Still, they want all civilians to leave the area. However, Rob insists on saving Beth even though military people advise against it. Upon hearing this, military personnel surprisingly do not interfere. Instead, they let the would-be rescue crew continue, warning them not to miss the last helicopter flights to safety. Ominously, a soldier also warns the group about something called the "Hammer Down Protocol." It seems to be the Pentagon's plan for a worst-case scenario and involves intentionally destroying Manhattan if they cannot otherwise kill the monster.

After many dangers and close calls, Rob and the others finally arrive at Beth's location. There, they discover that Beth is in an apartment on an upper floor of the complex. That presents a seemingly impossible challenge since the structure is extensively damaged, leaving no clear way to get there from the ground level. Rob and his party decide to try anyway. They subsequently climb the stairs to the thirty-ninth floor, encountering many obstacles along the way. Finally, they arrive at Beth's mostly destroyed apartment to discover she is injured and trapped under some rubble. With the giant creature looming nearby, they free Beth and begin the harrowing trek back to street-level Manhattan.

Despite long odds, they arrive at the military's designated meet-up point as the monster approaches. Boarding two separate helicopters, it seems as though Rob and the others will finally make it to safety. However, missiles strike the colossus just as they ascend into the sky. Amid much confusion, both helicopters are downed. The helicopter carrying Rob, Beth, and Hud crashes in Central Park. As they try to escape the wreckage, the monster appears overhead. Hud is killed, but Rob grabs the camera and runs for cover with Beth. Finding refuge under a bridge in Central Park, Rob aims the camera at himself and records a message for anyone who finds the camera later.

The film then gives viewers the impression that Rob, Beth, and the monster are destroyed in a massive explosion when the military implements its Hammer Down Protocol. However, viewers do not see confirmation of these details, thus ending the narrative in a somewhat open-ended fashion. Indeed, after lengthy end credits, a scratchy voice over a black screen says, "Help us." Although the voice presumably belongs to Rob, that is not confirmed.

For a film that primarily takes a straightforward approach to telling its story, *Cloverfield* has many ambiguities. The conceit of the movie—that it is a story told through what is supposed to be an unedited series of scenes captured on a found home video camera—means there are many gaps in the narrative. However, surface impressions aside, *Cloverfield* is very tightly edited. Often revealed through dimly lit and frenetic scenes, the narrative unfolds quickly. The film's quick pace, especially in the last hour of its 125-minute run time, gives viewers a very limited opportunity to catch their breath. In the words of writer Donato Totaro, it is a "bleak and wonderfully inconclusive"[10] movie experience.

On first viewing, some may not notice how much information is missing and how many details of the story are implied but not shown. Consequently, some of the presumptions that audiences may make about what is happening on screen may or may not hold up on a closer examination. But that is hardly unknown in filmmaking, and movies often lead viewers to conclusions not strictly supported by what appears on the screen.

Overall, *Cloverfield* provides food for thought in several respects. For one thing, the main characters often seem to have no idea about what they are doing. Their frequent cluelessness is more like baffled teenage characters in a low-budget horror movie than those in most giant monster films where the protagonists act with greater wisdom. By contrast, *Cloverfield's* main characters often appear dazed and uncertain about their actions. Even Rob, the nominal leader of the small band that tries to rescue Beth, has many doubts. He often seems to push forward more because he can think of no other alternative than because he is confident about what he is doing. Perhaps too traumatized to be any other way, Rob nonetheless veers very far from what is usually seen in a film "hero." His actions display some form of heroism—notably apparent in his desire to save Beth—but he remains an ordinary, uncharacteristically panicky screen protagonist.

The military personnel in *Cloverfield* are minor characters and have very little screen time. Yet, their inclusion is essential. What they are not is heroic in the sense of traditional movie heroes. Their heroism is measured and lies in their implicit humanness. They are shown as people simply doing their job under challenging circumstances. That may be a kind of heroism, but it differs sharply from the heroes that usually appear on the screen.

The story's inclusion of the Hammer Down Protocol—the Pentagon's plan to destroy the city if it cannot destroy the monster any other way—may suggest a cold and possibly heartless military angle to the narrative in the eyes of some viewers. Indeed, scholar Homay King writes that *Cloverfield* shows the military as "brutal, uncaring, secretive, and destructive" even if it is "ultimately effective, necessary, and right."[11] From one perspective, there is little to quibble about in this assessment.

However, from a more nuanced viewpoint, one can interpret *Cloverfield's* portrayal of the military in a somewhat different light, especially regarding the ordinary soldiers appearing in several scenes. For the most part, these characters seem less like "brutal" and "uncaring" automatons than regular people just trying to cope with a bad situation while performing their tasks as they understand them. They may seem imperfect, but they come off as real people. And while military characters make hard choices under conditions of ambiguity, their portrayal seems far less grotesque than the actual behavior of some of those involved in the Abu Ghraib scandal that made headlines in 2004.

From a broader perspective, when portraying many of its characters, from Rob and the members of his immediate group to the film's military characters, *Cloverfield* usually avoids the macho, reactionary heroics that often appear in American movies. For a production that is hardly an exercise in literal realism, the film presents many of the characters in a refreshingly realistic way. In this respect, *Cloverfield* takes a different path than audiences see in *The Mist*. David Drayton, the lead character thrust by circumstance into a would-be hero's role in *The Mist,* may ultimately be unsuccessful in saving the day, but it is not for lack of trying. Indeed, the character takes charge, forges ahead, and makes tough choices, even if the result is unsuccessful. By contrast, *Cloverfield's* Rob, though still leading the way, is much less explicitly heroic. The others do not necessarily go along with him because he displays leadership qualities. Instead, they sympathize with Rob's mission to rescue Beth, possibly because the other options do not seem much better than what Rob suggests. Indeed, Rob has more in common with the hapless yet kind-hearted Park Gang-du in *The Host* than with *The Mist's* David Drayton. Rob and Gang-du are heroes in a certain sense. However, they are hardly in the mold of traditionally heroic movie characters, which could be seen as a refreshing development.

That said, *Cloverfield* is, in most ways, a very American film, fully embracing and reflecting a U.S. mindset and the particular way the Americans experienced the world post–9/11. Though the United States' far-flung War on Terror was ongoing, U.S. society was still trying to process and make sense of the attacks that had shaken the country to its core.

American audiences may forget that while the War on Terror sometimes defined much of the 2000s in the United States, that was simply not the case in Japan, South Korea, or much of the world, where it was felt much less directly. Given those conditions, it would have been unusual for movies made primarily for markets outside the United States to focus on the subject in the same raw, emotional way that a U.S. production might if its makers chose to acknowledge those real-world circumstances.

Of course, given the prominence of the United States and its global influence, the rest of the world could not entirely avoid at least some occasional and vicarious references to post–9/11 American fixations. And sometimes, even kaiju movies from outside the U.S. reflected those conditions. Still, such references probably did not affect audiences elsewhere the same as in the United States. For example, despite obvious references to 9/11 in *Gamera the Brave,* the power of imagery depicting a towering building with a gaping hole was unlikely to have been as strong—or even as perceptible—to audiences outside the United States for whom the War on Terror mainly was something happening far away in a wholly different culture.

As a giant monster movie, *Cloverfield* can be compared to then-recent films such as *The Mist* and *The Host*. In this respect, the film is part of one strand of kaiju movie-making in which giant monsters are portrayed as pure destructiveness, not as humungous characters that might have redeeming or even positive qualities. (That second strand of kaiju movies includes many Godzilla sequels, in which viewers see Godzilla and a few other creatures—most notably Mothra—as humankind's ally. The same is true in most of the Gamera movies.)

But *Cloverfield* also invites comparison to something even more apparent than then-recent movies like *The Mist* and *The Host*. Indeed, as Andrew Housman writes in the online publication *Screen Rant*, "Among all of Hollywood's attempts at bringing an Americanized *Godzilla* movie to the big screen, it's still *Cloverfield* that most purely captures the terror and dread of a giant monster attack."[12]

Despite stylistic differences, *Gojira* (the original Godzilla movie) and *Cloverfield* have fundamental similarities beyond their storylines. Housman notes each film is rooted in "a sense of psychological trauma" and that each evokes the "nightmarish feeling of trying to survive an apocalyptic event."[13] These things are missing from the 1998 American *Godzilla*, a film that never fully establishes a sense of urgency and instead gets bogged down in a complicated narrative reminiscent of a procedural. The same is also largely true in Toho's Millennium Godzilla movies, released only a few years before *Cloverfield*.

Of course, there are differences between *Gojira* and *Cloverfield*, too. *Gojira* possesses an overt political message. Its anti–nuclear weapons stance is a big part of the film and could hardly have been missed by original Japanese audiences in 1954 (That message is largely cut from the film's Americanized edit, *Godzilla: King of the Monsters!*). *Cloverfield*, by contrast, lacks a clear-cut political message. True to its conception as an informational (rather than advocacy-oriented) faux documentary, it reports the (fictional) events but does not tell audiences what meaning to take from them.

In any case, compared to the disappointing Sony-TriStar *Godzilla* movie that came a decade earlier, *Cloverfield* demonstrated that an engaging Godzilla-like film could be made by American filmmakers after all. Placing a giant monster more squarely at the center than had been the case with *The Mist* the previous year, *Cloverfield* was in some sense like an unintentional proof-of-concept film. That was significant since, in 2008, it was still not at all clear that giant monster movies had much of a future. In Japan, kaiju movies seemed to be at least a temporary dead end. Toho had placed its kaiju series in suspended animation, and Kadokawa Daiei Studio seemed in no hurry to make a follow-up to its *Gamera the Brave*. And internationally, Bong Joon-ho's *The Host* was the most recent film with a giant monster to have a broad impact, but it was clearly a freestanding, one-off production. No one expected it to launch a new era of kaiju movie-making.

In that context, the appearance of *Cloverfield,* a clear-cut giant monster movie that was open-ended enough to leave audiences wanting more, may have seemed poised to jumpstart the genre. However, a sequel was slow to come. And as before, the immediate future of giant monster movies remained very much unknown.

*Cloverfield* arrived in theaters after clever marketing efforts that were helped by Paramount's ability to launch the film in over 3,400 theaters, a substantial number. By the time of its January 2008 premiere, intriguing trailers and a mystique created by the film's intentional shroud of secrecy helped generate $40 million in ticket sales at a time of year when box office returns are typically slow.[14]

The initially strong audience interest was accompanied by many positive reviews from movie critics. Yet, the apparent enthusiasm during its first days in theaters did not last. Business dropped by an eye-opening 70 percent the following week, ultimately disappointing industry analysts who had projected a better performance. As noted by Angus Finney, *Cloverfield* may have "exhausted its core audience in the first weekend and never broke through to the wider public" at the time, though it later performed well in the home-video market.[15] In terms of theatrical success, it did not seem as though *Cloverfield* had solved the giant monster movie genre's long-term problem of widening its appeal.

# 8

# Improvising with Monsters
*Monsters* (2010)

British director Gareth Edwards had never directed a full-length movie before. Still, his 2010 film *Monsters* delivered a fresh take on the kaiju movie genre and showcased his considerable skills as a filmmaker. Working with limited resources, Edwards used his creativity to get the most out of what he had and succeeded in delivering a bold cinematic experience. When *Monsters* received an advance showing at the influential South by Southwest Festival in March of 2010, it was evident that Edwards had created a thoughtful, genre-bending giant monster movie that satisfied many viewers on multiple levels.

By thinking beyond conventional approaches to moviemaking, the novice director stretched his shoestring budget to get maximum results. His film demonstrated creative kaiju movies did not necessarily require massive budgets to be successful entertainments. The film also suggested that there were still untapped approaches for making kaiju movies in the 21st century.

*Monsters* has many of the beloved hallmarks of classic giant monster movies. However, it breaks new ground in several ways. Although still reflecting the real world and the post–9/11 environment, Edwards' film signaled that the genre could become more than that once again. Indeed, the film moves beyond blatant references to 9/11 and takes cues from political concerns that emerged a few years later. On a thematic level, it was a breath of fresh air.

Of course, in some respects, Edwards' film is still of its time. Audiences, especially in the United States, obviously had not forgotten about the 2001 terror attacks and the fraught cultural environment that emerged in its wake. However, as the decade passed, 9/11 and the War on Terror began to recede into the background. It was not that the many problems had been entirely resolved. But many Americans who initially were traumatized by the events had become used to the situation. With 2001's traumas increasingly in the rear-view mirror, new conditions captured the nation's attention. These included a major economic meltdown in 2008 and the coming of the historic but divisive presidency of Barack Obama.

As the U.S. public's focus shifted, popular culture moved on, too. In that context, the short period in which American kaiju movies served as allegories for post–9/11 cultural anxieties soon passed. If giant monster films were to continue being made and finding an audience, they would need to find new ways to stay relevant in a changing society, at least in the U.S. market.

The road to *Monster's* premiere was unusual and is a compelling story in its own right. Edwards aspired to make the film—or more precisely, a film somewhat like the final product—with little prior directing experience. Initially, he worked as a visual effects creator and digital artist. His assignments included work on several television productions, including *Seven Wonders of the Industrialized World* (2003), *Hiroshima* (2005), *UFOs: The Secret Evidence* (2005), *Perfect Disasters* (2006), and others. The latter series also provided him with the opportunity to move into directing. He helmed two episodes of *Perfect Disaster* for the Discovery Channel in 2006. Then, two years later, he landed a job directing an episode of the series *Heroes and Villains* for the BBC.

Edwards was already interested in making some sort of science fiction movie when he entered a contest that required making a short film in only two days. His industry background gave him enough experience to make *Factory Farmed*. At a breakneck pace, he made the film and, as he later reported, "did all the effects at home."[1] The film used only two actors, Jacob Court and Allen Leach, as well as the services of Zoe Elliott, who produced the film, and Daniel Pemberton, who provided the music. Otherwise, however, Edwards did everything else himself. The results were impressive enough to win the competition. His dark and futuristic short film put him squarely on the road to directing something bigger and more ambitious.

Edwards had long admired Steven Spielberg, Quentin Tarantino, and especially George Lucas, whose *Star Wars* movies enthralled him from a young age. Making films with some science fiction or monster angle seemed a natural fit for him. However, that did not necessarily mean that Edwards' making of a kaiju-style movie was inevitable. According to his account, his decision to make *Monsters* did not arise from a specific longing to enter the fray of giant-monster films but rather from a chance encounter that gave him an idea. In a 2010 magazine interview, he explained: "I remember being abroad on the beach and watching these guys really struggling to pull a fishing net from the ocean. I couldn't understand what they were saying, but you could tell they were teasing each other about it, and I thought it would be funny if, when they finally pulled it out, it had a giant sea creature on the end or something."[2]

As he began thinking of a story loosely inspired by that encounter, Edwards thought about a scenario in which people were already living in a world threatened by monsters. Since they could not do much about it, he imagined, they would probably simply try to carry on with their daily lives despite the danger. Scary behemoths were essential to the film he envisioned, but his story would mostly be about how the characters would cope—or not cope—with that situation. As his ideas started to gel, Edwards approached a small London-based outfit called Vertigo Films, a relatively new company that produced and distributed independent movies.

Vertigo was interested, providing that the proposed film could be made with modest means. During discussions, Vertigo's James Richardson, a producer, recommended an extremely inexpensive film to Edwards as an example of how to complete a film at a minimal cost. Although, at that point, it seemed he would have to work with a small budget if things worked out, Edwards was enthusiastic about moving forward.[3]

When Edwards watched *In Search of a Midnight Kiss*, the film Richardson had mentioned, he not only was able to gauge what someone else had done with a shoestring production budget. He also discovered actor Scoot McNairy, one of *In Search of a Midnight Kiss's* stars. When Edwards subsequently made a deal with Vertigo, he was already in contact with McNairy as his male lead for the project.

One of the most surprising things about *Monsters* is that despite a large cast of characters, nearly all of whom perform well, only McNairy and one other person came from the ranks of professional actors. The other professional was Whitney Able, who was then in a real-life relationship with McNairy. As it turned out, they had good chemistry on screen. Between the two, they anchored the film with enough power so that the production was not diminished even though the remainder of the cast consisted of complete amateurs, all of whom were non-actors discovered and hired on location.

Many viewers who see *Monsters* for the first time would be surprised to learn just how much cost-cutting Edwards undertook to create the film. Indeed, the final result looks far more expensive and polished than many might think possible, given the tiny budget at Edwards's disposal. Part of the reason Edwards could accomplish such impressive results with so little money was due to his background. In his decade-long career behind the scenes, he had become very familiar and skilled with many aspects of filmmaking. He also learned how to get the most out of the limited resources he had available. Those skills and experiences probably led to his success

## 8. Improvising with Monsters 97

with some of the most unlikely production circumstances a person can find in a successful movie.

One of Edwards' critical decisions was to film on location in Central America and southern Texas, sometimes reportedly bypassing official channels in arranging filming sites.[4] In practice, this entailed Edwards, McNairy, Able, and the film crew driving around the region in a van and looking for existing locations that would suit the scenes Edwards envisioned. Although this would have been entirely unwieldy for a typical production with a sizeable crew, it was workable since the total number of people involved was minimal. Edwards served in multiple roles (including director, writer, cinematographer, and special effects creator), and the rest of the crew consisted of only James Richardson (producer), Ian Maclagan (sound), Verity Oswin (whom Edwards described as a "Mexican fixer"),[5] and "various drivers."[6]

However, the process was even more unusual than these details might suggest. Indeed, before beginning this atypical road trip to undertake principal photography, Edwards decided against working from a conventional or formal script. Instead, he worked up a story, divided it into various scenes, and then left open the words that would be spoken by whatever actors, aside from McNairy and Able, the crew could round up to bring the given scene to life. McNairy and Able were professionals who could handle this open-ended, improvisational approach. Meanwhile, Edwards believed that the absence of a formal script might result in better performances from the amateur members of the cast. He reasoned that giving those people guidance about what general type of things to say, rather than specific words to say, would be easier for them and yield more natural performances.

Going without a script may seem risky, but the results suggest that Edwards' gamble mostly paid off. McNairy and Able gave solid performances and demonstrated excellent screen chemistry. They are professional actors, and possibly that could have been expected. What is more surprising, however, is that the non-professional actors also turned in solid performances. In some cases—most notably in a scene where McNairy's character tries to buy boat tickets from a local vendor—the ticket seller's performance is so accomplished that even seasoned viewers could be forgiven for thinking they were seeing an experienced actor. But that was not the case. Indeed, Mario Zuniga Benavides, who plays the role, was discovered on-site and apparently never acted before or since. Yet, he steals the scene and gives a memorable performance that would have been more expected in a high-priced production.

Edwards' reliance on dialogue that the actors would create at the spur of the moment was not without potential pitfalls. Not knowing how much would be usable, he ended up filming much more than could be edited into the final production. It was undoubtedly not easy to coax suitable words and actions from actors, especially in the cases of those without prior experience. Yet, the method mostly worked. Much of that success probably can be attributed to Edwards' previous work making quickly-produced cable television documentaries. Those had similarly demanded the ability to put together watchable and narratively compelling works built from sometimes less-than-ideal pieces. Such is the nature of low-budget screen production.

The giant creatures in *Monsters* remain offscreen for much of the time. However, in a kaiju movie, the monsters eventually would have to appear before the audience. In some low-budget monster movies—as in some science fiction films with similar budgets—filmmakers sometimes squeeze savings from other aspects of the production to make more resources available in creating their star attraction: the monsters. Indeed, designing and executing movie sequences featuring giant monsters can significantly drain a budget. Yet, fans of that type of film have high expectations in this regard, which can justify the expenditure of so much time and money.

Edwards, however, was able to make a different choice. With his experience in generating convincing computer-generated visual effects efficiently and effectively, the director decided to create the visual effects himself. Working somewhat on the fly with a laptop computer loaded with Adobe After Effects software, he created and animated the monsters (as well as the film's other CGI effects) and then integrated them into the film himself.[7] This procedure required knowledge and resourcefulness. One problem surfaced when Edwards discovered that no off-the-shelf plug-in could animate the monsters' limbs. However, since the creature he designed somewhat resembled a cross between an octopus and a squid, he used a program that modeled ropes in motion and simply adapted it to stand in for the creatures' arms and legs.[8]

The film begins with a brief explanation. The government had inadvertently brought giant, mysterious aliens to Earth six years ago. After crash-landing in Mexico near the U.S. border, the creatures embarked on a path of destruction. Since then, the two governments cordoned off the entire region, and the United States built a massive wall to keep the aliens from venturing beyond Mexico. Meanwhile, the military's ongoing struggle is presented as a "new normal." Everything that happens in the film occurs against that backdrop.

Next comes a brief prologue that jumps immediately into a nighttime military mission in a Texas town along the Mexican border. A truck carrying soldiers and civilian passengers races through town. One of the

## 8. Improvising with Monsters　　　　　　　　99

soldiers joyfully sings the melody of "Ride of the Valkyries." (That famous piece originates from Richard Wagner's opera *Die Walküre*, but modern audiences know it from its prominent use in Francis Ford Coppola's *Apocalypse Now*.) Suddenly, the scene erupts in gunfire and explosions, and the camera catches a brief glimpse of giant monsters overhead. After a few seconds of chaos, another explosion seems to kill everyone in the trucks.

Following this prologue, the film's first act opens with much less on-screen excitement. Indeed, despite the unfolding crisis, people appear to accept that fact as they try to cope and go on with their everyday lives. American photojournalist Andrew Kaulder (played by Scoot McNairy) is in a remote Mexican town when his boss calls him with a special assignment. The boss's daughter, Samantha Wynden (Whitney Able), is near where Andrew is staying. The boss wants Andrew to accompany the daughter, a free spirit in her mid-twenties, back to safety in the United States. Although Andrew is initially reluctant to accept the assignment, the boss offers him a sum of money too large to turn down.

From this point forward, *Monsters* is essentially an escape story. In some respects, it is an unusual road picture in which two superficially incompatible people—Andrew and Samantha—are thrown together and then start to bond as they face a series of dangers. In one sense, the events on screen represent a journey to safety. Yet, from another perspective, it is quite the opposite. Indeed, to reach their destination, the would-be couple must travel along a perilous route. And in this way, much of the film shows the trials and tribulations that Andrew and Samantha face as they increasingly encounter new dangers and unknowns. As the soldier's signing in the prologue foretold, it is a trip more than slightly reminiscent of *Apocalypse Now* (and one of that film's primary sources, Joseph Conrad's 1899 novella, *The Heart of Darkness*).

The first leg of the journey requires complicated negotiations with locals and dealing with the problems entailed in such an undertaking, even if giant monsters were not lurking somewhere far offscreen. The pair have trouble getting transportation, and looking like American tourists, they become easy targets.

Eventually, after they hitchhike to a small coastal fishing town, Andrew haggles with a local boat owner and agrees to pay an inflated price for passage by sea to the United States the next day. But before the scheduled departure, their passports and funds are stolen. The man balks when they later plead with the boat's owner to let them pay later. He says the best he can do without full payment in advance is to arrange for the couple to travel by land and river to the U.S.-Mexico border. It is a harsh route that will take Andrew and Samantha through the deep forest and force them to trust an assortment of mercenaries who may not be trustworthy. In this part of the film, which is the section that most closely resembles the frighteningly absurd up-river journey in *Apocalypse Now*, the travelers increasingly come across evidence of the alien monsters, some of which are giant and others of which are much smaller.

Finally, however, luck runs out for Andrew and Samantha. As they travel by truck through the thick forest with paid-off mercenaries, a monster detects their presence and attacks. As a result, the mercenaries, who try to fight the menace, are killed. Fortunately, Andrew and Samantha have taken cover and survived the ordeal.

Now alone, the couple presses on, traveling by foot and coming across dead bodies and increasing evidence of recent monster attacks. At one point, they stop to climb the ruins of a pyramid hidden in the forest. Taking a moment to rest, they reflect on their lives and try to make sense of everything they have recently experienced together.

Finally emerging from the dense vegetation, they are now very close to the border, and the area is eerily desolate. Looking ahead, Andrew and Samantha see the immense border wall that is supposed to keep the monsters from entering the United States. They eventually make their way through an abandoned border-crossing gate, finally arriving in a small unpopulated Texan town. It is immediately apparent that the monsters have recently been in the area. After walking along a dusty road, they come across an abandoned gas station. Finding that the telephone there still works, they call for help.

While waiting for help to arrive, Andrew and Samantha see a nearby encounter between two giant creatures. They do not quite understand what they are seeing. Is it a fight of some sort? Or is it a courtship ritual? It is hard to say. They do not know whether they are witnessing something beautiful or terrifying.

Soon, military vehicles arrive. Andrew and Samantha board separate trucks that race off, presumably heading for safety. Careful viewers will note that the film has returned to where it started. (This point is easy to miss if one is not attentive.) The trucks whisk through town with passengers Andrew and Samantha. Then, the soldier from the film's first scene is again heard singing "The Ride of the Valkyries," and a giant creature appears out of nowhere. The film ends abruptly as the monster attacks.

The ending of this film has been the subject of speculation. Many viewers at the time did not realize how directly the first and last moments of the film are connected. Indeed, due to the darkness and chaotic nature of those scenes, it is difficult to sort out precisely what Edwards is showing the audience. Placed side by side, however, it becomes clear that these are not two separate but similar incidents but rather one incident that has been split in two and placed to serve as bookends for the movie.

Many viewers may not notice, at least initially, that the first and last scenes are a single scene split into two pieces, however. Much has happened between the film's first moments and the conclusion, so unless a viewer is attentive, it may not be evident that the first and final moments of the film show the same event. Once the connection is made, however, the fate of the lead characters changes from ambiguity to unhappy certainty. The first scene reveals that all the characters die in the explosion.

Many people did not notice these details when the film first circulated. Among fans of the movie, there was some online discussion about whether Andrew and Samantha could have survived. Some even wondered if the couple might appear in a sequel. However, Edwards was never coy about what happened to the film's lead characters. When asked about the ending in a published interview, he did not elaborate but bluntly said, "We cannot do a sequel with Scoot [McNair] and Whitney [Able], and that is my interpretation." Without making his reply into an overt spoiler for those who had not seen the film, which had only recently been released, the director indirectly confirmed the movie's downbeat ending.

Interestingly, though *Monsters* was a small production that in most ways differed from the then-recent movies *The Mist* and *Cloverfield*, it was the third giant monster movie to have a grim ending that includes the death of all (or, in the case of *The Mist,* most) of the lead characters. Moreover, in each of these cases, the characters who perish are not sacrificing themselves in acts of film heroism. Indeed, there is no such satisfaction for the audience. Instead, prominent characters in all three films abruptly die after almost surviving their ordeals. Ultimately, they exert no control over their fates and fall victim to bad luck.

*Monsters* shares another plot element with *The Mist* and *Cloverfield*, too. Unlike what happens in many kaiju films—especially those in the Toho tradition—these three American monster movies show the military as only partially effective. In each case, armed forces only make a difference in the fight against the monsters late in the proceedings.

In Edwards' film, the U.S. government's colossal border wall is supposed to keep the alien creatures from crossing the border from the dubiously labeled "infected zone" (mainly in Mexico and Central America) into the United States. However, as the movie's final section reveals, the massive wall, presumably built at great expense, has not worked. While the northern areas of the United States remain free from invasive monsters, the borderland region is now, in the language of the film, "infected."

The film's final sections blatantly raise comparisons with immigration, which was already a hot-button political issue in the U.S. at the time. That type of reference was not necessarily a novelty. In many kaiju-style films, the giant creatures metaphorically stand in for one kind of issue or another. Seldom, however, have the beasts so obviously called to mind an entire category of people. Although it is an obvious point, it should be mentioned that Edwards is not even remotely implying that migrants are monsters. That is evident even if a person knows nothing of the director's political beliefs. Indeed, Edwards carefully constructs the monsters' story as one in which the monsters are more victims than monsters.

According to the narrative, the vast creatures did not intend to come to earth but were brought here inadvertently by the United States. Edwards' creatures howl and behave in sometimes scary and even deadly ways. However, they are not portrayed as particularly angry or evil creatures bent on killing humans. Instead, although very little is revealed about them, the monsters may just be reacting to circumstances. They might have been utterly benign if they had not been spirited away from their home planet. Indeed, the frightening kaiju in *Monsters* may not be much more than very large, misunderstood victims of circumstance.

Over its hour-and-a-half running time, *Monsters* jumps from a more or less traditional kaiju film with road-trip and love-interest angles to a movie that also serves as a political parable. Though many, perhaps most, giant monster movies have a political subtext, *Monsters* is particularly upfront about it. It calls to mind not a generalized political climate but something specific: immigration. And although that issue was perhaps not as divisive and polarizing in 2010 as it would be a few years later during the presidency of Donald Trump, it was already a hot-button issue.

Immigration into the United States, especially from Mexico and Central American nations, had been a long-standing source of controversy, but it took on a new life in the post–9/11 era. American xenophobia was hardly a recent phenomenon, but it gained new life in the wake of the 2001 terror attacks. Then, the issue exploded when an economic crisis abruptly emerged in 2008. As financial distress increased, some Americans complained that immigrants were taking away what they called "American jobs." Anger focused mainly on the many migrants who entered the United States unofficially. American policy about undocumented immigrants quickly became a lightning rod issue.

In places such as Texas, the issue was hotly debated. Many wanted much stricter enforcement of federal immigration laws than had been the case for years. Amid such controversy, George W. Bush signed the Secure the Border Act of 2006 into law. It authorized the construction of hundreds of miles of fences and new technologies to police the southern U.S. border. Some aspects of the policy were always controversial, and construction of the new fencing was slow.

In 2009, with the Act yet to be fully implemented, John Carter, a Republican member of Congress, offered a glimpse into the passion and intensity that the issue aroused. "Our border problem has always been one of lack of enforcement," he wrote in a newspaper guest column. "There is more at stake here than just immigration," he continued. "Since our founding, a key principle of our republic has been our national commitment to living under the rule of law.... So we fight for more than a border fence. We fight for the rule of law and democracy against those who flaunt both."[9] As those words suggest, immigration that did not go through officially recognized channels was already a deeply emotional issue.

*Monsters* acknowledges this divisive topic unabashedly. Yet, its critique of the situation is less overtly political than practical. In the film, the wall the U.S. government builds to keep the monsters out of America is technologically advanced and genuinely imposing. Yet, despite the presumably monumental effort and enormous expense required to make it, it simply does not work. It is as if to say that the American government can do all it wants; the border will still be breached. That message implicit in the movie (whether intentional or not) was probably not a welcome one for some people on each side of real-world American immigration policy. And audiences obviously could have chosen to disregard the real-world implications of the *Monsters* story if they wished. However, it is a surprisingly pragmatic commentary nonetheless.

In any case, audiences never really learn whether the human campaign against the alien monsters is ultimately successful. When the story ends, humankind seems to be winning, but there is no indication of what might happen next. However, because the focus of Edwards' film is mainly on the small-scale personal story of Andrew and Samantha, that may not matter. The enormous creatures are never far from the action, but the fight against giant monsters is not the film's focus. Instead, the struggle of ordinary people trying to live in dangerous times takes center stage. Interestingly, that is roughly the same attitude Americans had come to have as the tenth anniversary of 9/11 approached.

From the perspective of some viewers, such considerations are beside the point. Although the movie is an impressive accomplishment in many respects, the director is aware of criticism that the monsters are not on screen enough to suit some fans of the genre. Regarding that point, Edwards said, "There is more time of the monsters [in his movie] than the shark in *Jaws*. *Jaws* is obviously a far superior movie, but that proved to me that it's not a simple matter of the more monsters you have shown the scarier it'll be.... It doesn't work that way."[10]

Although it is a movie with colossal beasts, many reviewers at the time did not simply regard it as another kaiju film. Critic Roger Ebert, for example, compared it to the work of director M. Night Shyamalan, the maker of *The Sixth Sense* (1999), *Signs* (2002), *The Village* (2004), and other popular films. According to Ebert, *Monsters* similarly focuses on "characters, relationships, fear, and [a] mostly unseen menace."[11]

Some aspects of *Monsters* raised comparisons to other works, too. For example, some parts were reminiscent of *District 9*, Neill Blomkamp's well-regarded 2009 science-fiction film. In that movie, humans agree to give extraterrestrial aliens refuge on Earth. Some also drew comparisons to *Jurassic Park*, the 1993 Steven Spielberg blockbuster, which, like Edwards' movie, features large, terrifying creatures lurking in a jungle-like forest.[12] Writing for *Deep Focus Review*, Brian Eggert even saw elements reminiscent of Werner Herzog's *Aguirre, The Wrath of God* (1972), about a Spanish conquistador's grueling quest for treasure in Peru.[13] And, of course, parallels to Francis Ford Coppola's *Apocalypse Now* were difficult to miss and widely noted.[14]

That *Monsters* called to mind such varying films is a testament to Edwards' vision. He had managed to create a multifaceted movie of potential interest to audiences beyond kaiju film enthusiasts. Interestingly, however, it could easily have turned out very differently. Indeed, when he first considered the project, he had been thinking about a more straightforward tale of scary alien monsters invading Earth. That tried-and-true storyline has been used many times since it was popularized by H.G. Wells' book *War of the Worlds*. However, when Edwards learned that *Cloverfield* would have a similar plot (though in an urban setting), he changed course and retooled his story.[15]

That unplanned change led to a vastly different film that focused more on humans coping with a world in which monsters are ever-present than battling the creatures. The completed film's story primarily centers on Andrew and Samantha's evolving relationship against a frightening backdrop. From one perspective, it was a fascinating and arguably very successful change in direction. Yet, the shift took *Monsters* far from what some viewers may have expected. One writer noted that the movie "is almost the antithesis of a sci-fi action film, and that is likely to frustrate and anger people who come in expecting *War of the Worlds* or *Aliens*."[16]

Edwards' change in direction is mainly one of emphasis. Many giant monster movies feature human romances as subplots. That is hardly new. But Edwards somewhat reverses the situation in *Monsters* by bringing Andrew and Samantha's story to the foreground. And with that, the film transformed from what could have been a straightforward kaiju movie into what Edwards describes as "a tragic love story."[17]

Edwards reportedly spent only $15,000 for the equipment he needed to shoot the film. Although post-production expenses cost much more, he made the entire film for $500,000 or less, a shoestring budget for a feature film. Early reactions to the movie were sufficiently positive for it to earn a screening at the famous and influential South by Southwest Festival. The positive response there led to a U.S. distribution deal with Magnet Releasing, a unit of Magnolia Pictures.[18] As a small-scale, independent feature, *Monsters* was never sent to a wide theatrical release. But it eventually earned more than $5.5 million globally,[19] a respectable figure given its budget and provenance but hardly a sum that would set the film world on fire.

Yet, despite its modest impact in financial terms, *Monsters* accomplished at least two noteworthy things. It offered surprising realism for a kaiju movie, attracting serious attention from many critics in the process. It also established Gareth Edwards' reputation as a gifted director. Indeed, shortly after *Monsters'* debut, Edwards was hired to helm a new American-made Godzilla film backed by Warner Bros. and Legendary Pictures. As a new decade brought changes to the giant monster genre, it appeared that at least some dormant traditions were about to be reawakened. But before Godzilla returned to the screen, more changes were to come.

# 9

# For the Love of Kaiju
*Pacific Rim* (2013)

Action-oriented blockbuster franchises were all the rage among movie-goers in the 2010s. With emphases on increasingly spectacular and bombastic digital effects, these movies wowed audiences and racked up huge box office numbers. Superhero movies were front and center in this trend. The genre had been around for decades, but now these productions gained new respectability as they garnered enormous profits on their march to box-office domination.

As early as the late 2000s, it was already evident that superhero movies were poised to take a central place in the film marketplace. A look at the top-grossing films from 2008 drove home that point. That year, two superhero movies—*The Dark Knight*, the latest in a string of films based on the DC Comics Batman character, and *Iron Man*, based on the Marvel Comics character—captured the first and second place at the U.S. box office.[1]

Then, in 2009, a staggering business deal fueled further growth in the rising superhero movie genre. Unexpectedly, Disney purchased Marvel Entertainment for a whopping $4 billion. Although Marvel had previously doled out movie rights to some of its characters (including *Spider-Man*, *The Fantastic Four*, and *The X*-Men) to other studios, the deal meant that most of Marvel's vast inventory of characters came under Disney's control. With this substantial new supply of intellectual property, Disney planned to create a major franchise, the Marvel Cinematic Universe (MCU). By 2012, when *The Avengers* decisively commanded the U.S. and international box offices, the plan seemed to be working.

The immense popularity of superheroes tantalized the film business in some ways. With its long history of imitating success, Hollywood had a track record of producing movies to satisfy what it perceived as consumer demand. Indeed, the industry had seldom failed to jump on the latest trends. But the rush to cash in on the popularity of superhero movies had consequences for other types of films. As the decade progressed, a glut of superhero movies seemed poised to crowd different kinds of films out of the market. For the makers of kaiju movies, this turn of events suggested that to be successful, they would have to find ways to carve out space for their productions.

The 21st century's new breed of superhero movies possessed characteristics that had long been part of kaiju movies. Emphasizing spectacle, destruction, and epic battles, traditional giant monster films aimed to wow audiences with special effects and melodramatic plots. Most superhero movies aim to entertain by emphasizing those same elements. Both genres sometimes also function as morality plays or films with a message, but first and foremost, the traditional goal has been to meet, more than challenge, audience tastes and expectations. That often results in movies that are visual extravaganzas, rich in over-the-top mayhem.

Mexican director Guillermo del Toro's 2013 blockbuster *Pacific Rim* aimed to make a place for kaiju movies in the superhero-dominated film market in much the same way. He was no stranger to films inspired by comic book characters. Some contemporary audiences are more familiar with his movies *Pan's Labyrinth* (2006) or *The Shape of Water* (2017). However, in the first decade of the new millennium, he directed a string of inventive movies based on comic-book heroes: *Blade II* (2002), *Hellboy* (2004), and *Hellboy II: The Golden Army* (2008). As a lifelong comics fan, these works made sense within his growing filmography. He approached them with the same sincerity and commitment as with his other work. Intriguingly, Blade is a superhero immersed in the world of vampires, and the Hellboy character *is* a monster. So, although often categorized as comic-book movies, these films also overlap the realm of monster movies.

By then, del Toro had already developed a deep and lifelong passion for monster movies. Indeed, he has been passionate about monsters in popular culture—and in movies, especially—since childhood. Even a quick scan of his resume as a director reveals that in far more than an incidental way, his love of the topic has informed nearly the entirety of his career as a filmmaker.

In some ways, del Toro was a natural fit for directing a new, big-budget giant monster movie. His prior experience handling complex, big-budget productions featuring beloved comic book franchises provided good preparation, and he had a natural affinity for all cinematic things monster-related. However, the path to his involvement in *Pacific Rim* was not as direct as might be imagined. Indeed, were it not for serendipity, it might not have happened at all.

After *Hellboy II* was complete, del Toro wanted to make a film faithfully based on Mary Shelley's *Frankenstein*. He spent some months working on such a film, hoping to add it to Universal's rich catalog of monster movies. That did not work out, but in the meantime, director Peter Jackson had suggested that del Toro would be an excellent choice to direct a film version of J.R.R. Tolkien's *The Hobbit,* a planned two-part prequel to Jackson's *The Lord of the Rings* trilogy. However, after some months of work and delays, del Toro also left that project. (The project eventually morphed from a two-picture project into a new trilogy, with Peter Jackson directing each part and del Toro credited as one of the screenwriters.)[2]

Despite some hard work and initial interest from Universal, a third project also failed to pan out. The director envisioned a big-budget film version of H.P. Lovecraft's horror story *At the Mountains of Madness.* That possible film also drew interest from James Cameron, a friend of del Toro, who seemed interested in being a producer on the project. Due to the potential R-rating of the film and other concerns, however, it did not come to fruition.[3]

After these false starts, del Toro was searching for a viable project. By coincidence, he had a meeting at Legendary Pictures, where he discovered that screenwriter Travis Beacham had recently been talking with them. Beacham was exploring ways to bring a giant monster movie he had been developing to the screen. When Legendary officials brought up the subject, del Toro took an immediate interest. Beacham was an old associate del Toro liked, and the proposed movie had an angle that attracted del Toro's interest—giant monsters.

Indeed, del Toro had been a fan of kaiju movies since childhood. As a boy, he was especially fond of *The War of the Gargantuas,* a 1966 co-production of Toho and the American studio United Productions of America (UPA).[4] His memories of that movie, and others similar to it, had remained vivid over the years. Thus, the decision to join Beacham on the project was easy to make for multiple reasons.

With pieces quickly falling into place, Legendary rounded up funds to secure a considerable budget—reported in various sources as between $150 million and $200 million—and secured a distribution deal with Warner Bros. At this point, del Toro was finally on his way to his next directorial project and one of the biggest giant monster movie productions in recent memory.[5]

Although the original idea was Beacham's, both men worked closely and cordially on developing the script once del Toro joined the project. Each of them contributed ideas, changes, and refinements to flesh out the treatment that Beacham had brought to Legendary. Ultimately, the final script was a joint effort. They worked on it "for about a year," according to del Toro.[6] Yet, as a film, *Pacific Rim* would be easily identifiable as a del Toro picture. It is probably not much of an exaggeration to say that his cinematic vision and formidable attention to detail are evident in nearly every frame of the end product.

Many fine directors had made kaiju movies with good intentions, often hoping to keep the genre's reliably enthusiastic core audience happy while also aiming to expand the viewership base. But although some directors had a positive relationship with kaiju movie fans, del Toro's case was different. He and Beacham were not just making a film with fans in mind. Both men were themselves enthusiastic fans of the genre. As Beacham later said, "We speak the same fanboy vernacular. He [del Toro] has a level of enthusiasm for this sort of thing that I really haven't seen in a lot of directors."[7]

When the script was finished, Beacham and del Toro had created a monumental tale. It featured numerous battles between mysterious kaiju that attack Earth in waves and humankind's defense forces, who rely on colossal humanoid robots—called Jaegers in the film—that are so big and complex that each needs two human pilots to operate. At del Toro's insistence, the kaiju are original and fearsome in design and present a menacing appearance. (Despite del Toro's love for classic kaiju movies, Ian Nathan reports that the director "instituted a strict policy that neither beast nor robot would reference any pre-existing movie giant."[8]) While developing the distinctive look of the monsters, del Toro followed his usual practice of overseeing everything over a process that took "many, many months."[9]

The giant, human-piloted robots also have an original look. In some respects, they superficially resemble the similarly colossal mechanized heroes in *The Transformers* movie franchise, which Michael Bay had been directing since 2007. Yet, the Jaegers also call to mind Ultraman, the super-sized character at the center of numerous television series and movies from Japan's Tsuburaya Productions, which began in the mid–1960s.

The kaiju villains and Jaeger heroes appear on the screen throughout the film. Their highly orchestrated action scenes are points of emphasis throughout the production—so much so that 1700 visual effects (VFX) shots were needed. Lucasfilm's Industrial Light and Magic unit created these effects for the film's standard and 3-D versions.[10] (In that respect, *Pacific Rim*, with its heavy reliance on special effects from high-end VFX production houses, is about as far from Gareth Edwards' essentially homemade special effects experience as is imaginable.)

The project's substantial budget meant del Toro could afford the actors he wanted to hire. That said, it would not have been unusual if Legendary had wanted concrete assurances—and even veto authority—regarding del Toro's casting decisions. Given the massive money to be spent on making the movie, that probably would have been understandable. However, according to the director, he was given much freedom in casting choices and in essentially every aspect of the production. According to del Toro, Legendary said to him, "Cast anyone you want." He was surprised by this degree of freedom. However, taking Legendary officials at their word, del Toro said that he "cast actors I really wanted to work with—not just Charlie [Hunnam] and [Kikuchi] Rinko, but Idris Elba, Charlie Day, Ron Perlman, Burn Gorman."[11]

British actor Charlie Hunnam had met the director some years earlier, in 2008, when del Toro was choosing the cast for *Hellboy II*. That did not work out, but the actor made a good impression on del Toro. Hunnam subsequently achieved considerable fame starring in the FX television series *Sons of Anarchy*, which began its long run in 2008. So, when it came time to assemble the cast for *Pacific Rim*, Hunnam quickly came to mind.[12]

Japanese actor Kikuchi Rinko was not well known in the United States. However, several years before *Pacific Rim*, she had earned many accolades for her performance in Mexican director Alejandro González Iñárritu's *Babel* (2006). The film earned a Golden Globe award, and Kikuchi's performance was widely acclaimed. A subsequent Academy Award nomination substantially raised her visibility in the U.S. film industry. More significant in terms of her eventual casting in *Pacific Rim, Babel* was the work of del Toro's close and long-time friend, Iñárritu. That connection undoubtedly played some part in del Toro's eagerness to cast the actor, whom he placed in a pivotal role.

Idris Elba, the most recognizable name to American audiences when *Pacific Rim* debuted, was by then an in-demand actor who could essentially pick and choose the parts that interested him. He and del Toro seem to have admired each other's work, and his addition to the cast in a significant role helped solidify the movie's growing reputation even before filming had begun.

Many of the remaining cast members were familiar to U.S., British, and some international viewers of their work on popular movies and television shows. Of those actors, Ron Perlman, who appears in a small but amusing part, already had a long history of being a del Toro favorite. He had appeared not only in the title role throughout del Toro's *Hellboy* series but also in del Toro's *Cronos* (1993), the Mexican horror movie that was del Toro's first feature film.

In its finished version, *Pacific Rim* tells an apocalyptic kaiju story that is rich in detail and has a new and fully developed mythology. Like some previous giant monster movies, the Earth has already been attacked by mysterious kaiju as the story begins. The strange colossi seem to have come to Earth via an interdimensional portal at the ocean floor and have destroyed many of the planet's cities. In response, Earth's defense forces

## 9. For the Love of Kaiju

have developed the enormous, twin-piloted robots they call Jaegers. These mechanical behemoths equal the kaiju in size, strength, and agility. They are powerful and effective, provided they have excellent pilots guiding them.

The two pilots in each Jaeger can do their job only if they work at a fundamental level in unison. To do that, they must link their minds by using neurological "drifting." That technique deeply connects the pilots to the point that they share memories and consciousness during the process. It is intimate and profoundly emotional, requiring highly compatible pilots to work.

As the story unfolds, earth's governments have grown weary of funding the Jaeger program. They seem convinced that building walls around major population areas would better serve humanity's long-running war against the kaiju. Consequently, they want to close the Jaeger operation and switch to a conventional technique. That is despite intense opposition from defense officials, most notably including Stacker Pentecost (played by Idris Elba), who strongly cautions against that decision.

Officials tell Pentecost that the few remaining Jaegers can be used until the new defensive wall initiative is completed. With that news, the last operational Jaegers are sent to Hong Kong. From there, Pentecost, who is skeptical of officials' new plans, decides to use the Jaegers in a last-ditch effort to destroy the kaiju's undersea portal with a nuclear bomb.

At the Hong Kong base, a small and unlikely group of Jaeger pilots train for their final missions. Raleigh Becket (Charlie Hunnam) is a new arrival, but he is not a novice in the Jaeger program. Indeed, he and his brother were ace Jaeger pilots a few years earlier, and both were highly admired until a mission went wrong. When his brother died due to that incident, Raleigh walked away from the program, planning never to return to it. But now, long after those tragic events, the situation is desperate, leading Pentecost to bring Raleigh back even though the pilot is still reeling from his sibling's death.

The current pilots, who are not enthusiastic about welcoming back a pilot who had previously turned his back on the program, make life difficult for Raleigh. The returned pilot's only supporter (other than Pentecost) is Mako Mori (Kikuchi Rinko), a woman who was taken in and protected by Pentecost after her family died in a kaiju attack. Now Mako is a trusted advisor. She is keen to see Raleigh return to action, and when events lead to a pilot shortage, she yearns to become a pilot herself. Pentecost resists that idea, but he has little choice.

As it turns out, Mako is a good match for Raleigh mentally and psychologically. Indeed, even though they are strong-willed and clash about many things, tests show that the two are compatible to drift well together, which is essential for a successful Jaeger operation. Soon, they begin training together, a process that culminates when Raleigh and Mako engage in physical combat with one another. Breaking the genre's conventions, Mako emerges as the victor. Now, it seems, a powerful new pilot pairing is ready for action. However, when she finally operates the Jaeger unit with Raleigh, Mako's painful memories of her traumatic kaiju encounter in childhood cause the system to malfunction, nearly destroying one of the few remaining Jaegers. Fearing the worst if Mako were to continue as a pilot, Pentecost grounds her.

Meanwhile, two scientists on site continue to research the threat. One of them makes a startling discovery: the kaiju are biological weapons—clones sent by intelligent beings on the other side of the portal who intend a wholesale invasion of Earth. Several more battles between the Jaegers and increasingly powerful kaiju follow. The Jaegers have trouble holding their own against the increasingly powerful monsters. Having no choice, Pentecost reactivates Mako and sends her and Raleigh out to battle a kaiju that is attacking Hong Kong. They eventually subdue the beast.

In the movie's final act, Pentecost and his team prepare to destroy the portal. As planning is underway, Raleigh discovers that Pentecost is terminally ill. Yet, when one Jaeger is in dire need of a second compatible pilot for the mission, Pentecost takes the job himself, alarming Mako, who is unaware that her guardian is dying.

In a development familiar across action-oriented genres, the planet's defenders embark on a final battle on the ocean floor. As the Jaegers approach the target area, the situation is ominous. After several plot twists, it becomes evident the Jaegers are walking into a trap. A brutal undersea battle erupts. Finally, it becomes apparent that the humans can achieve victory only by making the ultimate sacrifice. Pentecost and his co-pilot do so, allowing Raleigh and Mako to finish the job. At last, the portal is closed, the invasion stops, and the kaiju are defeated. Mako and Raleigh have survived the ordeal, and humanity is saved.

In many ways, *Pacific Rim* is a classic giant monster movie, which is not surprising given the enthusiasm and warm feeling that del Toro has for the genre. Therefore, it is not surprising that throughout much of the film, monsters, and meticulously staged action, are front and center. *Pacific Rim* presents first-rate special effects and a believable, detailed fictional world in which to place them. There are many scenes of spectacular kaiju action, an inclusion that typically pleases the kaiju fan base and might also appeal to fans of action- and spectacle-oriented films.

But as long had been an issue for kaiju movies, an important question remained. Was there enough here to appeal to the types of viewers who already liked the genre and expand the audience base to include general audiences? On that front, the results seem less certain. A film review published in *Variety* immediately after the production's premiere is enlightening. In the piece, critic Justin Chang makes a relevant observation. "While the director's love for his material is at once sincere and self-evident," he notes, "it's the sort of devotion that winds up holding all but the most like-minded viewers at an uninvolving remove."[13] The result, he adds, is an "overall experience if not unlike that of watching someone play a highly elaborate videogame."

Indeed, the film's primary emphasis on battles between the Jaegers and kaiju—the single thing that fans may find among the film's best features—may be problematic for those not already immersed in those types of movies. That, at least, appears to be the verdict that film critic Matt Zoller Seitz reached in a 2013 review. He was saying what numerous other viewers may have also believed at the time: that the "fight scenes are often shot too close-in for my taste, and they go on for too long." Of course, that criticism could also be made of numerous special-effects-laden blockbusters of the era. On that point, Setiz says that similarly overly long fight scenes "also afflicted *Iron Man 3* (2013), *Star Trek Into the Darkness* (2013), *Man of Steel* (2013), and other recent summer films,"[14] so his critique does not single out del Toro's movie in that respect.

Based on what appears on screen, it is evident that much of del Toro's time and attention—as well as much of the movie's budget—went into planning, designing, and executing the impressive CGI battle sequences. However, *Pacific Rim* is more than just that. Even critic Seitz seems to agree when he writes, "*Pacific Rim* knows what sort of film it wishes to be; it is that film and much more. In its clanking, crashing way, it's real science fiction, a play of ideas."[15] *Variety* critic Nathan Ian agrees, writing that "for all its mayhem, *Pacific Rim* is a film with more emotion than its trailers could have led you to expect."[16]

Some may have expected this "emotion" to emerge from some sort of romantic subplot involving the two lead characters, Mako and Raleigh. After all, romantic subplots involving the hero(es) are so common as to be a trope in the genre. So, when they first appear on screen together, viewers may have thought that is where del Toro was also taking the Mako and Raleigh story arc. The two show hints of that sort of screen chemistry in their scenes together. But interestingly, del Toro does not take the film into romantic territory when dealing with his two leads' emotional relationship.

In a turnabout from standard expectations, in which some sort of romantic entanglement between the male and female characters would have seemed inevitable, del Toro upends things and does so in multiple ways. He and co-screenwriter Beacham not only avoid a romantic storyline; they also invert the relative position of the two lead characters.

Again, first impressions may be misleading. For example, many viewers might initially surmise that the film's main hero is Charlie Hunnam's character, Raleigh. That presumption would be understandable given that he is the male lead in an action-oriented kaiju movie, and overwhelmingly, such films—like nearly all hero-oriented genre movies—historically have presented the male lead as the main hero. To the extent that women are included in the ranks of the heroic at all, they usually have been relegated to second-tier, second-class status in terms of heroism.

However, Kikuchi Rinko's Mako character is as heroic as Raleigh—more so when looking at the storyline overall. In some ways, Mako holds the multi-faceted narrative together as arguably the central character in the film and as the one whose transformational life story is most fully revealed to the audience. In that sense, Mako is at the emotional core of the film. Indeed, from one perspective, *Pacific Rim* can be described as the story of Mako's journey from a terrified young girl, revealed in a flashback, to a full-fledged hero.[17]

This reading of the film is far from idle speculation. Based on what he said in a post-premiere interview, it is very close to what the director had in mind. As much as del Toro set out to make a kaiju movie that harkened back to and honored the films he loved so much as a child, he also had something in mind beyond that. He later said, "I thought of *Pacific Rim* as a Russian Doll, with a hurt girl at the center, and then Mako, and then a giant twenty-five-story robot. And finding that the strength came from the fact that at some point as a child, she was afraid, and she's not afraid anymore. Which I think is essentially a metaphor for all our lives."[18]

Mako thus provides the nucleus around which the rest of the movie is constructed. She gives a human center to what could have been just a long series of scenes showing giant monsters and robots. That del Toro succeeds in doing this is undoubtedly partially due to the strong performance from Kikuchi, who, in the words of one reviewer, "manages to render her character's shrinking-violet reserve as intriguing as her sudden displays of physical prowess."[19]

That is not to say that *Pacific Rim* offers a flawless viewing experience completely devoid of problematic representations. Writer Brooke Jaffe, for example, observes that the entire film has only two named female characters, and of those, only Mako is central to the story.[20] Yet, Jaffe also notes del Toro's success in "smashing gender-based action movie tropes."[21] And that is not something that could be taken for granted in many blockbuster-style movies of the time. Jaffe further notes that del Toro avoids presenting Mako in a way that is "sexualized for fanservice." Admittedly, that is a very low bar indicative of the dismal slowness that has characterized meaningful reform in the film business. (Or, as Jaffe says, "It's a sad state of affairs when *not* sexualizing any woman who walks on screen is [seen as] a rare and commendable act."[22])

Yet, regardless of the director's intentions, some writers conclude that *Pacific Rim* falls short of the mark in treating gender issues. Jason Barr, for example, notes that the Mako character lacks full autonomy and that the character's "destiny is deeply affected and manipulated by male characters." In addition, Barr observes that Mako and the only other significant named female, a character named Sasha Kaidonovsky (played by Heather Doerksen) "never interact" at all. Based on these and other considerations, Barr concludes that *Pacific Rim* is "not female-friendly or even [a] female-acknowledging film."[23]

Undoubtedly, people will continue to debate this issue not only with regard to *Pacific Rim* but also concerning genre movies and cinema overall. However, regardless of where such discussions might eventually lead, it seems clear that from the start del Toro intended to approach the film (and the Mako Mori character, specifically) in a way that broke with sexist conventions. According to del Toro's account, he wanted Mako to have "equal force" with the male characters and to be a "real, earnestly drawn character."[24] Whether del Toro successfully fulfilled this ambition may be in the eye of the beholder. However, the director seems successful in steering clear of any overt or implied romantic subplot, offering audiences a rare example of a "close, emotionally intimate male-female friendship that never turns physical."[25]

The human element is integral to *Pacific Rim*, but the kaiju are its primary focus. That contrasts markedly with *Monsters* or *The Mist*. In those films, the giant monsters theoretically could be replaced with a different type of threat without altering the story too much. In *Pacific Rim*, these colossal creatures are not only essential; substituting something else for them would dramatically change the entire story.

Whether it is necessary to dwell on whether the movie's giant beasts have some deeper meaning beyond simply being monsters is an open question. For example, Jason Barr summarizes the film's story as basically a tale of shock and awe. His impression of it as a movie that introduces threatening beasts early on and continues "the destruction and violence with little interruption for the entirety of the film" seems reasonable, at least from a certain point of view.[26] Still, Barr also notes that the film's imagery evokes natural disasters, ecological emergencies, and the looming climate crisis.[27] *Mother Jones* writer Asawin Suebsaeng reaches a similar conclusion, going so far as to write that "the true culprit in *Pacific Rim* isn't actually a sea monster from another dimension. It's pollution."[28]

However, while *Pacific Rim* contains tacit environmental and climate change messages at some level, such themes seem mainly incidental to the production overall. Jason Barr may be essentially correct in seeing *Pacific Rim* as "standard kaiju fare," filled with "big, blockbuster battles that have little semblance—and do not wish to provide semblance—to modern realities."[29] As he argues, it is primarily the type of film that seldom veers from "familiar territories." There may be "sermonizing about pollution, climate change, or nuclear disaster," but the movie avoids "commenting on other current events such as terrorism."[30]

Although that view may be overstated, it seems true that del Toro was mainly interested in making a kaiju movie similar to the escapist, entertainment-focused films from his youth. Using *Pacific Rim* to comment on post-9/11 life or other pressing world issues does not appear to have been high on his agenda. The film is undoubtedly a product of its time, as movies, by their nature, are. But it is a film that reflects an interest in film, *per se*—not only classic kaiju fare but also many other types of motion pictures. Scholar Nicholas Bollinger goes so far as to label *Pacific Rim* a "cult movie" that is "full of self-aware intertextuality."[31] There is something to that perspective. Indeed, del Toro makes liberal use of references to numerous other works. As Bollinger notes, "The sheer number of references to other movies … is staggering."[32] Indeed, beyond references to kaiju movies, various scenes are reminiscent of films from the James Bond and *Star Wars* franchises, among others.

With its hefty budget and the high expectations that undoubtedly came with it, there was much pressure for del Toro to deliver a movie that would perform well at the box office. As it turned out, however, it did not do quite as well in the U.S. theatrical market as expected, generating only about $102 million in ticket sales domestically. However, published sources indicate it did much better internationally, yielding over $309 million in other markets—more than three times the domestic U.S. total.[33] That meant that given the production budget and typical marketing and distribution costs, *Pacific Rim* was likely at least a moderately profitable undertaking for its backers, Legendary and Warner Bros. Whether it was successful enough to warrant the launching of a new franchise—an idea that had been much discussed throughout the filmmaking process was not yet clear. (Eventually, a sequel did materialize. *Pacific Rim Uprising* was released in 2018, but by then, del Toro had mostly diminished his role, remaining on board mainly as one of several producers.)

*Pacific Rim* was a rarity in some ways. It launched a fully blown kaiju world with a rich, textured backstory at a time when big-budgeted, blockbuster-style giant monster movies usually relied on previously established kaiju characters with global recognition. Both del Toro and the studios may have hoped for greater financial returns and more critical acclaim, but the film did respectively well and was far from a failure as a film.

In any case, Legendary seems to have been undaunted by the genre. Indeed, during most of the time *Pacific Rim* was in process, it was moving forward with a new kaiju movie for which it had even loftier ambitions.

# 10

# Hollywood Tries Again
## *Godzilla* (2014)

By the time *Pacific Rim* was introduced to global audiences in 2013, Legendary Pictures and Warner Bros. had already planned another kaiju movie for which they harbored even greater ambitions. A few years before *Pacific Rim*, Legendary had acquired rights to make a new movie that would bring Godzilla back from a long hiatus.[1] (The previous rights deal between Godzilla owner Toho Studio and Sony-TriStar had since lapsed.) With Warner Bros. co-producing and providing additional financial backing, Legendary was now clear to make a new Hollywood-style Godzilla movie. Hoping it would be the first in a new franchise effort, the studio partners wanted to launch it as soon as 2012.[2] Ultimately, that proved to be slightly too ambitious, but by 2014 it was finally ready.

Given the disappointment generated by Roland Emmerich's 1998 *Godzilla*, it may seem odd that U.S. studios expressed interest in the famous kaiju character. However, executives at Legendary, which spearheaded the project, were undaunted by TriStar's 1998 misfire. They knew it would be essential to get things right in their production and not repeat TriStar's mistakes. However, they were confident they could leverage the monster's global fame in a top-quality release.

That self-assurance was apparent in a 2010 statement issued shortly after Legendary completed its deal with the Japanese rights owner. "Toho's Godzilla franchise boasts one of the most widely recognized film creatures worldwide,"[3] it said, adding: "Legendary intends to approach the film and its characters in the most authentic manner possible. The company will, in the near future, announce a filmmaker to helm the film for an intended 2012 release. The film will fall under the company's co-production and co-financing deal with Warner Bros. Toho will distribute the film in Japan."[4]

Like studio leaders in Hollywood, Toho's president also expressed high hopes for the new agreement, saying, "We are delighted in rebooting the character together to realize its much-anticipated return by fans from all over the world."⁵ Given the lofty expectations expressed by all involved, the stakes were high. If Legendary–Warner Bros. failed to deliver anything short of a blockbuster, there was every reason to think their movie would be judged as another failed American attempt to tame Toho's most famous monster.

Determined to succeed, Legendary and Warner Bros. agreed on a generous budget to ensure the new Godzilla film would not be hampered by insufficient resources. Yet, if the history of filmmaking has shown anything, it is that money alone does not assure a successful production. In this project, as in others, the most crucial factor would be the creative team making the film. And in assembling that team, the most critical decision would be selecting a suitable director.

In a somewhat surprising move, that key position went to Gareth Edwards. At the time, Edwards had only one feature-length feature on his resume—the very low-budget film, *Monsters*. However, that 2010 production had won numerous accolades and impressed many, a remarkable feat considering that it was made on a shoestring budget. Although the choice of Edwards had some degree of risk, he had solid skills and proven know-how. Most importantly, in his debut movie, he had already shown an affinity for using special effects in service to a film's story rather than relying on effects for their own sake. He also demonstrated that he knew how to bring a focus on human characters to a production in which giant monsters played a key role. And more than that, he proved he could get a quality movie to the finish line even under challenging circumstances.

With a director on board, one of the next major tasks was to finalize a script. Legendary had hired David Callaham to prepare a preliminary version of the story. When it came time to convert this early work into a workable script, Edwards worked with screenwriter Max Borenstein. Much of their collaboration was accomplished via long-distance phone calls, with Edwards in Great Britain and Borenstein in California.⁶

Borenstein grew up watching Toho Godzilla movies. He especially admired the original 1954 classic, which he has described as a "masterful" film and "an intense sociological document of its time," a reference to its clear reflections of the early, fearful days of the Atomic Age.⁷ Unsurprisingly, his work on a new Godzilla feature carried forward one of the original's central premises: "When you fool with nature, you get untold consequences."⁸

As the process continued, writer David S. Goyer, and later Drew Pearce, also worked on the screenplay. Eventually, Legendary also brought in Frank Darabont to develop the script's final version. Darabont was known as a skilled writer and no stranger to working with complex screenplays. Perhaps just as importantly, he was the screenwriter-director of *The Mist*, the 2007 adaptation of Stephen King's story with a giant-monster angle.

If the new Godzilla movie were to achieve blockbuster status, it probably would need a solid cast to bolster its chances. Ample funds were available, but finding the right actors to fill each role was essential. And since Edwards was intent on making a serious film, securing the services of actors who could bring a sense of gravitas to their performances was crucial. Edwards realized that many top actors might not think a Godzilla movie would do anything to enhance their reputations. Indeed, they likely would think the opposite. So, to be sure that potential actors knew he was intent on making something worthwhile, he told them he would not make a "popcorn blockbuster."[9] For the actors who signed on to appear, he said, "We need a performance that is as a strong as in an Oscar-bait drama."[10]

Ultimately, the project attracted what the United Press International dubbed "an A-list cast."[11] Aaron Taylor-Johnson and Elizabeth Olsen were cast as Ford Brody and Elle Brody, the married couple whose story is at the heart of the human drama aspects of the film. Bryan Cranston, who had recently finished the hit television series *Breaking Bad*, agreed to appear as Joe Brody, Ford's father, and award-winning French actor Juliette Binoche signed on to play Sandra Brody. For one of the film's other prominent roles, veteran Japanese actor Ken Watanabe, well-known to global film audiences, was selected to play scientist Dr. Ishiro Serizawa. The remainder of the large cast was similarly filled out with accomplished actors, including Sally Hawkins, David Strathairn, Zhang Ziyi, Richard T. Jones, and Hironobu Kanagawa.

Regardless of the positives the human cast could bring to the screen, the movie needed much more than that. The Godzilla creature needed a convincing design that passed muster with kaiju movie fans and general audiences. As has been the case with most kaiju movies, the final character design was achieved only after exploring many possible options. With his interest in respecting the character's origins in *Gojira*, some may have presumed that Edwards would select something closely patterned on that precedent. However, the director realized that being too literal in borrowing from the 1954 version of the creature could cause problems. Too much of a "retro-Godzilla" look could feel "a little cartoony," he thought, so he instead chose a design that would give the monster a look that was "a bit more angular."[12] Working with Weta, Peter Jackson's famous special effects company in New Zealand, it took months of what Edwards called "trial and error" to reach a final design.[13]

Next came special effects, another facet of the production that could make or break it, depending on whether audiences found the visuals convincing. With a budget massively larger than was available for Edwards' previous film *Monsters,* many options were on the table, including the latest and most expensive effects. Hardcore kaiju fans would be demanding, but Edwards also had to consider the broader audience of general viewers. They would want to see visual effects that equaled or surpassed those in blockbusters like the Marvel movies they knew and loved and routinely drew huge crowds. Still, with years of experience doing special effects before becoming a director, Edwards knew that the visuals would have to be handled judiciously. Overuse could be counterproductive. As he later said, "You get battle fatigue quite quickly when you have these fight sequences at the end of the movie. And you can easily peak and then hit a plateau and then there's nowhere else to go."[14]

To lead this aspect of the production, Edwards brought in a heavyweight special effects expert. Jim Rygiel, who won an Academy Award for the *Lord of the Rings* trilogy, brought top-notch experience and a contemporary sensibility to the production. He oversaw effects work farmed out to numerous specialty companies, including Weta and other special effects outfits. With multiple effects firms on board, Rygiel and Edwards worked to show the audience the kaiju as realistically as possible, portraying the creatures as living beings that interacted with their natural surroundings.[15]

Some months after principal photography wrapped up the previous summer, *Godzilla* was finally ready to debut in early 2014. Now, its makers would see if Edwards had made a movie that could live up to its public relations hype.

A montage during the opening credits reveals that giant monsters have been around for a long time and that reports of atomic bomb testing in the Pacific after World War II were cover stories designed for multinational efforts to defeat a terrifying monster.

The scene then jumps ahead to a Philippines jungle in the late 1990s, where something huge seems to have recently emerged from a crater. Dr. Serizawa, a Japanese scientist brought in to investigate, is not sure what. Meanwhile, nuclear engineer Joe Brody worries about recent tremors threatening the power station he oversees in Japan. The worsening situation leads to a reactor failure that leads to the tragic death of scientist Sandra Brody, Joe's wife.

Flash forward 15 years. Ford Brody, the now-adult son of Joe and Samantha, has just returned to his home in San Francisco, where he reunites with his wife, Elle, and their young son after an extended tour of duty in the U.S. Navy. Before he can get settled, however, Ford receives a call. His estranged father Joe has been arrested in Japan and needs Ford's help. With mixed emotions, Ford heads to Japan to sort things out.

After he is released, Joe insists that Ford accompany him to the home they abandoned 15 years earlier. Complicating the situation further, their former home is deep inside a no-entry zone, said to be contaminated by radiation from the earlier crisis. The two men secretly go there anyway, only to discover that the area is not actually contaminated. Concluding that they had stumbled on some sort of coverup, Joe and Ford continue to their destination, where Joe retrieves research documents that he left there many years earlier.

As they are about to leave the area, the two men are detained by a security detail and taken to the nearby power station. Before the situation is resolved, radiation levels at the plant abruptly go haywire. In the resulting turmoil, Joe and Ford are released from custody just as a colossal creature emerges from beneath the surface. The giant monster, dubbed a MUTO (Massive Unidentified Terrestrial Organism), destroys much of the complex. Shockingly, Joe Brody is seriously injured and dies a short time later. Before long, American soldiers arrive at the restricted zone to inform Dr. Serizawa, who is running a secret project at the former power station, that the U.S. military is assuming control. After reviewing the situation, the U.S. military commander and Dr. Serizawa realize that Joe Brody might have had valuable information.

Officials tell Ford about a secret kaiju crisis that erupted in the Cold War and that recent events seem related. With this glimpse of the big picture, Ford tells the officials his father suspected there was more than one MUTO and that the creatures were communicating. Ford heads home, but the MUTO from Japan arrives on the scene during his stopover in Hawaii. Godzilla, which has returned after a long absence, closely follows the other creature, evidently in some sort of response to the MUTO threat. The two kaiju soon battle in the Honolulu area before abruptly leaving.

Finally, military authorities realize what is going on. The MUTO from Japan is heading to California to mate with another MUTO headed in that direction. Godzilla appears to be in pursuit, presumably to destroy the two MUTOs, as Dr. Serizawa had already suspected. The three kaiju converge in San Francisco, where spectacular new monster battles commence. The military wants to prevent widespread devastation and, over Dr. Serizawa's objections, decides to lure the kaiju out to sea with a nuclear weapon intended to destroy them.

As the military attempts to deliver the nuclear weapon to the ship for that purpose, many problems arise. In one incident, Ford's son and other children nearly die. In another, the atomic bomb somehow ends up in the middle of the city. That latter incident causes Ford and his team to parachute into the area to deal with the problem. They eventually manage to retrieve the weapon and deliver it to the ship. In the film's final section, the kaiju fights intensify, and Godzilla finally displays his full power using his atomic breath against the MUTO creature. Godzilla is temporarily victorious but weakened in the process. When MUTO reawakens, and attacks, Ford is still aboard the boat carrying the nuclear device. But Godzilla suddenly reappears for a final battle that brings the creatures back to the city.

After an epic fight, Godzilla prevails but seemingly dies in the process. Meanwhile, a helicopter rescues Ford just before the bomb explodes. In the film's last moments, Ford is finally reunited with Elle and their son, but the city lies in ruins. Across town, Dr. Serizawa gazes at Godzilla's lifeless body when Godzilla suddenly reawakens. The film closes as the giant creature heads back out to sea.

With a "ride off into the sunset" finale, Edwards gives viewers a nostalgia-inducing conclusion. He also sets up the studio's clear intention to produce at least a sequel and, most likely, a new, American-centric franchise. Initial responses suggested that the director had delivered a production that seemed to make Godzilla's future more secure than had been the case in many years.

In resuscitating *Godzilla* for a theatrical release, Edwards faced the same issues as other recent kaiju filmmakers. Although he, like some other directors (including luminaries such as Peter Jackson and Guillermo del Toro), was a fan of classic giant monster movies, Edwards' challenge was to make something that would do more than cater to kaiju fans. Although the movie included some nostalgic aspects, Legendary and Warner Bros. were banking on Edwards' making a film that would appeal to the same sort of broad, largely youthful audiences that flocked to the latest blockbusters from Marvel and other studios. His mandate, therefore, was to create a contemporary movie with wide appeal.

He seems mostly to have accomplished that goal. Upon Godzilla's release, many more people were satisfied with Edwards' film than in previous American-made attempts to create a blockbuster-style kaiju movie.[16] It probably helped that Edwards brought his unique storytelling style to the project. Although still a novice director in some respects, he was not afraid to break audience expectations or to include an edgy sensibility to his work.

That said, an average U.S. viewer was probably more than a bit surprised when Edwards killed off not only the Sandra Brody character but also her husband, Joe Brody, early in the proceedings. Indeed, many people likely presumed that actor Bryan Cranston—then exceedingly popular due to his role in the hit television series *Breaking Bad*—was Godzilla's main star. To have his Joe Brody character perish scarcely 30 minutes into the film was a calculated jolt. However, people who had seen *Monsters* and paid close attention to it may have realized the director had shown a willingness to kill off the main characters before. (Edwards would do so again in his following project, *Rogue One: A Star Wars Story*, which had a plot that proved to be a virtual bloodbath.)

From the beginning, Legendary's *Godzilla* was planned and conceived foremost as a kaiju movie, meaning that the human story could not overwhelm the focus on giant monsters. However, Edwards wanted to offer an engaging human drama that would run throughout the movie and help hold things together. However, despite those intentions, reactions to the film's human storylines were decidedly mixed.

*Washington Post* critic Michael O'Sullivan was among those who were not won over by the human dimensions of the story. To him, the kaiju seemed "way more interesting than any of the human characters."[17] O'Sullivan questioned the production's minimal use of Juliette Binoche and Bryan Cranston, and he was unimpressed by Aaron Taylor-Johnson's performance. Another drawback, according to the critic, was "casting Ken Watanabe, Sally Hawkins, and David Strathairn, and then giving them nothing to do."[18] Some viewers may also have been surprised at the minimal screen time given to Elizabeth Olsen, whose character, Elle, plays a mostly secondary role in the story. (None of the women characters are much more than window dressing in the film.)

Some viewers had a very different and more positive reaction. For example, famous film critic Leonard Maltin wrote, "While some of these characters are genre archetypes, I'm happy to say that the writing and acting never sink to the level of cliché."[19]

While some found the human story somewhat lacking, others were less than happy with the amount of screen time devoted the film's kaiju star, Godzilla. In the eyes of some, Edwards does not pay enough attention to Godzilla and the other kaiju to give audiences a satisfying experience. As a result, some people thought the movie was "dull."

Jason Barr, who argues that many kaiju films are influenced by Kabuki theater, attributes some of the audience complaints to unfamiliarity with the slow start that is typical in that traditional form.[20] From a different perspective, however, the film can serve as an exercise of the less-is-more approach. By limiting the screen time of Godzilla and other kaiju characters, Edwards arguably adds additional weight and significance to the scenes in which the monsters appear. That had been the apparent approach in several then-recent kaiju films (including *Gamera the Brave, The Mist, Cloverfield,* Edwards' *Monsters,* and others), which used kaiju screen time sparingly. Interestingly, it is the exact opposite of what had appeared in *Godzilla: Final Wars*, which, though providing a hit parade of kaiju battles, had been a disappointment to viewers and Toho Studio ten years earlier.

Even if concerns about kaiju screen time are set aside, the question

## 10. Hollywood Tries Again

remains: what type of giant monster movie was Edwards trying to make? It is not an exercise in nostalgia (though it has some nostalgic elements) aiming to revisit the campy kaiju movies that were popular in the later 1960s, 1970s, and 1980s. Nor is it an attempt at parody or dark humor, two approaches that Edwards carefully tried to avoid. On the contrary, Edwards seems to have sincerely intended to make a serious movie that honored the source material—meaning Godzilla had to be the focus— while avoiding the pitfalls of a patronizing rehash.

That seriousness of intent can be seen when Edwards ties the proceedings in his movie to the source material, especially to the original *Gojira*. The character of Dr. Serizawa is an obvious nod to the 1954 original, which also features a leading character by that name. More significant is the somber tone and gravity Edwards intends to bring to the screen. Indeed, as with the Toho classic six decades earlier, Edwards aims to present a movie that can be taken seriously. Despite occasional moments of nostalgia, his *Godzilla* is a film that tries to avoid anything that could be interpreted as camp. Instead, it imagines a scenario in which the massive creatures and scenes of apocalyptic destruction, which in other contexts could look absurd and far-fetched, are portrayed as realistically as he could manage. One could argue whether the director successfully reached that lofty goal, but his sincere intentions seem evident.

The 1954 *Gojira* movie was a thinly veiled allegory about the folly and potentially nightmarish implications of atomic weapons. That aspect of the film had been abundantly clear in the Japanese release at the time. However, it is essential to recall that very few Americans saw that version of the film. Instead, American audiences mostly knew the substantially recut version of *Gojira* that U.S. distributors released in 1956 with the new title, *Godzilla, King of the Monsters!* More than simple trimming, the U.S. version substantially altered the original narrative and included some entirely new scenes featuring American actor Raymond Burr, who had not appeared in the original. When the changes for the American edition are considered, the anti-nuclear theme, which is thoroughly woven into *Gorjia*, is far less noticeable. (Given the centrality of the U.S. nuclear arsenal in 1950s Cold War politics, it is easy to see why U.S. distributors would have been interested in toning down the original's anti-nuclear stance.) The result was that in 1956, and for decades that followed, many U.S. viewers likely were oblivious to the anti-nuclear theme of the Japanese version. Indeed, in contrast to the impression many Americans may have gotten from Godzilla's first cinematic appearance in the United States, the Japanese version was "much darker in tone, with the monster working as a clear metaphor for nuclear menace."[21]

Probably no one expected, or perhaps even considered, that Edwards would bring the anti-nuclearism of mid-century Japan's *Gojira* to his 21st-century production, and indeed, he did not do so. However, in many respects, the 2014 movie does harken back to *Gojira* in tone and, in some cases, substance. Like *Gojira*, for example, Edwards' film is infused with some dimensions of horror. Many Toho sequels substantially deemphasized the horror angle to the point that that dimension is difficult to spot in later entries in the series. However, Edwards not only brings horror back; he makes it central and broadly organizes his film around it. It is evident in the overall darkness of the visual design, in the scenes of terror and death, and in the starkness of the story itself.

These psychological considerations are probably most apparent in the many scenes where Godzilla and the other kaiju are shown in low-light situations and at night. Doing so meant that the dimly lit environment sometimes partially obscures bravura effects. Yet, the dark atmosphere emphasizes the horror aspects of the narrative. Interestingly, that same atmosphere is one of the hallmarks of the original 1954 *Gojira*, in which many scenes similarly are filmed to emphasize darkness.

Edwards had included much mayhem and death in his previous feature, *Monsters*, going so far as to kill off his two lead characters. (Interestingly, *Monsters* is filmed and edited in a way that largely obscures the lead characters' off-screen fate, so much so that some initial viewers seem not to have realized that they perish.) Yet, *Monsters* presents its kaiju sparingly and with a sense of awe and strange beauty. The film focuses on the human characters and their evolving relationship, but it only mildly evokes horror roots or connections. That all changes in Edwards' *Godzilla*.

The monsters in the 2014 *Godzilla* seem remorseless and deadly in a way that is similar to the 1954 classic. That is entirely the case for the MUTOs in Edwards' film, and, except for Dr. Serizawa, the film's human characters presume it is the case for Godzilla, too. Indeed, aside from Serizawa, the human characters are not in awe of the creatures. They are terrified by them. And like many classic horror films, the fear they cause is especially frightening due to intense danger and unnerving uncertainty. Edwards seems to have gone to considerable lengths to heighten the film's sense of dread. For the most part, he takes the story's premises very seriously, and to keep the audience in a somber mood, he carefully tries to avoid camp.

Edwards' film is partially a throwback to *Gojira* in another way, also. In the 2014 movie, Godzilla is more than a huge but otherwise straightforward monster. Indeed, like the creature in *Gorjira*, the 2014 Godzilla is not only a force of nature. It is the restorer of the natural order, appearing suddenly to rebalance the world when things have gone terribly wrong. Of course, the causes of imbalance differ in the two films. In *Gojira*, humans have unleashed atomic weapons that rupture that balance. In the 2014 *Godzilla*, the MUTOs are the culprits, though there are some hints that humans have inadvertently made things worse. Despite these differences, Godzilla does not engage in destruction for its own sake or because it is an agent of evil. Instead, Godzilla is a force intent on setting the earth, or perhaps the entire cosmos, right. Its destructiveness, which admittedly causes much collateral damage and death, is a side-effect of that overarching purpose, not an end in itself.

In positioning Godzilla as the restorer of balance, Edwards evokes some themes prominent in Toho's *Godzilla, Mothra, and King Ghidorah: All-Out Monsters Attack* from 2001. As in that production, Edwards' Godzilla is not an agent of good or bad but a powerful natural force that stands guard and preserves the natural order. Even though roughly the same theme appears in both films, there is at least one significant difference. Compared to the 2001 film, Edwards takes a more generic approach to Godzilla-as-force-of-nature. The 2001 movie situated Godzilla's behavior within a framework deeply rooted in traditional Japanese cultural beliefs. Edwards abandons that approach. In his version, the monster still exists to reassert nature's balance, but that angle of the story lacks the overt moral framework that director Kaneko Shusuke established in his 2001 movie. It is a subtle difference that portrays Godzilla as an agnostic rather than a supernatural being.

General moral questions appear somewhat more frequently than nuclear issues, though treatment of them is vague. For example, various high-stakes situations force characters to make difficult choices. One of the first occurs early in the film when Joe Brody must decide whether to follow protocol and close the safety doors before his wife escapes from danger. (He does close the door and then heartbreakingly watches his wife and others perish on the other side of a protective window.) Then there is the matter of whether officials should admit the existence of the kaiju or keep the public in the dark. (They choose to keep the secret.) Characters must also decide whether to sacrifice some members of the public to save others and use a nuclear weapon to defeat the kaiju, even though that would pose significant consequences. In these and other parts of the story, people face a series of choices in which no good options exist.

Some people have noted the prominent role of the U.S. military throughout the film. Indeed, Aaron Brody, who is probably intended to serve as the main character, is a U.S. Navy armaments expert, which is a departure from many giant monsters features that have a civilian protagonist. The U.S. military remained mainly in the background in Edwards' previous feature, *Monsters*. In that film's story, American troops and firepower were no more than marginally successful in the long and drawn-out fight against alien kaiju. Contrastingly, the U.S. military is front and center in his version of Godzilla. Not only is Ford Brody, one of the main characters, an active member of the U.S. Navy, the film overall depicts a mighty U.S. military at the center of the struggle.

In a related matter, the kaiju threat is presumably something all humankind would need to address. In the 2014 movie, however, only the United States seems to play much of a role. Indeed, the United States takes a go-it-alone strategy in which it seemingly has little use or respect for any other country. In many ways, Edwards' *Godzilla* can be seen as a very Americanist movie. It is U.S.-centric to the point that it simply presumes the United States will naturally take the lead in important matters as if there is no other possible way.

However, such nuances probably did not play much of a role in the movie-going public's reception of 2014's *Godzilla* or any other giant monster movie. Such concerns seem far removed from the interests and expectations of hardcore kaiju fans or the general movie-going public, at least in the United States, where neither the Godzilla character nor the genre is associated with deep meaning. What *Variety* critic Peter Debruge said in his review of the film could be applied to the genre overall: "Godzilla movies, like wrestling matches, are ultimately judged by the quality of the mayhem, and Edwards excels at blowing things up."[22] From that vantage point, as long as Edwards delivered a film that found an exciting and engaging way to win fans over using the traditional formula, the film could be judged a Hollywood success.

Edwards' *Godzilla* entry did respectable business at the box office. Against an estimated production budget upwards of $160 million,[23] the film reportedly grossed $529 million. More than 60 percent of that total came from the international market. The $201 million domestic total represented a respectable if not entirely spectacular theatrical performance. (An additional $45 million in subsequent home video sales added to the film's success.)[24]

Interestingly, that domestic total was insufficient to earn a place among the top earners in U.S. theaters that year. With a flood of blockbuster rivals—including Marvel-Disney's *Guardians of the Galaxy*, Lionsgate's *Hunger Games: Mockingjay, Part I*, and Marvel-Disney's *Captain America: The Winter Soldier*—Edwards' movie failed to earn a spot among the top-ten highest-grossing films in U.S. theaters that year, instead placing eleventh.[25] Still, the film did well enough to keep dreams of a sequel— and perhaps a new franchise—alive.

Regardless of how one looks at the film's performance and reputation, Edwards seemed to have erased the bad memories that many film-goers, and especially kaiju fans, had harbored for Roland Emmerich's 1998

## 10. Hollywood Tries Again

movie. Some had faulted certain aspects of Edwards' 2014 film, but the complaints were mostly mild overall. It was, therefore, not surprising that his name was attached to the planned sequel soon after it became apparent his *Godzilla* mostly satisfied crowds and was on its way to generating substantial box-office numbers.

In the meantime, however, producers at Disney had also become interested in the director. That interest became a commitment when Disney's Lucasfilm unit signed Edwards to direct *Rogue One: A Star Wars Story*. With the director's services now tied up elsewhere, Edwards exited the Godzilla sequel, leaving the unanswered question of who would be the next filmmaker to tackle Toho's famous monster.

# 11

# Reclaiming a Monster's Legacy
## *Shin Godzilla* (2016)

Legendary Pictures' *Godzilla* earned enough at the box office to secure 14th on the list of top-performing films worldwide for 2014.[1] Taking in over $500 million, it was a solid success financially. Yet, this achievement should be taken in the context of the film industry of the time. The pressure to produce outsized box-office receipts had become a fact of life for directors of big-budget features. In the blockbuster-dominated era, insiders regarded big numbers like those generated by *Godzilla* as ordinary. Only truly massive ticket sales could impress them. So, while *Godzilla's* numbers looked good in some sense, they were overshadowed by the highest-grossing movie that year, *Transformers: Age of Extinction*. That film took in more than a billion dollars across all markets, nearly double *Godzilla's* total.

Still, although the 2014 *Godzilla* did not break the top-ten films or yield spectacular financial success, it drew a large audience due to its solid, if not stellar, box-office performance. In Tokyo, Toho studio executives took notice of the American production's success. It had been a decade since *Godzilla: Final Wars*, the studio's most recent entry in its series featuring the monster. Now that Edwards' film showed pent-up interest in the giant green monster, Toho officials decided it was time to revive their franchise. Since the company wisely had retained the right to continue making Godzilla movies in-house even if the character was also licensed elsewhere, the path to a new Toho movie featuring its most famous kaiju was wide open.

It did not take long before the wheels were set in motion. Toho announced that it would soon bring its new Godzilla to the screen at a press conference on December 5, 2014. No director was attached to the project yet, and few details were available. However, Toho's Ueda Taichi promised the work would be completely original and thus not tied to Edwards' Hollywood movie. "We have developed the technology to create

## 11. Reclaiming a Monster's Legacy

a new Godzilla," he said. "I want it. I can now do what I couldn't do in the past with that level of quality. I want to make a work that can compete with Hollywood!"[2]

Toho spokespersons did not reveal what approach the studio would take to achieve the goal of producing a film that would be competitive with Edwards' computer-generated visual spectacle. Would Toho forego heavy use of CGI, a feature of most then-current blockbusters, and instead continue to rely on actors in traditional costumes (use of so-called "rubber suits") to create giant monsters on screen? He did not say. However, he emphasized that Toho wanted to develop a series of kaiju movies for modern audiences. And as an additional indication that the studio was taking the franchise very seriously, the producer also revealed that Toho had established an internal Godzilla Strategy Team to look at ways to bolster the studio's storied franchise in screen media and beyond.[3]

More information was forthcoming several months later, in the spring of 2015, when Toho revealed that the company had selected two directors for the project. Anno Hideaki was to write and serve as the overall director of the film. The studio named Higuchi Shinji as the director of special effects and co-director.

Anno was mainly known at the time for creating and directing the popular Evangelion franchise, an influential post-apocalyptic anime series of films and television shows, and for a few other productions. Interestingly, Anno also made a documentary about the 1999 movie *Gamera 3: The Revenge of Iris*.

Anno was initially reluctant to accept the directing offer. He was working hard on other projects and was unsure about taking on a potentially vast and daunting new project at the time. Eventually, however, he had a change of heart. In a 2015 interview, he said he had been "moved by the sincerity of Toho and the enthusiasm of director Higuchi Shinji" and therefore decided "to take on this new, one-time-only challenge."[4] When he spoke to the press in 2015, Anno already knew the direction he would take the new Godzilla film. "The science fiction world in which Godzilla exists is not only a dream and aspiration but also a caricature, satire, and mirror image of reality," he said. "It is also a reckless attempt to depict it in present-day Japan."[5]

Meanwhile, Higuchi Shinji already had a long association with making kaiju movies, having started his career in the special effects department for *The Return of Godzilla* (1984). After that, he directed live-action films, including the war film *Lorelei* (2005) and the award-winning historical drama *The Floating Castle* (2013). He also helmed *The Sinking of Japan* (2006), a disaster movie based on Komatsu Sakyō's best-selling novel *Japan Sinks* (1973). As it would turn out, experience in making a disaster movie would prove to be a valuable background for telling the type of story that Higuchi Shinji's colleague, writer-director Anno Hideaki, wanted to tell.

Indeed, Anno's final script essentially framed the new Godzilla story as a tale of a large-scale disaster. To tell that type of story, the filmmakers would require the services of many actors. Indeed, even before the film's debut, a Toho spokesperson revealed that the forthcoming production would boast a cast of 328 actors, which was said to be the most actors ever to appear in a Japanese movie.[6]

Major roles were filled with experienced performers, led by Hasegawa Hiroki, Takenouchi Yutaka, and Ishihara Satomi. All came to the project with many years of professional experience. Of those filling out the supporting roles, some cast members had recently worked on co-director Higuchi Shinji's 2015 movie *Attack on Titan*. Many others, including long-time actors Emoto Akira and Kunimura Jun, had appeared in earlier Toho Godzilla productions.

As with previous movies in Toho's Godzilla series, details about the monster's character design drew intense curiosity, especially among hardcore kaiju fans. Although the earliest advance reports did not give details about either Godzilla's character design or the method they would use to produce kaiju sequences in the film, by the spring of 2016, the studio released more information. The filmmakers enlisted Maeda Mahiro, who had previously collaborated with Anno, to work on Godzilla's design.[7] It was a multi-faceted assignment since the monster mutates several times in the story. In a break from Toho tradition, the studio heavily relied on motion capture and computerized special effects to render the monster on screen. However, throughout the creature's evolution, the effects were designed to be somewhat reminiscent of the actor-in-a-rubber-suit look from Toho's earlier run of kaiju movies. It was only one example of the directors' efforts to honor tradition while making a work that would be anchored in the 21st century. This old-and-new approach is evident throughout the production's two-hour running time.

In the film's opening scene, Japanese officials investigate an abandoned boat in Tokyo Bay when an undersea explosion damages a major tunnel. The blast throws Tokyo into a panic and paralyzes the government bureaucracy. However, unlike the other bureaucrats, the youthful Yaguchi Rando (played by Hasegawa Hiroki) is determined to cut through the red tape. As others seem unsure about what they should do, Yaguchi says what he thinks is obvious: A monstrous sea creature must have caused the explosion. Although the others are skeptical, Yaguchi turns out to be correct. A new report indicates that a colossal creature has emerged from the bay. Shocked by this development, officials debate whether to kill, capture, or drive it back out to sea. As they argue about the best option, the creature moves into a narrow tributary leading into the city, causing significant destruction.

Government bickering continues as the strange monster moves ashore, shedding its previous eel-like skin and morphing into a colossal amphibian. As the creature moves along the shore, it levels entire buildings and causes much carnage and mayhem. Although they remain indecisive, officials decide the monster must be killed. But they worry about civilian casualties and temporality delay the plan until an evacuation is complete. Finally, however, the Prime Minister feels he must authorize an attack. But as soon as the operation begins, the monster unexpectedly stops. When it awakens, it has transformed and has a larger, more powerful form. At first, the creature is more destructive than ever, but then it abruptly returns to the sea.

Though the situation has stabilized, officials fear the monster will return. They soon recognize the existing bureaucracy cannot cope with the crisis. So, they create a new task force composed of "lone wolves, nerds, troublemakers, outcasts, academic heretics, and general pains-in-the-bureaucracy" to deal with it. With Yaguchi at the helm, the task force adopts a scientific approach to solve the monster problem.

Meanwhile, the government learns that the United States and other world governments plan to act on their own. Then, a U.S. envoy unexpectedly arrives on the scene. Kayoko Ann Patterson, the daughter of a U.S. senator and also the granddaughter of a Japanese Hiroshima victim, informs Japanese officials that the United States is investigating the disappearance of a Japanese professor who had worked on a U.S. energy project. He secretly predicted that a monster, which he named Godzilla, would eventually appear.

Before long, the creature, which everyone now calls Godzilla, rises and comes ashore just outside of Tokyo. The monster heads to the city center and looks much larger—like Godzilla in the original 1954 film. U.S. airpower joins the fight when the new prime minister orders the military to resume the attack. The assault starts well but quickly worsens. Godzilla has a new superpower—atomic breath—which it uses to destroy attacking aircraft, causing much additional destruction. Many people escape during the chaos, but the prime minister and other officials die. Meanwhile, Godzilla eventually weakens and again becomes inactive. The battle temporarily halts, but the area is on fire and bathed in deadly radiation.

A new prime minister and aides from the old guard take over, but the young upstart Yaguchi retains a prominent role. His task force soon succeeds in developing a chemical coagulant to immobilize and freeze Godzilla, which makes a conventional military assault unnecessary. However, the U.S.-led international alliance is unimpressed. They want to finish off Godzilla using a nuclear missile even though that would have disastrous consequences for Tokyo.

Fearing the worst, Japanese officials widen evacuation orders, hoping to save the population before the U.S. launches its missile. Meanwhile, Yaguchi's team works to produce its new coagulant. When enough of the substance is ready, Japanese defense forces use train bombs as part of a plan to administer it. That awakens Godzilla, which again has evolved into a larger and more powerful form.

A lengthy battle ensues, during which Godzilla displays more new powers. The fight continues until Japanese forces finally administer enough coagulant to freeze the monster in place and stop Godzilla in its tracks, just as Yaguchi's team predicted. With the creature immobilized, the U.S. nuclear attack is suspended, and the worst seems to have passed. However, a final close-up of Godzilla's frozen tail reveals numerous smaller, mutant creatures emerging from it, suggesting that a deadlier mutation may be in the offing.

It did not take long for home audiences to embrace Godzilla's return to theater screens in a Japanese-made movie. In what must have been a satisfying development for Toho executives, *Shin Godzilla* topped the Japanese box office during the first two weeks of its run, significantly outperforming the much-touted *Godzilla: Final Wars* more than a decade earlier. For traditional kaiju enthusiasts, directors Anno and Higuchi delivered an experience that largely matched or bettered expectations. Some viewers quibbled about the monster's multiple designs and some of the special effects. Some others expressed disappointment about Godzilla's relatively modest screen time and that no other kaiju appeared to create more extensive and spectacular battle scenes. Yet, despite these perceived shortcomings, the film generated interest and enthusiasm among the genre's devotees. More surprising to some was that it attracted massive support from its home audience, extending well beyond the kaiju fandom's confines.

Although *Shin* Godzilla's great popularity with Japanese audiences may have surprised outsiders, even a cursory look at the film reveals much of the reason for its success in its home market. Indeed, while the movie functions nicely as a freestanding kaiju movie, it is also an obvious allegory with a unique appeal to the Japanese public. That is because director-screenwriter Anno crafted a script that contains many reminders of the terrifying, real-world earthquake that struck Japan on March 11, 2011. That event, often called "3/11" in Japan, also resulted in a massively destructive tsunami. The disaster led to 15,000 deaths and left 450,000 without homes. The earthquake, which at the time was the most powerful on record in Japan, also caused the Fukushima nuclear disaster, one of the worst nuclear power station accidents in history.

## 11. Reclaiming a Monster's Legacy

The connection between *Shin Godzilla* and the 3/11 disaster is more than incidental. Co-director Higuchi explained in a later interview that he and Anno "tried to use monsters to reflect the social problems of the time.... The Fukushima meltdown and the Tohoku earthquake are the sort of natural disasters that we haven't seen in several hundred years. In a way, those disasters are the *kaiju* of our day."[8]

More than most giant monster movies, the reference to a specific crisis with a nuclear dimension places Anno's script squarely and explicitly in the tradition of Toho's *Gojira* sixty years earlier. In more than a superficial way, the Fukushima disaster is to *Shin Godzilla* what the Lucky Dragon 5 incident is to *Gojira*. (The Lucky Dragon 5 was a small Japanese fishing boat that inadvertently was caught in the fallout of a hydrogen bomb test near Bikini Atoll in 1954. The tragic incident was well-publicized and became a major inspiration for *Gojira*, which Toho made later that same year.)

The widely felt effects of the 3/11 earthquake and tsunami threw most of the country into crisis. As events passed, recovery efforts began. However, conditions at the Tepco company's Fukushima nuclear power station did not improve. In fact, the problem worsened. Partial cooling system failures caused partial meltdowns in three of the station's four reactors. The situation proved extremely difficult to resolve and continued to deteriorate amid radiation leaks and the evacuation of over 150,000 area residents.

A 2012 review of the Fukushima accident published in the *Bulletin of the Atomic Scientists* faulted not only the station's owners. According to the review's authors, "The Japanese government's unpreparedness also played a role in exacerbating the Fukushima disaster."[9] The report's writers take the country's Nuclear Safety Commission (NSC) and the nation's nuclear community to task. In their view, the Japanese nuclear community's overconfidence led them to "not take the need for improvement of safety regulations seriously before Fukushima."[10] So, when the accident occurred, a combination of "unclear jurisdictions, complicated turf wars, and mountains of red tape" significantly complicated efforts to address it effectively.[11]

For example, when the Tepco company, the power station's owner, said it was considering abandoning the failing building and evacuating workers on March 14, Japan's prime minister and other top government leaders "stormed into Tepco headquarters."[12] The officials then warned workers on duty that the consequences would be dire if Tepco followed through with its plan to abandon the station. The result would be "10 to 20 sources of radiation" and the release of "two to three times the contamination discharged at Chernobyl." Under the circumstances, the prime minister insisted that abandoning the station was inconceivable. Moreover, the prime minister reportedly "mentioned that the United States or Russia would not have any choice but to intervene in the Japanese government's effort to control the nuclear disaster" if it withdrew from the station. Of course, the government did not have the authority to order the employees to stay and possibly die, so it eventually turned to Japan's Self-Defense Forces, whose members had little choice in the matter but to obey orders.[13]

An attack in the fictional world of a monster movie is obviously far different from the real-world emergency of 3/11 and the Fukushima disaster. However, as the brief discussion above reveals, the bureaucratic confusion in *Shin Godzilla* is reminiscent of what happened during the 3/11 crisis and the Fukushima case. As in the historical events of the disaster, the officials in *Shin Godzilla* face a situation they had not anticipated and for which they were unprepared. The red tape, as well as the confusion about exactly what to do and about who should do it, are hallmarks in both the fictional script and the real-world events. And interestingly, the expectation—or perhaps fear—that an external power would intervene and act on its own is common to both. In some ways, *Shin Godzilla* encapsulates the reality of bureaucratic politics in a time of crisis, a topic that might otherwise seem arcane and undramatic, into a compelling fictional story. In other words, the film dramatizes a subject that is not easy to dramatize and, astonishingly, manages to do so within the context of a kaiju film.

Including social, political, and environmental themes in otherwise conventional kaiju movies is not new. However, when that happens, a giant monster is usually presented as a straightforward symbol of something else—some real or imagined threat or danger. In other instances, social, political, or environmental themes are simply added as textures to enrich a main story that is in other respects familiar kaiju tale. These different themes exist along with (but remain subsidiary to) the main story. In other words, many kaiju movies just happen to include other topical references that sometimes appear thrown in merely to provide topicality; the different themes have little bearing on the story.

However, in *Shin Godzilla*, something different is happening. Typically, when giant monster movies refer to real-world themes, those references either appear sporadically here and there rather than throughout the entire production, or they are presented in a very general way that does not have much influence on other screen events. In contrast, the echoes of 3/11 and Fukushima in *Shin Godzilla* are thoroughly woven into the film and permeate its whole story. Unusually, the film treats the traditional kaiju elements of its story and non-kaiju themes (3/11 and Fukushima, in this case) more or less equally, with neither aspect overwhelming the other. It is as if two films—one about a giant monster and the other about government bureaucracy—have been merged into one. Of course, depending on an individual's interests and background, a viewer might pay far more attention to one element or another. In any case, two readings—one rich in allegory and one a straightforward monster story—are there for those who choose to see them.

The movie's references to specific real-world details are probably not as apparent to viewers outside Japan who are unfamiliar with the events the film references. They would probably find it much harder to connect the movie as directly to government actions in 3/11 and Fukushima as domestic Japanese audiences. But that is understandable. Although people outside the region may be aware of 3/11 and the Fukushima disaster to some degree, most probably never knew about the details and difficulties of the Japanese government's response to them.

This type of locality in perspective and understanding is a broad topic. Still, it has significant implications for internationally distributed films (and other media). Indeed, the varying responses to *Shin Godzilla* demonstrate how differently a movie might be read depending on the local context in which it is seen. The world may now resemble Marshall McLuhan's "global village," but most people still seem focused on matters close to home. They know and understand far less about how people experience things elsewhere.

That is something that filmmakers need to consider when making a work that will be distributed globally. It is not simply a matter of editing a movie in a way to pass the requirements of censors elsewhere (though that is sometimes a consideration). It is also that audiences elsewhere, who come to films with their own cultural inclinations, will not necessarily notice or interpret things in a movie the same way a production's home audience likely would. For example, while most people outside the United States did not feel the effects—especially the emotional effects—of the September 2001 attacks as intensely and in the same way that people in the United States did, Americans seldom realize this. Instead, many in the U.S. presume that the entire world felt 9/11 just as they did. The point is that even significant crises that receive global news coverage—whether Japan's 3/11, the United States' 9/11, or something else—are not seen the same everywhere. It is an obvious point but one too often forgotten.

As mentioned above, some in the fandom were critical of the relatively modest amount of screen time the film's directors gave to the various incarnations of Godzilla. And to be sure, if one were to judge the movie based on how much time it devoted to showing the monster and related action scenes, disappointment seems likely. Yet, the horror genre, within which kaiju movies are often located, frequently employs that same strategy. Horror filmmakers often dole out images of their monsters judiciously to keep audiences on edge and to create narrative tension. Whether or not one wishes to categorize *Shin Godzilla* as a horror film—or something closely related to that—is an open question. (A good case could be made for identifying it more as a disaster procedural than a work in the horror genre.) Regardless, *Shin Godzilla*'s directors were in good company when they minimized the mighty kaiju's time on screen. As it stands, each appearance of the monster is impactful and somehow is related to moving the story along. Scenes of gratuitous destruction and vapid spectacle— scenes that routinely appear in many blockbusters, especially in kaiju and superhero movies—are kept to a minimum.

With its focus on the ineffectiveness of the established government bureaucracy, the procedural elements of the plot have a Kafkaesque quality. The world of red tape and the confusing complexity of the bureaucracy it portrays could apply to a multitude of governments across the globe. But other parts of *Shin Godzilla*'s story are unique to Japan's post–World War II political identity. Those can be found in the film's raising the questions of its relationship to the United States and the related matter of the role of Japan's Self-Defense Forces in the 21st century.

One of the most striking aspects of *Shin Godzilla* is that while its central premise—the existence of a colossal monster—is very obviously fictional and bears no actual connection to reality, the world in which the story is set is not. In its political and social aspects, the version of Japan depicted in the movie is a realistic, albeit exaggerated, portrait of the country in the 2010s.

Since its disastrous experience in World War II, which culminated in the United States dropping atomic bombs on Hiroshima and Nagasaki, the Japanese government has been wary of directly engaging in international conflicts militarily. And for obvious reasons, the Japanese people have generally opposed nuclear weapons. However, while Japan, as of the early 2020s, is often still described as pacifist, the country has long maintained an active military defense posture.

Still, as scholar Narushige Michishita notes, "the Japanese government maintains that the Self-Defense Force is not a military force." Why? "It is because Article 9 of the Japanese constitution stipulates that Japan shall not possess land, sea, and air forces."[14] People outside Japan may look at the precisely named Self-Defense Force and see it as equivalent to a traditional military establishment. However, within Japanese society, it has not been quite that. The difference, which may seem merely rhetorical if taken out of the Japanese context, is that in Article 9, Japan renounced using the military to settle international disagreements. In theory, then, at the time of this writing, the SDF still exists only for actual self-defense.

Over the decades, some people in Japan became disenchanted with the limitations of Article 9 and advocated that Japan adopt a more global and forceful outlook, possibly expanding the scope of the military in the process. Among the advocates for this change was the late Abe Shinzo, the long-serving Japanese prime minister.

Although it is highly unusual for a government leader to comment on a kaiju move, in September 2016, Prime Minister Abe did just that. "I hear that the Self-Defense Forces are very active not only in the real world but also in the movie *Shin Godzilla*," he said, adding that he understood that "the characters, from the Chief of Staff of the Joint Staff to the members of the Self-Defense Forces, are well drawn. I believe that such popularity is also due to the unwavering public support for the Self-Defense Forces."[15] It therefore appears that intentionally or not, Anno's script was seen as relevant and reflective of an important issue—the role of Japan's military—at the time, enough so that a national leader talked about it in the context of his administration's political agenda.

A subtext to this is Japan's relationship with the United States, which Anno's script characterizes as one of subservience. Throughout the story, Japanese officials attempt to deal with the situation before the United States acts unilaterally. In more than one scene, Japanese officials lament their seeming powerlessness in the face of the United States, which treats Japan as a subordinate. Therefore, in the film, and perhaps in real life, the drive for increased Japanese defense capability is not simply about the nation's ability to defend itself. It is also closely related to reducing inequality in its relationship with a critical ally, the United States.

In a different realm, *Shin Godzilla* markedly differs from nearly all other kaiju movies in one respect. Here, despite the fear and carnage that the monster inflicts in the story, the human characters approach the problem as a technical problem to be solved. The government paralysis here does not result from people being so terrified that they cannot act. Indeed, the main problem is not that people are paralyzed with fear—instead, the overly complex rules, protocols, and multiple layers of decision create the problem.

Interestingly, in contrast to many U.S. monster and horror films, *Shin Godzilla* is a very bright film visually. While the U.S.-made *Godzilla* of 2014 is cloaked in darkness, for example, most of the events in *Shin Godzilla* happen in broad daylight or in blandly lit conference rooms. (A prominent exception is a nighttime battle scene in which Godzilla rages against its attackers with laser-like rays emanating from its dorsal fins.

In that sequence, the darkness is needed as a backdrop to emphasize the eye-catching special effects.)

Despite the film's emphasis on bureaucracy and officialdom, many viewers were satisfied that *Shin Godzilla* provided an experience that did not veer so far from expectations to detract from it as an entertaining kaiju movie. Writing for *Forbes*, Luke Y. Thompson summed up what many probably thought. He notes that "the bureaucratic satire can get a little too repetitive…. But that's not why you come to a Godzilla movie, is it? You want to see Tokyo get trashed good, and it does, more cinematically than in most of the recent franchise installments."[16]

Taking in $75 million in the Japanese market, *Shin Godzilla* received a far better reception in Japan than the most recent movies in Toho's Godzilla series more than a decade earlier. Although the box office totals outside Japan were minimal, *Shin Godzilla* attracted enough attention in markets such as the United States to gain notice. The worldwide community of kaiju fans took the production seriously, which undoubtedly enhanced Toho's reputation. *Shin Godzilla* clarified that the studio could make a modern, relevant kaiju movie at a fraction of a typical Hollywood budget by emphasizing compelling ideas as much as spectacle.

Astonishingly to some, *Shin Godzilla* received significant recognition from the industry. It won the top "Best Work" prize from the prestigious Japan Academy Film Prize Association. In addition, Anno and Higuchi shared the Academy's "Best Director" award, and the film also garnered awards for art direction, sound, editing, lighting, and cinematography. *Shin Godzilla* also was named "Best Film" by the Association of Tokyo Film Journalists, which awarded it the 2017 Blue Ribbon Ward. Taken together, all of this was stunning proof that it was possible for a kaiju movie to gain respect and approval among film professionals and the mainstream market, at least in Japan. Whether a giant monster movie anything could attain anything approaching that level of recognition in the U.S. or international markets was debatable.

# 12

# A Monster Within
## *Colossal* (2016)

When director Nacho Vigalondo's movie *Colossal* was screened at several festivals in 2016, it made a splash as one of the most atypical and intriguing giant monster movies in a long time. To some, its eclectic, genre-defying mix of romantic comedy, social commentary, and kaiju elements had the potential makings of a hit movie. Yet, the reception was tepid when the film went into general release in the spring of 2017. Some critics and film-goers raved about it, but the Spanish filmmaker's movie barely made an impression among the wider audience. These mixed results aside, in most respects, *Colossal* was one of the most original giant monster films to come around in many years. It is an instructive example of what can happen when filmmakers try to extend kaiju conventions beyond traditional boundaries.

In the world of giant monster films, *Colossal* is an unusual case that intentionally deviates from the giant monster movie tradition. It is so atypical that it raises fundamental questions about what kaiju films could or should be in the 21st century. Indeed, the director's unique vision defies so many of the genre's conventions that it may cause some fans to question whether it should be classified as a kaiju movie at all.

On the surface, there might not seem much to debate in this regard. Although scenes featuring the film's main giant monster are few, *Colossal* unambiguously builds its story around a massive beast. However, the giant monster often recedes far into the background of the narrative as the film unfolds. Vigalondo instead focuses on the human characters and their complex, troubled relationships. And while there are some scenes of massive urban destruction, most of the screen time is devoted to an all-too-human story involving substance abuse, relationship issues, and toxic masculinity, leaving the film's terrifying monster mostly a sideshow. It does not give the impression of being a film that bows to the expectations of kaiju fans.

Yet, the director developed the project with a deep appreciation for the giant monster genre and its fans. Vigalondo had at least one important reason to avoid disrespecting the genre's legacy or the relatively small but intensely loyal community of kaiju fans: he grew up watching kaiju movies and is one of those fans, too. Indeed, although *Colossal* often seems to drift far from the genre's typical conventions and emphases, he wanted to respect the kaiju audience. "I didn't want to make a comment on those [earlier kaiju] films," he told an interviewer. "I understand people get that impression before they see the film, but I don't want the movie to feel like we're mocking kaiju-eiga films."[1]

Growing up in Spain, where access to kaiju movies was not always easy, Vigalondo enjoyed giant monster films and often sought them out. The 1986 version of *King Kong* made a particularly powerful impression on him when he was very young. Throughout his youth, he enjoyed monster movies of various kinds, especially those featuring giant robots. However, his viewing did not include a steady diet of classic Toho films since Asian productions were distributed in Spain infrequently.[2]

Becoming a director was not a career path that occurred to Vigalondo as a boy. For a long time, he had no frame of reference to even dream about that occupation. For one thing, his small hometown in northern Spain did not have a movie theater. What he knew of the cinema was mostly from television. So, it was a revelation to him when, during his teenage years, he gained access to a VCR, then the prevailing home video technology.

By the time he went to university in Bilbao, Vigalondo's interest in filmmaking had blossomed, and he was serious about pursuing it as a career. While studying visual communication, he became acquainted with others with similar interests. Eventually, he and some of his peers began experimenting with making short films. After his university studies, Vigalondo made a short film entitled *7:35 de la Mañana* (2003), drawing attention and an Academy Award nomination in the Best Short Film category.[3]

Within a few years, he was making feature films. *Truecrimes* was released in 2007. *Guardian* writer Andrew Pulver described it as "an enterprising Spanish time-travel thriller."[4] Although it did little at the box office, it drew some attention from critics and science fiction fans alike. Two more films, *Extraterrestre* (2011) and *Open Windows* (2014), did not draw huge crowds, either. However, they were reasonably well received by those who saw them and added to his modest but growing reputation as a filmmaker with an original perspective.

When he began writing *Colossal* in 2015, he did not have secure financial backing or a definite plan. However, he knew he "wanted to make a monster movie"[5] and to do so on his terms. He had a simple but compelling premise for the story: a "crazy idea about this monster mimicking the movements of someone as a giant avatar on the opposite side of the world."[6] That, he believed, could be the basis for a "realistic take on a monster movie."[7] By design, it would be a "smaller and more humble" film, and, not unimportantly, one that could be made with a modest budget.[8]

From the beginning, Vigalondo envisioned a film in which the story of the human characters would be central. The emphasis would not be on monster battles or filling two hours of screen time with electrifying special effects. In other words, spectacle would play a lesser role than the human story the director wanted to tell. Given this vision, the film's success would largely hinge on the actors filling the leading roles.

Vigalondo developed a script that was true to his vision, but initially he lacked a clear path to getting the film made. With neither significant financial backers nor a deal with a big studio, it was not clear how he could move the project forward. Before long, however, the project's fortunes took a turn for the better. A version of the script was circulated among some agents on speculation. Then, in a surprising turn of events, the director received good news. The project had come to the attention of Anne Hathaway, the famous Academy Award–winning actor, who was then known mainly for appearances in romantic comedies.

"You can imagine my face when I got the news that she was interested in it,"[9] Vigalondo later said. "She read the script through her agent and just showed her interest. It was as simple as that. She approached us—me and Nahikari Ipiña, my long-time producer since the short films."[10] Hathaway later explained some of the reasons for what could seem to be an unlikely project for her. "It's just exactly my sense of humor,"[11] she said. "It's the way I like to think about things without being made sad by them. I love genre subversion." As she understood the project, it would be a movie she "would be first in line to see whether or not I was in it."[12]

With Hathaway's unexpected interest, the film's fortunes looked much brighter. She was not an actor even remotely associated with kaiju movies, but once her enthusiasm for Vigalondo's script became known, the project began to attract potential backers. Because Vigalondo had never seriously considered that *Colossal* would be a film in the blockbuster vein, he did not need to attract vast resources. Conceived as a more personal, indie-style movie than as one of the era's blockbusters, he knew his film could be completed with a modest budget. So, when Hathaway's name became attached to the project, it was enough to put together a viable plan. As the director said, "With a star of Hathaway's magnitude on board, *Colossal* had no trouble securing financing."[13]

The financial package relied on funding partners in the United States, Spain, South Korea, and Canada. These included Voltage Pictures, which signed on early. Eventually, other funding sources came together, as well.

The final list of participants included Neon,[14] Legion M, Toy Fight, Brightlight Pictures, Sayaka Producciones Audiovisuales, and Route One Entertainment. All that added up to an estimated budget of about $15 million. That was an extremely modest sum for a contemporary film but not much different than the budget of *Shin Godzilla,* the Japanese kaiju feature released in 2016.

Although she undoubtedly did raise the visibility of the project in the eyes of potential backers, Anne Hathaway's importance to the film was primarily due to her credentials as an actor who could deliver a solid performance. Unlike some kaiju movies in which spectacle overwhelms the work of the actors, *Colossal* placed Gloria, Hathaway's complex character, at the center of the narrative. The film has many demanding scenes, ranging from the comedic to the dramatic, that call for an actor with Hathaway's range.

With Hathaway's interest in playing the lead role secure, there was then the matter of filling out the rest of the cast. The other pivotal role of Oscar, the film's male lead, soon attracted Jason Sudeikis, then mainly known as a long-time cast member of NBC's *Saturday Night Live* and movie comedies such as *Horrible Bosses* (2011). Like the Gloria character, Oscar changes during the movie and displays a range of emotions and behaviors, some extreme and damaging. The opportunity to play Oscar thus gave Sudeikis a chance to show audiences something new. Filling out the rest of the cast, Vigalondo turned to actors such as Dan Stevens, Austin Stowell, and Tim Blake Nelson. All of them had solid credentials.

Although the human story is the film's focus, Vigalondo knew the kaiju's design was critical and that the design of the giant creature needed to be taken seriously. As would later be obvious when posters and promotional graphics for the movie were released, the final creature design was highly reminiscent of the kaiju in the 1985 North Korean feature *Pulgasari.* The monster's relatively brief appearances at various points of the film were created using digital effects that were executed by Intelligent Creatures, a special effects production house based in Toronto.

Most of *Colossal's* principal photography took place in Vancouver over six weeks in the fall of 2015. The production was ready to be showcased at the Toronto International Film Festival the following September. The movie was then marketed for a traditional release in April 2017. Before its general release, *Colossal* attracted strong interest and good reviews on the festival circuit. Part of that was because of Vigalondo's reputation. In retrospect, some of his earlier works provided hints of the direction Vigalondo would take when he began working on *Colossal* in 2015. For example, *Extraterrestrial,* like *Colossal,* experiments with combining elements from disparate genres. (*New York Times* critic Jeannette

Catsoulis described it as a film in which an "alien invasion is just an excuse for romantic farce."[15]) Similarly, *Open Windows* also mixes "high-concept sci-fi and kitchen-sink relationship comedies"[16] while adding dimensions of a psychological thriller.

Yet, before *Colossal's* debut, its director's modest but growing reputation was only one part of the reason for public curiosity about the movie. Indeed, the film made headlines soon after it was announced in the spring of 2015 when Toho Studio sued over its production. It turned out that even though he did not plan to include Godzilla or any other Toho kaiju properties in his film, Vigalondo reportedly had said his film would be "the cheapest Godzilla movie ever made."[17] He may not have meant that literally, but that statement, among others, was enough to raise eyebrows at Toho, which seems to have suspected possible copyright infringement.

In addition, the lawsuit alleged that Voltage had distributed an email "to potential investors … which included a publicity shot from Gareth Edwards's recent Hollywood *Godzilla* reboot and several further images from other Toho films about the monster."[18] Unsurprisingly, that did not sit well with officials at Toho, either. Despite the potential for a legal fight that could derail *Colossal's* release, the two sides reached an agreement by October. Reports indicated that "the producer of the new film will clarify that it is not remaking *Godzilla*."[19] The legal challenge was undoubtedly a hassle for Vigalondo and Voltage, but the controversy brought unexpected publicity to the still-unfinished film, heightening public awareness of it.

When it was finally released, it was evident that *Colossal* was nothing like a Godzilla film. Indeed, in terms of narrative and intentions, its story is light years away from a Toho kaiju production. Visually, too, the film's kaiju character bears little resemblance to the famous Japanese studio's favorite monster. If anything, *Colossal's* creature is reminiscent of the giant beast in the unusual 1985 North Korean movie *Pulgasari*.

As was the director's intention all along, *Colossal* is a unique mix of straightforward kaiju elements and human drama. The film opens with a brief scene in which a child's doll is lying on the ground in South Korea. When a young girl picks it up, a giant kaiju appears.

Cut to an apartment building in New York City, where a drunk Gloria (played by Anne Hathaway) arrives home to find Tim (Dan Stevens), her disgruntled boyfriend, waiting to confront her. An argument and breakup follow.

When Gloria moves back to her hometown in the northeastern United States, she meets Oscar, whom she met in elementary school and has not seen in many years. As Gloria settles into life in the small town, she takes a job at the dive bar Oscar now owns. There she meets several of Oscar's regular customers, including Joel (Austin Stowell) and Garth (Tim

Blake Nelson), men who always seem to defer to Oscar (Jason Sudeikis) and possess little awareness of life beyond their hometown. Living alone in her former family home, Gloria has several nightmares about vague but troubling events from her past. After one disturbing dream, she awakens to news reports that a giant monster is attacking Seoul, South Korea, an event that causes a "global state of emergency."

Despite the kaiju attack in Korea, life goes on for Gloria and the others. Over time, however, Gloria slowly realizes that the actions of the kaiju, half a world away, seem to mimic her gestures and motions. She does not know how or why but realizes she somehow controls the monster. For the time being, she keeps that shocking discovery to herself.

Gloria becomes increasingly drawn into the toxic relationships between Oscar and his regulars as time passes. While drinking with them after hours one night, Gloria blurts out her strange connection to the kaiju. At first, they do not believe her, but she later demonstrates it, after which they accept it as true. Later, she talks with Oscar, who shares the news that a giant robot has joined the enormous monster in Korea. Surprisingly, Oscar claims he controls the giant robot just as Gloria controls the kaiju. As the tense discussion continues, Oscar reminds Gloria that a giant monster first appeared in Seoul when they were children.

Despite all this, life in the small town goes on. After another after-hours drinking session, Gloria and Joel spend the night together. The following day, Gloria awakens to discover that the giant robot is causing trouble in Seoul. She soon confirms that Oscar, who is visibly angry with her, controls the robot's movements.

It turns out that Oscar has been jealous of Gloria's "amazing life" for many years. He threatens to make the robot create more havoc in Seoul if Gloria does not submit to his vague demands. Soon after, he instigates a violent confrontation with Gloria at the nearby playground, which causes a simultaneous battle between the monster and the robot in Seoul.

After that short-lived episode, things settle down when Tim, Gloria's ex-boyfriend, comes to town, apparently to reconcile. However, he has a disastrous encounter with Oscar, after which another confrontation erupts between Gloria and Oscar.

Afterward, Gloria remembers an incident from her youth where Oscar destroyed her homemade diorama of a cityscape with a monster and robot. She also recalls ominous lightning had struck at precisely that time. Those events caused her to manifest a real-life giant monster—a colossal version of the toy in her diorama—in Seoul 25 years ago. Cutting from this memory to the present, another confrontation between Gloria and Oscar escalates into a violent, physical fistfight, immediately causing a deadly battle between the kaiju and the giant robot in Korea.

A break in the action and more soul-searching finds Gloria and Oscar in their separate domains. As Gloria thinks about how to de-escalate the situation peacefully, Tim calls to tell her he is going home. Oscar, meanwhile, has been drinking and is looking for Gloria. Just when it seems that Gloria is about to fly back to New York to reunite with Tim, it becomes clear that she has instead flown to Seoul. From there, she phones Tim to say she will never return.

Meanwhile, an out-of-control Oscar, still in his hometown, manifests the giant robot in the Korean capital. But the situation is different now. Gloria, in Korea, manifests the kaiju, which appears not in Seoul but in Oscar's small American town. In the film's climax, the kaiju suddenly grabs Oscar and hurls him far into the distance. In Seoul, the giant robot disappears across the horizon, too. With the end of the crisis in Korea, there is much jubilation. As Seoul's citizens celebrate in the streets, Gloria, still in Seoul, stops by a local haunt where she tells the bartender she has a fantastic story.

Within the context of the film, the giant monster and robot that plague Seoul are literal rather than metaphorical manifestations of Gloria and Oscar. The film's explanation for this bizarre phenomenon, mainly in flashbacks to the characters' youthful days, seems like something out of science fiction. According to *Colossal's* internal reality, a lightning bolt activated some freakish natural process that caused Gloria's (and later, Oscar's) thoughts to materialize in a gigantic form in a distant geographical location. Does it make sense or seem even remotely plausible? No, but in that respect, it is not very different from many other plot elements in popular science fiction. It hardly requires more suspension of disbelief than many other movie plots, whether in the science-fiction genre or something more down to earth. It is not much more outlandish than numerous elements in many other productions. It is simply a plot point viewers must accept as a given to enjoy the film. Accordingly, it is possible to look at the story as a straightforward science-fiction fantasy.

However, considering the film's emphasis on the main characters' toxic interrelationships and psychological issues, it also seems reasonable to consider other ways of looking at this aspect of the narrative. For example, a viewer could read the film as a tale that touches on psychological projection and the conditions that prompt that phenomenon. Although that concept is often associated with Sigmund Freud, whose work no longer holds sway in the academic world to the degree it once did, it is nonetheless an idea with a historical presence in Western societies and popular culture.

As described by scholar Yvonne Sherratt, "Projection is a psychoanalytic term for the placing of internal impulses onto the external world....

[It] can be a defense against a prohibited emotional impulse, a destructive wish towards a family member, etc." Following Freud, she further explains that "projection can consist of the placing of 'evil impulses into demons,' such that it appears to be demons wishing or enacting harm upon others rather than the individual himself."[20]

According to director Vigalondo, the impetus for *Colossal* began with his "crazy idea about this monster mimicking the movements of someone as a giant avatar on the opposite side of the world."[21] That gave him a "chance to make a realistic take on a monster movie without raising a huge budget." Still, it was not until he fleshed out the characters of Gloria and Oscar and "figured out why they were fighting [that] the whole movie became real."[22] Although there is no reason to presume that the director necessarily intended a literal invocation of the psychology of projection, that concept provides an illuminating way to think about bizarre events that transpire on screen.

In some aspects, *Colossal*'s use, intended or not, of projection as both a plot device and a plausible analytic framework is not unprecedented. Modern psychology and the cinema grew up together and have parallel histories, and many films have substantial psychological components. For example, one film with some similarities to *Colossal* regarding the projection idea was released more than a half-century earlier than Vigalondo's movie. That film is *Forbidden Planet* (1956), the classic American science-fiction movie starring Leslie Nielsen. The film is set on another planet and loosely based on Shakespeare's *The Tempest*.

One of the significant parts of *Forbidden Planet*'s story involves an invisible giant monster that appears intermittently and can only be vaguely seen when it encounters electricity. On the rare occasions when the beast emerges, it is always menacing and destructive. It never is depicted as a benign creature. Initially, it is unclear what the monster is or why it behaves as it does. Eventually, however, it emerges that it is a fearsome, unintended projection from the subconscious of a human scientist who had lived on the planet for a long time. According to the complicated story, ancient technology from a long-dead alien civilization had made elements of the scientist's subconscious into a real monster without the scientist's knowledge. The script provides a science-fiction explanation (the alien technology) for a plot element modeled on Freudian-style psychological projection. Indeed, unsubtle references to the famed psychoanalyst's theories and concepts appear throughout the film. According to scholar N. Megan Kelly, *Forbidden Planet* has a "psychoanalytic 'subtext' so omnipresent in the narrative that it could substitute for a Freudian reader."[23]

*Colossal* does not significantly allude to Freud in the way *Forbidden Planet* had many years before, and there are also many other significant differences between the two films. However, in both cases, the giant monsters are directly connected to the subconscious of the respective film's characters. The line between human and monster is more than just blurred; it is erased. In *Colossal*, as in the earlier movie, giant monsters only exist as extensions of human beings.

Given Oscar's increasingly violent and abusive behavior, it is likely that many viewers were pleased to see both him and his robot avatar tossed into oblivion at the end. However, spectators are hardly given any reason to wish for a similar fate for Gloria, even though the kaiju her mind subconsciously created was the first on the scene and equally destructive. Vigalondo appears to make a considerable effort to make the kaiju impersonal and to lessen any impulse to blame Gloria for the monster's violent actions. But the narrative does not give viewers the luxury of separating the two quite that easily. Gloria may not have intended to create the giant creature, and she certainly did not wish death or injury upon the innocent citizens of Seoul. Yet, intentional or not, those terrible outcomes are precisely what she had unwittingly caused. That presents audiences with a disturbing moral question, one with profound implications beyond the fantasy of a genre movie: To what extent should a person who unknowingly causes unintended negative consequences be held responsible for those tragic outcomes? After all, the people killed and injured are no less harmed just because Gloria did not mean for it to happen. It is a type of unintended harm that often appears in the real world in connection with alcohol- or substance-induced behaviors.

Many have interpreted *Colossal* as a hybrid of romantic comedy and kaiju genres. However, despite some overlap with romantic comedy tropes (mainly occurring in the early parts of the film), it would be difficult to conclude that the film is dominated by comedy or romance. The relationships depicted, especially those between Gloria and Oscar and Gloria and her ex-boyfriend Tim, are demeaning and fueled by alcohol-aided rage and dysfunction. Some amusing moments include a scene in which the kaiju in Seoul scratches its head and dances in response to Gloria's movements back in the United States. However, genuinely comic scenes are few and far between, and they primarily function as breaks in a story that is otherwise tense and violent.

In this respect, *Colossal* treads into somber, serious territory seldom addressed in giant monster films. Rarely has a kaiju movie offered its audience so little escapism. When Gloria's giant monster and Oscar's huge robot appear, they do not distract viewers from feelings about real-world problems and tragedies. The fight between the kaiju and the robot is competently presented, but the problematic relationship between the main characters remains at center stage.

Writer Alissa Wilkinson notes how much Vigalondo departs from the genre's conventions. In her view, "*Colossal* feels calculated to irritate audiences who insist on tidy explanations and clean finishes.... [It] is a surprisingly mature way to get at some really dark issues—addiction, unhealthy relationships, and self-sabotage—that purposely blunts its subject matters with a weird, seemingly nonsensical plot device."[24]

Vigalondo's vision for the film and his clever script allow him to delve far more deeply into such concerns than is expected for this type of film. And unlike many other giant monster movies that do bring in real-world connections (such as themes of anti-nuclearism, ecology, or the presumed immorality of nations), here the director keeps things personal. His giant monsters are constant reminders of situations many viewers would have seen or known about in their social circles or communities—situations that people often do not wish to talk about, let alone directly address.

The director believes his filmmaking reflects the cinematic "roots of indie films coming from the 1990s."[25] In other words, his aims—at least up to the point when he made *Colossal*—were not related to making tradition-bound cookie-cutter blockbuster-stye movies. Indeed, as his work up to and including *Colossal* demonstrates, Vigalondo does not create homogenized, easy-to-digest motion pictures. He did not shy away from controversial subject matter early in his career. He also showed a willingness to radically shift tone, even when that happens midway through a film, as is the case in *Colossal*.

The director had consistently demonstrated an interest in challenging audiences and giving spectators something substantive to think about, even if that was at the cost of defying audience expectations. So, it was probably never the case that Vigalondo would set out to make a routine giant monster movie that would check off all the boxes in a kaiju fan's wish list for ingredients in such a movie.

As a creative way to tell a sadly relevant story, many viewers judged that Vigalondo had made an original, thought-provoking movie. Yet, it did not produce waves of enthusiasm beyond a relatively small audience. When released in the autumn of 2016 at the Toronto International Film Festival, it was generally well received and generated some publicity. However, its general release some months later, in April 2017, did not impress. At its opening weekend, fewer than 400 theaters in the United States (the film's primary market) showed the film.[26] It grossed only $3.2 million during its official run in the U.S. and slightly under $1.3 million in the international market. Even with another half million dollars from the home video market, the total was only about $4.5 million,[27] far below an amount that would recoup the estimated production budget of $15 million.[28] (For comparison, the previous year's *Shin Godzilla,* which had a similar budget, yielded a much healthier $75 million overall box office revenue across multiple markets.)

Many hardcore fans of giant-monster movies seem disappointed in Vigalondo's approach to making *Colossal*. He may have veered too far from average kaiju fan expectations despite his sharing of the fandom's affection for the genre. It is also possible his film was too unorthodox for general audiences to accept and possibly too hard to categorize for marketing purposes. Whereas *Shin Godzilla* had demonstrated that an audience for kaiju films continued to exist, *Colossal* may have shown that audiences would not readily embrace a production that took too many liberties with convention. If so, that situation would not be wholly surprising. Throughout cinema history, the makers of many types of films have struggled with the question of how far they could push genre boundaries without losing the audience. Although *Colossal* is a compelling film in some ways, its lukewarm reception by kaiju fans may have answered that question.

# 13

# Reimagining the Beginning
## *Kong: Skull Island* (2017)

At the annual Comic Con event in the summer of 2014, Legendary Pictures founder Thomas Tull revealed that the studio was working on something big. He then showed the crowd a foreboding video clip featuring a rough sea, remote wilderness, and menacing creatures. The narration suggested something ominous. "Going up that river was like traveling back to the beginning of the world when the plants ran wild, and the trees were kings," the voice said. "We penetrated deeper and deeper into the heart of darkness." If those words sounded familiar, it was because they were.[1] It was a passage from Joseph Conrad's famous 1899 novella, *The Heart of Darkness*. That story partially inspired Francis Ford Coppola's 1979 Vietnam War epic, *Apocalypse Now,* and, to a lesser extent, Gareth Edwards' *Monsters* in 2010. Here, the quotation was used to promote something else: a new Kong movie with the tentative title of *Skull Island*.[2]

Reports indicated that Max Borenstein, who had written the screenplay for Legendary's 2014 *Godzilla,* was already working on the script. More surprising was the director reportedly attached to the project at the time. Previously, rumors suggested that *King Kong* (2005) director Peter Jackson had hoped that Guillermo del Toro would helm the next movie featuring the colossal ape, but that was not to be. Instead, new 2014 reports indicated that Legendary had invited Joe Cornish to direct the new feature.[3] It may have seemed an unlikely choice since, to that date, Cornish had only directed one film, the science-fiction comedy *Attack the Block* (2011).

Ultimately, that did not work out, either. The project moved forward without Cornish, and a while later, Legendary announced that Jordan Vogt-Roberts would direct the new Kong film. He also had limited directing experience, but his feature *Kings of Summer* (2013) garnered positive attention at the Sundance Film Festival.[4]

Legendary had partnered with Warner Bros. to make Godzilla in

## 13. Reimagining the Beginning

2014, but it was working with Universal, which had made the most recent King Kong film in 2005, for the new movie. But soon, the plans changed. In early September 2015, Legendary announced it was also moving the *Skull Island* project to Warner Bros. According to an article in *Deadline*, the purpose was "to unite the property with Legendary's other giant franchise, Godzilla."[5] Writer Mike Fleming, Jr., called the move a potentially "epic pairing," noting the Legendary-Warner "*Godzilla* sequel that is in the works will be followed by a movie that pits the giant ape versus the giant fire-breathing reptile."[6]

After the studio settled on a director, casting decisions for the new Kong feature moved along relatively quickly. The final roster included superhero movie notables, perhaps indicating Legendary's desire to create a blockbuster that could compete with that increasingly dominant genre. For example, actors Brie Larson (*Captain Marvel, 2019*, and others), Tom Hiddleston (*Thor*, 2011, and others), and Samuel L. Jackson (*Iron Man*, 2008, and numerous others) were well-known for their work in Marvel Cinematic Universe projects. And actor Tony Kebbell had starred in one of Fox's Marvel movies (*Fantastic Four*, 2015) before the Fox-Disney merger. Other famous actors also appear in prominent roles. John Goodman, John C. Reilly, Corey Hawkins, and others are among them. Notably, the cast also includes actor Jing Tian. She appeared in several U.S.-based films but is much better known in China, where she has starred in historical epics and action films.

As other elements in the project started to come together, the script, though well underway, had yet to be finalized. Borenstein was working on the first draft and had many back-and-forth discussions about the story elements with Legendary officials. One critical decision involved deciding in which era the movie would be set. Borenstein thought about several options. One idea was to place the action in 1917, which would have been earlier than the time setting of the original 1933 *King Kong*. He also considered the Vietnam War era.

When Vogt-Roberts officially joined the project, he liked the Vietnam idea and pitched it to Legendary executives. They agreed with this general approach, but after some discussion, they decided to set the movie not at the height of that war but just after the United States announced it was withdrawing from the conflict.[7]

With that aspect of the film established, it was time to make progress toward a final screenplay. In a move that was not unusual, Legendary brought in other writers to move things along. One of the new writers was John Gatins, who had been nominated for an Academy Award for his *Flight* (2012) screenplay. Another was Dan Gilroy, who wrote scripts for such films as *Freejack* (1992), *The Bourne Legacy* (2012), and *Nightcrawler*

(2014). Both took part in revising and fine-tuning Borenstein's version of the script.[8] However, the studio felt there was still more to be done, so they brought in Derek Connolly, whose most recent experience had been as the co-writer of *Jurassic World* (2015). (According to reporter Borys Kit, Connolly was primarily involved in "last-minute work."[9])

Although each writer undoubtedly contributed something unique, in a post-production interview, Borenstein said he was "the first writer" and "also the last writer."[10] Indeed, much of the film's way of framing the updated Kong story was his. For example, he seems to have been primarily responsible for setting aside what he calls "the Beauty and the Beast" angle woven throughout the original *King Kong* movie and most of its sequels.[11] That represented a significant change. He also had concerns about portraying indigenous populations in the origin stories of earlier Kong movies, which he described as "archaic."[12] Instead, Borenstein said, "What popped into my head for the paradigm of the movie was *Apocalypse Now*. That's obviously a war movie, but I liked the idea of people moving upriver to face a misunderstood force that they think of as a villain, but ultimately, they come to realize is much more complicated."[13]

Reaching a workable and imaginative script that matched what the director and studio envisioned was a significant milestone. However, a movie featuring a giant monster as its main character would need more than a solid script. Special effects would be vital to the film's potential success, especially in an era where audiences seldom accepted anything less than first-rate visuals. Peter Jackson's 2005 Kong movie relied primarily on motion capture and digital animation techniques, most of which were created at the Weta special-effects studio that Jackson co-founded. Those results pleased many, though some believed that the "compositing of the computer-generated imagery (CGI) and live action is clunky,"[14] especially in scenes with significant motion.

More than a decade had passed since then, and audiences had become even more discriminating about visual effects in the intervening period. So, at the outset, Vogt-Roberts and studio executives knew they would need to pay close attention to rendering Kong convincingly and naturally. Recognizing the possibility that the effects could make or break the film, they turned to Industrial Light & Magic, a firm long known for its innovative work.

Vogt-Roberts wanted his Kong to differ from previous versions in at least one crucial respect. Jeff White, the production's visual effects supervisor, recalls, "For Jordan [Vogt-Richards], it was really about getting back to this sense of a movie monster rather than just a giant gorilla."[15] In other words, the director's vision called for a creature design that was "not a gorilla" and "not something we've necessarily seen in previous Kong iterations but certainly looking for the most inspiration from the original '33 *Kong.*"[16]

Vogt-Roberts wanted to pay homage to tradition and also do something new. That meant retaining enough of the giant beast's visual appearance to acknowledge the earlier movies, particularly the RKO original. However, he also wanted to revise Kong's character design to make it consistent with Legendary's overall vision. The new version of the beast would need to fit seamlessly into the shared cinematic universe the studio was developing in tandem with its Godzilla movies. Indeed, before Vogt-Richards' film was even released, Legendary made no secret that *Kong: Skull Island* was to be part of a multi-movie story arc that eventually would see the giant primate battle with the king of the monsters. That news had been in circulation since at least 2015.[17]

The redesign helped make Kong truly monstrous, as the director envisioned. For example, Vogt-Richards's concepts required an agile warrior beast. So, the creature's proportions were altered to lengthen the torso and to diminish any sense that Kong used his hands when walking about as real-world gorillas do. That and a few other changes gave Kong the silhouette of a human superhero.

Fictional Skull Island, where the movie is set, is populated by many fantastic creatures, of which Kong, though the most important, is only one. The other monsters are also designed to maximize the aura of menace as the story unfolds.

One problem in all kaiju films—and in special-effects-laden movies, in general—may seem less obvious to casual viewers, but it is critically important. Whether rendering monsters or anything else, the special effects must be convincingly combined with the other material to make a seamless whole. Indeed, it is often in the compositing of special effects and traditional footage that such movies sometimes go awry.

A central task facing the special effects team was to bring together all sorts of imagery—some live-action, some digital—in a way that did not detract from the viewing experience. As part of that effort, much time and effort were devoted to matching camera angles used in location filming and the angles used by digital special-effects animators. When this type of compositing is done well, viewers may not be aware that it has even been done. When done poorly, however, it can be a jarring visual experience. Successful attention to those sorts of details is essential to holding an audience's attention and keeping them involved in the story.

When the film was finally released in March 2017, fans and other movie-goers could see how much the new work did or did not change or add to the well-known Kong legend. It begins with a short prologue set on a remote Pacific island during World War II, where two downed fighter pilots chase each other from the beach to a dense jungle. As they reach a cliff, Kong suddenly appears, and the scene ends.

After the opening credits and montage, the scene switches to Washington, D.C., in 1973, as the United States ends its participation in the Vietnam War. Members of the top-secret Monarch project, led by Bill Randa (John Goodman), have come to the capital seeking funds for a secret trip to an uncharted island rumored to be the home of colossal creatures. The mission is approved, and a small unit of U.S. soldiers under the command of Lt. Col. Preston Packard (Samuel L. Jackson) is assigned to accompany the Monarch personnel. After Monarch rounds out its team with expert tracker James Conrad (Tom Hiddleston) and photographer-journalist Mason Weaver (Brie Larson), the group sets sail for fog-shrouded Skull Island.

Upon arrival, the stated plan is for the helicopters to drop explosives on the rugged terrain for supposed geological research. Of course, that is just a cover story, and the real purpose, known only to Monarch leaders, is to draw out giant monsters. Almost as soon as the helicopters are airborne, an angry Kong appears, swatting the copters down like flies. Many of the aircraft crash or are destroyed. One downed chopper was carrying Packard, who is enraged that the creature has injured and killed many of his soldiers.

The commotion has left different groups of the expedition widely separated in unknown terrain. Eventually, Packard catches up with Bill Randa to ask what is going on. After an angry exchange, Randa admits the expedition's true purpose is to find giant monsters. Elsewhere, a ground team of Conrad, Weaver, and a few soldiers see various enormous creatures. As they travel deeper into the jungle, they encounter Hank Marlow (John C. Reilly), one of the pilots who had crashed on the island in World War II. Marlow has been cut off from the outside for years. However, he has since been accepted by the island's indigenous people.

The following scenes tell about the indigenous population's struggle to live in a place dominated by angry giant beasts. After fully realizing the urgency of escaping the island, Conrad, Weaver, and their group, now joined by Marlow, hatch a plan to head to the other side of the island, where they hope to be rescued by Monarch's awaiting ship. (Interestingly, the film mostly ignores the fate of the indigenous people.) Then, in a sequence similar to *Apocalypse Now*, Conrad's group takes a makeshift boat along the river. En route, they re-establish radio contact with Packard, and the two groups meet. All does not go well.

The two leaders have different goals. Although Conrad still plans to head for safety and Packard wants revenge against Kong, they travel together for a while. Along the way, they encounter more giant monsters, one of which kills Bill Randa. The groups then separate again. While Conrad's group rests, he and Weaver unexpectedly come across Kong. The beast engages with them peacefully, but Kong is soon drawn away by an explosion in the distance. It turns out that the explosion is part of Packard's plan to lure the giant ape into a trap.

When Kong arrives, Packard prepares to finish him off. However, Conrad and Weaver followed Kong. They confront Packard, but before the situation is resolved, a new monster suddenly appears and kills the officer. Kong and the other beast fight. Then, unexpectedly, in a nod to the cavalry trope in old Western movies, two members of Conrad's group arrive on the scene in the mission's armed boat. (They had stayed with the boat while the others traveled on foot and were just catching up with them.) With machine guns blazing, they give Kong the advantage. The other monster is quickly defeated.

In the film's final scenes, Conrad, Weaver, and the other survivors quietly head downriver to the ocean, where they are rescued. Back in the island jungle, Kong triumphantly roars. A closing montage shows Marlow at home after all his lost years. The film fades to black, and after an on-screen warning that more monster trouble is yet to come, the end credits roll.

As this brief recap suggests, *Kong: Skull Island* does significantly differ from not only Peter Jackson's 2005 Kong film but also from nearly all other Kong films before that. (Two glaring exceptions to that observation are Toho's 1962 feature *King Kong vs. Godzilla* and its *King Kong Escapes* from 1967.) These differences are far more than superficial changes to the character's visual design. Instead, Vogt-Roberts' movie offers a much more thorough reimagining of the great ape and the fictional universe it inhabits than in any previous Kong film.

As he intended, the director successfully eliminates almost all traces of the Beauty and the Beast concept. This idea is a linchpin in the 1933 original movie and most of its sequels, including Jackson's 2005 remake. There are a few minutes of screen time in which Kong seemingly empathizes with Weaver. Still, nothing of a genuine relationship between the two characters is implied with any significant force, let alone the type of unusual, if the not outright troubling, interspecies romance of more traditional Kong stories. Kong is presented sympathetically as a creature wronged by the Monarch organization's dubious mission and generally an ally of Skull Island's inhabitants. But beyond that, he lives in his own world and mostly pays little attention to humans.

Despite some updates, Kong's great size, general appearance, and outward ferocity mostly survive from the previous movies. The director shows audiences a few personality traits that make Kong a sympathetic protagonist. However, Vogt-Roberts removes most of the sentiment found in the earlier films (excluding the two Toho features) and mainly reframes the creature squarely as a powerful kaiju. The character exists in this film primarily to be a mighty warrior, not a soft-hearted and misunderstood beast, even if a few traces of that remain.

As Borenstein had envisioned, much of *King Kong: Skull Island* evokes *Apocalypse Now,* Francis Ford Coppola's 1979 Vietnam War movie. Viewers first get a hint of this when Tom Hiddleston appears early in the proceeding playing a mysterious character named Conrad, an apparent nod to author Joseph Conrad, author of *The Heart of Darkness,* which inspired Coppola's epic. The connection to *Kong: Skull Island* is even more evident when it becomes clear that it will feature an expedition deep into an unexplored jungle where something horrible will appear. That same story element is central to the Coppola film and the Conrad novella.

Reminders of *Apocalypse Now* do not stop with plot similarities, however. In terms of cinematography, numerous shots involving helicopters are highly reminiscent of Coppola's film. So, too, is Vogt-Roberts' use of 1970s-era popular music to evoke the era. He includes several period pop songs in the background at different points, such as during a battle between Kong and military helicopters.

As much as *Kong: Skull Island* leans on *Apocalypse Now* in some obvious ways, it also evokes other works. In the most obvious example, Samuel L. Jackson's character, U.S. Army Lieutenant Colonel Preston Packard, comes across as a reworking of Ahab, the single-minded sea captain in Herman Melville's novel *Moby Dick*. Like Ahab, Packard is an obsessive character whose thirst for revenge overwhelms his judgment and leads to his death. In *Moby Dick,* the captain is motivated by his memory of a violent encounter with a great white whale years earlier. Ahab lost a leg as a result, after which he became fixated on revenge for the rest of his life. In *Skull Island,* Packard's quest for revenge arises after the deadly encounter with Kong, in which many of the soldiers under his command perish, and one soldier goes missing.

As a seasoned combat officer in the Vietnam conflict, the Packard character would presumably have lost soldiers before. Yet, it is seemingly only the encounter with Kong that leads him to become completely unhinged. It prompts him to take actions that endanger the surviving soldiers in his unit under his command, and, in the end, it costs him his life. Some writers have suggested that within *Skull Island's* worldview, Packard's Ahab-like behavior is a metaphor for something more than the dysfunctional psychological state of the character. Indeed, just as the giant-protagonists in many kaiju movies symbolize something more than straightforward monsters, the Packard character in this film appears to be

## 13. Reimagining the Beginning

a stand-in for a much bigger idea. Writer Matthew J. Theriault notes the significance of the Vietnam War period in which the movie is set.[18] However, it also raises much broader ideas than that divisive story. According to Theriault, director Vogt-Roberts uses the backdrop of the war as a "metaphor ... [in which] the American empire is entrapped in a violent cycle of developing new weapons technologies to win wars and engaging in new conflicts to justify its arms buildup and bloated defense spending."[19]

It is not necessary to accept such an overtly political reading of the film to see that *Skull Island* includes many scenes of spectacular military firepower. However, as the film portrays, possessing all that advanced weaponry does not necessarily lead to a military or any kind of victory; in fact, it can worsen matters.

In pitting the U.S. military forces against the giant Skull Island monsters, Vogt-Roberts adds another layer of symbolic meaning to the production. More than monsters versus people, *Skull Island* presents a battle representing the modern technological world versus an admittedly frightening and romanticized version of nature writ large. In that respect, *Skull Island* takes an approach like the original 1933 *King Kong*, where the contest between allegedly civilized humans and the rest of the natural order is a dominant theme.

Of course, it is not as simple as that. Consider, for example, that many kaiju films, including most in the Japanese tradition, are set in modern industrial and post-industrial societies. That allows for scenes of massive urban destruction and large, chaotic crowds. Because they focus on the contemporary world, people residing in non-technological communities seldom appear in those films.

However, dating back to the original 1933 film, the Kong tradition is less clear-cut than that. For example, the original 1933 movie, Peter Jackson's 2005 film, and 2017's *Kong: Skull Island* all feature stories in which the colossal ape lives on a remote island populated by people in small, pre-industrial societies who have had little contact with the modern world. That may add what is supposed to be a quaint angle to the story in each of these films. However, how these productions addressed the inclusion of pre-industrial indigenous people presented some issues.

Matthew J. Theriault makes an important point about this when he observes the "technological hubris" the Packard character exhibits in his behavior on the remote island. In Theriault's view, the 2017 film takes a different approach to this aspect of the story than Peter Jackson's 2005 movie. Jackson portrayed the indigenous inhabitants of Skull Island as having a "fearsome visage and feral demeanor," and this gives viewers the impression that "without technology and civilization," humankind "descends into brute animality."[20] By contrast, according to Theriault, director

Vogt-Roberts takes an almost opposite view in the 2017 movie. The absence of technology and "civilization" on *Skull Island* has not resulted in indigenous people becoming brutes. Instead, it has allowed them to remain closer to a pure state of nature that the film portrays "according to the tired trope of the 'Noble Savage.'"[21]

The debate about whether *Skull Island* portrays the islanders as brutes, noble savages, or something else may never be settled. However, there can be little doubt about one point: they are mostly relegated to the role of window dressing in the film. They are depicted as a hazy, amorphous group. Members of the group have no individual identity and have little-to-no agency. The human characters of the industrialized-world essentially ignore them. For example, the native islanders know much about the kaiju. However, the newcomers express little interest in any of that. True, Hank Marlow, who had lived with the islanders since he crash-landed there in the 1940s, respects the indigenous people who had saved his life. But the newcomers, with their ego-affirming firepower, have no interest in learning any more than the absolute minimum about the islanders. Their curiosity about what the islanders may know about the monsters is no more intense. In these ways, an innate tension between the conflicting goals of discovery and conquest lurks not far below the film's surface.

As for the Kong character, *Skull Island* retains some of the 1933 film's ideas about the giant ape. Both films place the exploitation of Kong, including forcible removal from its natural habitat and bringing the creature under human control. The goal of the expedition in the 1933 movie is to transport Kong to the United States, where the beast will be put on display as entertainment. Monarch's intentions in *Skull Island* are equally exploitative but not in the same way. They want more than simply putting the creature in shackles. Their aim is nothing less than to subdue and weaponize Kong, which raises the exploitation to a new level. In the end, the secretive Monarch group and its borrowed military forces fail to bring Kong under their control. The giant ape resists and manages to stay free, at least for the moment.

The extent to which audiences have thought about some of these and other issues the film raises is debatable. But these matters are apparent to those willing to see them. However, the director constructs the film to make it easy to overlook such problems if a viewer so wishes. In line with classic kaiju movie characteristics (common in some other genres), *Skull Island* emphasizes shock and awe for much of the run time. That arguably provides ample distractions for those not interested in the film's potentially deeper meanings.

Indeed, Vogt-Roberts offers much on-screen excitement in the form of battles and derring-do, which, combined with dazzling special effects, do not guide an audience into a state of contemplation. Of course, contemplation is hardly the intent. Instead, *Kong: Skull Island* was always intended to be a mass-appeal blockbuster. As such, it focuses on entertainment values. Given the substantial cost of making the film, that was probably the only approach that made sense from a business perspective.

The pressure to secure a significant financial return on a large investment seemed to dictate that Vogt-Roberts would have to aim for something spectacular to attract a vast audience. The film's production costs had soared far above those of more modestly budgeted giant-monster movies (say, for example, *The Host*, *The Mist*, and *Colossal*). Consequently, if Vogt-Roberts' film failed to draw crowds in theaters, the losses could be disastrous. And while *Skull Island* needed to perform well at the box office to recoup its costs, it also required an outsized performance to keep the studio's hopes for a franchise alive.

The people behind movies such as *The Host*, *The Mist*, and *Colossal* undoubtedly hoped their productions would be profitable. However, slimmer budgets meant less risk. So, while lower budgets may have been a drawback in some ways creatively, the correspondingly lower financial stakes meant their makers could aim for works that were far more personal projects than *Skull Island*. They could hope for a smash hit, but they surely knew their respective films would probably not become international blockbusters. Approaching their work with different aims and realistic expectations, they aimed for broader-based measures of success.

Much of the critical reaction to *Kong: Skull Island* was positive. Although it would overstate matters to call that an unexpected development, the reviewers' support was certainly nothing that could be taken for granted beforehand. On the contrary, given the track record of giant monster movies, there was a strong possibility that *Skull Island* would be dismissed and found lacking in the professional press.

Writing for *The Guardian*, Wendy Ide described it as "a robust ripping yarn ... [that is] enjoyable enough, if a little overblown."[22] *Variety's* Owen Gleiberman said the production had "a lot going for it ... [and that it is] a rousing and smartly crafted primordial-beastie spectacular."[23] Meanwhile, *Time* writer Stephanie Zacharek described the movie as "great fun ... [that is] grand and nutty and visually splendid."[24]

As with many other professional reviews, these examples responded favorably to the escapist entertainment and spectacle aspects of Vogt-Roberts' film. In those respects, some, perhaps many, people seem to have experienced *Kong: Skull Island* in the way they would experience a Marvel or other superhero film. It is the type of reaction that, from at least a market perspective, validates the notion that even if a kaiju film has larger aims than simply being a monster smash-up, that is hardly the point. That may be especially true if the film's producers have franchise aspirations.

As in the past, most potential viewers in the 21st century do not necessarily expect—or even desire—giant monster movies to spend too much time exploring big ideas with any depth. Straightforward entertainment and spectacle, with not too much emphasis on the human aspects of the story, appear to be more in line with what many movie-goers want from such productions.

Indeed, in the late 1910s, there seemed to be ample demand in the U.S. film marketplace for entertainment-oriented giant monsters movies. Warner Bros. distributed a different but competing film the following year that also featured a giant ape. *Rampage* (2018) is a family-oriented vehicle highlighting the likable star, Dwayne Johnson. It was directed by Brad Peyton, who had previously worked with Johnson on *Journey 2: Mysterious Island* (2012). The story of Rampage involves a sinister outfit that uses gene manipulation to make wild animals, including a friendly gorilla, grow to a monstrous size. Reportedly made for about $120 million,[25] *Rampage* grossed about $428 million globally, a healthy three-and-a-half times its production budget.

That was a year after *Kong: Skull Island* pulled in $567 million at the box office.[26] *Skull Island* easily outperformed *Rampage,* but the production budget for the Disney movie was also much higher than the Dwayne Johnson vehicle. (*Skull Island* is said to have cost about $185 million.[27])

The interesting point is that while the 2017 Kong film was a solid financial success, achieving slightly more than three times its budget at the box office, it was not so successful as to completely overshadow the success of a different kind of giant ape movie in the following year. Legendary's somewhat dark and apocalyptic style of kaiju movie seemed to be building an audience base. However, the similar success of *Rampage* suggests that audiences were still willing to pay for something much lighter in tone and substance. The two films epitomized two starkly different, possibly somewhat incompatible, approaches to making movies featuring giant monsters. Whether either direction would overpower the other at the box office in the long term remained to be seen.

# 14

# To a Battle Royale

*Godzilla: King of the Monsters* (2019) and
*Godzilla vs. Kong* (2021)

In the waning months of the 2010s, Disney ruled the box office, mainly on the strength of its juggernaut Marvel franchise. For example, in the U.S. market in 2018, three of the highest-grossing movies were Disney properties, including its Marvel unit's *Black Panther* and *Avengers Infinity War*, which held the top two spots. The following year, Disney took all five places in the list of top-grossing movies with its lineup of *Avengers: Endgame, The Lion King, Toy Story 4, Frozen II,* and *Captain Marvel*. Disney also cemented its leading position in the global film market. It boasted the top two highest-grossing movies internationally (*Avengers: Infinity War* and *Black Panther*) in 2018 and four of the top five (*Avengers: Endgame, The Lion King, Frozen II,* and *Captain Marvel*) in 2019.

On the few occasions when movies from beyond Disney production houses managed to break into the upper ranks of box-office hits, those films also tended to be superhero movies or major franchises from other studios. Those types of movies remained massively popular, and the studios were happy to satisfy the public's appetite for them. On the downside, such productions almost always cost a fortune to make. Production budgets of well over $100 million were typical, and budgets closer to $200 million no longer seemed as unusual as in earlier years.

In that environment, it is easy to understand why Legendary and Warner Bros. wanted to ground their budding kaiju movie franchise firmly. The moviegoing public no longer seemed to have much appetite for standalone movies or, for that matter, for dramatic films that appealed to mature sensibilities. The public's preferences had not changed overnight, but by the late 2010s, it was apparent that many of the older tastes and appetites had faded. In addition, during the "peak television era," cable and streaming television platforms had changed viewing habits and production patterns. To compete seriously in that environment, movie studios needed to adapt to the new realities of the U.S. theatrical film market.

In the changing entertainment landscape, the films that held sway in movie theaters were mainly works highly engineered to meet blockbuster expectations. Although there continued to be exceptions, big, loud, recognizable, and easy-to-consume (and to market) productions were the new norm for so-called "A-list" movies. In some ways, that type of environment was seemingly perfect for a franchise starring famous and well-loved giant monsters.

Despite the stiff competition, Legendary Pictures already had made a credible showing with its efforts to build a new kaiju cinematic universe centering on Godzilla and Kong. Elsewhere, Toho created a sensation in the Japanese market with its modestly budgeted *Shin Godzilla* in 2016. That could have led some people to think Toho was planning to restart its most storied franchise. However, any thoughts of making a sequel to that had been placed on hold, partly to avoid scheduling conflicts with Legendary's next movie featuring the beast. And indeed, in 2019, about two years after *Kong: Skull Island's* premiere, Legendary brought *Godzilla: King of the Monsters* to theaters worldwide.

It had been nearly five years since the debut of Legendary's *Godzilla* in 2014. Since then, the studio had considerably refined its kaiju cinematic universe plans. *Kong: Skull Island* had gone a long way toward creating an original unifying mythology for the franchise. The world-building fleshed out the Monarch organization, the hollow earth, and the origin story of the ancient kaiju called Titans.

It was no secret that Legendary planned for Godzilla to eventually square off against Kong in a blockbuster-style movie that would be very different from Toho's campy but entertaining *King Kong versus Godzilla* (1963). Considering that the studio's intentions were well known, some people were probably surprised when Legendary squeezed another solo Godzilla movie into its lineup before the Kong-Godzilla match-up.

But from Legendary's perspective, the individual Godzilla and Kong story arcs were not yet fully aligned. *Kong: Skull Island* had paved the way from the colossal ape's side of things. But there was more world-building and calibration to do in preparation for Legendary's reimagined Godzilla story. *Godzilla: King of the Monsters* (2019) was intended to finish that work and set up a spectacular battle between the world's two most famous giant monsters in a subsequent film.

Legendary chose Michael Dougherty to helm the new Godzilla standalone movie. At the time, Dougherty's reputation as a director was mainly based on his movie *Krampus* (2015), which also involved Legendary. That low-budget film was an offbeat mix of fantasy, horror, and comedy. Though it lacked mass appeal, it generated a respectable financial return. In addition to that experience, Dougherty had been one of the story writers for two superhero movies, the somewhat forgotten *Superman Returns* (2006) and *X-Men: Apocalypse* (2016).

Since *Godzilla: King of the Monsters* was to act as a bridge between the 2014 Godzilla movie and the yet-to-come Kong match-up, it is unsurprising that it mostly picked up where the 2014 movie left off. (The storyline completely ignored Toho's intervening *Shin Godzilla*.) It acknowledges much of the plot from the 2014 outing but ignores or downplays most of the previous edition's human characters. (Only a few characters from the 2014 film—such as those played by actors Ken Watanabe, Sally Hawkins, and David Strathairn—reappear in the 2019 film.) The 2019 movie's main characters are primarily new additions, including Mark Russell (played by Kyle Chandler), Emma Russell (Vera Farmiga), and Madison Russell (Millie Bobby Brown).

The human story largely centers on the fractured relationships between scientists Mark Russell and Emma Russell, now divorced, and between Emma Russell and her adolescent daughter, Madison, who is caught in the middle of her parents' bitter split. The formerly married couple had previously worked with Monarch, the mysterious organization researching Godzilla, Kong, and the other Titan monsters. Mark Russell tried to put the monsters behind him after the events of 2014, but Emma Russell had since gone rogue. Now working with eco-extremists, she is determined to bring other Titans back to life as part of a mad-scientist-like scheme to heal the planet. Not unexpectedly, things quickly go wrong, which eventually pits Mark Russell, who again joins forces with Monarch, against ex-wife Emma Russell, whose plans go awry.

The complicated narrative about the human characters is soon overwhelmed by battles between newly awakened Titans and Godzilla. (Of interest to kaiju fans, the "new" monsters, Rodan, Mothra, and King Ghidorah, are long-time fan favorites licensed from the Toho stable.) A series of kaiju fights ensue, with Godzilla eventually emerging victorious.

Legendary delivered a U.S.-made movie for the international market, updating and further Americanizing a classic Japanese kaiju movie formula. Some critics liked it. One such reviewer, Scott Cullura, described it as "a fun exercise in giant monster madness."[1]

Others, however, were far less charitable. A review posted in *The Guardian* gave the film a dismal one-star rating and succinctly summed up the major complaints. According to the writer, *Godzilla: King of the Monster* suffers from loud and "tedious" sound. It has too many dimly lit scenes set in severe weather conditions, making much of the film visually "indecipherable." The reviewer also found the human characters, which take up much of the screen time, are "devoid of wit and barely functional in communicating the story."[2] Whether the film suffers from those issues more than many other kaiju movies is debatable. Nonetheless, the review is evidence that the 2019 entry in Legendary's still-new franchise did not strike some viewers as different enough in the right ways to overcome some audience objections.

Despite muted enthusiasm in some quarters, *Godzilla: King of the Monsters* was a credible American-style kaiju movie in most respects. It fulfilled its primary role in solidifying the foundations of Legendary's Monsterverse. After its release, the studio remained committed to continuing its giant-monster franchise.

Yet, there was also a reason for some trepidation. *Variety* reported that *King of the Monsters'* production budget was $170–200 million.[3] That is a substantial sum, even in the context of astonishingly high production costs that had become commonplace in the late 2010s.[4] Hollywood accounting practices are notoriously obtuse, but widely accepted formulas suggest that, in general, big-budget films need to clear much more than their production budgets at the box office to become profitable. (This is due to significant costs associated with marketing and distribution, which in some cases are thought to equal or surpass the production expenses.) Given such considerations, *King of the Monsters'* box-office performance was not comforting from the studio's perspective. In any case, V*ariety* reported that the receipts from the film's opening weekend were "middling" and "well below" the opening domestic totals for its 2014 *Godzilla* or 2017 *Kong: Skull Island*.[5] In the words of *Variety's* Rebecca Rubin, "Those diminishing returns are troubling given that these movies are only getting more expensive to make. That should concern Warner Bros. and Legendary as the studios wrap up production on *Godzilla vs. Kong*.'"[6]

Indeed, a movie that would pit Kong against Godzilla had been central to Legendary's Monsterverse vision for many months and was always regarded as *the* main event. That probably explains why work on that film started long before *Godzilla: King of the Monsters* had wrapped. In some ways, the opportunity to showcase the world's two most famous and storied giant monster characters in one film provided the rationale for their still-new Monsterverse. The whole point of undertaking the complicated arrangements to get the rights for both characters under one studio roof was primarily to bring attention to the franchise that a high-profile fight between the two kaiju would provide.

Legendary had been stoking fan expectations for many months. In May 2017, the studio released information to further intrigue kaiju fans. Around the same time that *Kong: Skull Island* opened, the studio announced it had established a "writers' room" to develop essential story elements for what *The Hollywood Reporter* termed "the big prize: the eventual *Godzilla vs. Kong* movie."

Executives selected *Pirates of the Caribbean* co-writer Terry Rossio to lead the effort. He was to be joined by a large group, including Patrick McKay (co-writers of *Star Trek Beyond*). Other writers included Lindsey Beer, Cat Vasko, T.S. Nowlin (who was involved in *Pacific Rim*), Jack Paglen, and J. Michael Straczynski (known for the *Babylon 5* television series and work on *World War Z*).[7]

The road to a finished script proved lengthy, even with a sizeable writing staff. Eventually, Michael Dougherty, director of *Godzilla: King of the Monsters*, and Zach Shields, who had co-written that film, made contributions. After more work, the final version of the script was credited to two writers with experience writing blockbusters: Eric Pearson, then best known for work on Marvel's *Thor Ragnarok* (2017), and Max Borenstein, who had already worked on Legendary's 2014 *Godzilla* as well as *Kong: Skull Island* and *Godzilla: King of the Monsters*.

Work on writing the film was just starting when, in May 2017, the studio announced it had picked a director, Adam Wingard, for the Kong-Godzilla match-up. At that point, Wingard was known mainly for "low-budget horror thrillers,"[8] including the modestly funded *Blair Witch*, Lionsgate's sequel to the phenomenally successful movie, *The Blair Witch Project* (1999).

One complaint about *King of the Monsters* was that it was weighed down by "too much human drama," as a review in the *Los Angeles Times* concluded.[9] Yet, press reports during the development of *Godzilla versus Kong* suggested that the sequel was also likely to feature a potentially huge cast of actors, a possible indication that this would be another movie where humans and kaiju competed for screen time. Some *King of the Monsters* cast members—notably Millie Bobby Brown and Kyle Chandler—were slated to appear in the sequel to help tie the story together. On top of that, an extensive roster of talent was added.

The new cast members included Swedish actor Alexander Skarsgård, who had been appearing in U.S.-based films since 2008's *Zoolander*. He was assigned the role of Monarch scientist Nathan Lind. Other significant parts went to Rebecca Hall (as Ilene Andres, another Monarch specialist), Brian Tyree Henry (as Bernie Hayes, a tech specialist and conspiracy theorist), Oguri Shun (as Ren Serizawa, son of a late Monarch scientist), and many others.

As the cast was assembled, work on the visual design of the monsters was ongoing. Since it would be a sequel, the designs for the main kaiju characters, Kong and Godzilla, were similar to their previous Legendary appearances. Moving Pictures Company, Scanline, and Weta were hired to handle special effects. Filming began in late 2018 at locations in Australia and Hawaii[10] and was completed a few months later in April 2019,[11] a month before *Godzilla: King of the Monsters* (the film to which it would be a sequel) had even opened. Much post-production work remained unfinished, but at the time, Legendary and Warner Bros still aimed to bring *Godzilla vs. Kong* to theaters in March 2020, only a year in the offing.

As things turned out, however, things did not go as initially planned. In November 2019, six months after *King of the Monsters'* less-than-stellar debut came the news that the Godzilla-Kong movie would be delayed until November 2020.[12] What, if anything, did that mean? In and of itself, pushing back the launch date of a major release is not unprecedented, and it is not necessarily problematic. It can and does occasionally happen for a variety of reasons. For example, a delay could be for something as innocuous as changing to a more desirable launch date. Even though many delays are unremarkable, a significant delay is sometimes taken as a warning sign of potential difficulties with the film itself.

Still, delaying the much-heralded next entry in the Monsterverse franchise was a worrying sign. According to a report in *The Independent* newspaper, the date was moved because *King of the Monsters'* generated "dismal reviews and disappointing box office."[13] (*The Independent's* earlier review of that film had gone so far as to call it a "dismaying" movie marred by "cartoonish, one-dimensional performances."[14]) That was hardly the strong lead-in to the Godzilla–Kong match-up the studio wanted. Considering the circumstances, it was not surprising that Legendary and Warner Bros. might want to take more time with the upcoming release. That would allow public memory of the previous outing to fade somewhat. It would also give the filmmakers more time to ensure the forthcoming film was exactly what they wanted. However, by pushing back the date, it was evident to people following the film industry that there were questions about the future of the Monsterverse. It seemed likely that another disappointing entry might sink any realistic hope of an ongoing franchise.[15]

But all was not lost. Even well-established franchises stumble occasionally, and a single disappointment does not necessarily bring them to a halt. In any case, the new release date at the beginning of the busy U.S. holiday season was, in theory, a good one. If nothing else went wrong, there was still good reason for studio executives to be at least cautiously optimistic.

But as the world knows, many things well beyond the filmmakers' control went horribly awry. The unexpected emergence of the worldwide Covid-19 pandemic wreaked havoc on everyday life and the global economy. Suddenly ordinary activities such as attending classes, dining in restaurants, and going to theaters, were limited or prohibited. The pandemic upended the film business. Regular film distribution was disrupted as theaters closed or radically reduced their schedules. Across the industry, numerous movies were ready, or almost ready, for release. The production money was already spent, but with theaters almost completely locked down, the usual avenue to recover those costs—let alone generate profits—had disappeared. To make matters worse, there was no clear indication of when things might return to "normal."

It was not long before it became evident that the pandemic would drag on in one form or another for much longer than most people had hoped. As time passed, some businesses got back on their feet with relatively minor adjustments, but the movie business continued to suffer. Audiences seemed reluctant to return to theaters with the same enthusiasm or in the same numbers as before the pandemic, which resulted in unpredictable and often anemic box-office business. The film industry was deeply rattled. Suddenly, running movie theaters seemed a much dicier proposition than before, and some venues closed. In that context, the entire industry was worried. An often-voiced fear was that the crisis might have permanently altered the film-going landscape. Perhaps audiences would never return to theaters in numbers close to pre-pandemic levels.

The situation might not have seemed so dire if less were at stake. However, over several decades, the traditional film business had become dependent on blockbusters. And the cost of making that kind of movie had soared. (This phenomenon was accompanied by a virtual shunning of mid-budget films, which exacerbated the situation.) Studios committed to producing blockbuster-style movies often spent $125 million to $150 million or even more just to make a single movie, not counting typically exorbitant marketing and distribution costs. Recovering those expenses and making a profit under the traditional theatrical-release model requires a large audience of paying customers. However, with theater attendance numbers looking weak due to the lingering influence of the pandemic, how realistic was it to expect a film to attract vast numbers of theater attendees?

Such questions plagued the release of *Godzilla vs. Kong*, which had cost well over $150 million to make. By the summer of 2020, when the pandemic was still raging, Warner Bros. announced it would postpone many of its upcoming releases. Under the new plan, *Godzilla vs. Kong* would be delayed again and scheduled for a revised release date of May 21, 2021.[16] That was not particularly unusual since other studios facing similar situations were doing the same thing.

However, controversy erupted when Warner Bros. subsequently changed the date yet again. It abruptly moved the *Godzilla vs. Kong* opening date from May to two months earlier in March, additionally indicating it would launch the film on its HBO Max television streaming service the same day. As reported by *Variety*, this change was made by Warner, with Legendary "largely kept out of the loop" even though Legendary had put up a substantial proportion of the money to make the film.[17]

The issue may seem like much ado about nothing to many fans and other ordinary viewers. However, it was troubling to many people involved in making the movie because of the "potential loss of profit participation" and implications for other payments calculated based on ticket sales.[18] (The thinking was that the simultaneous HBO Max release would deter many from seeing the film in a theater.) The disagreement was severe enough that Legendary threatened legal action against Warner Bros., though the two studios came to an agreement in early 2021.[19]

When the film finally opened in March of 2021, curious fans could see the long-awaited giant monster face-off. In its final edit, the film's plot offered new wrinkles but mainly covered much familiar territory. The title alone announced the movie's main event to audiences. The remaining questions were how the filmmakers would frame the climactic face-off and how the human characters would be involved.

Addressing these questions, director Wingard quickly sets up the coming conflict in opening scenes that portray Kong as essentially a sympathetic character and Godzilla as a heartless creature that has taken a destructive turn. The early sequences also introduce a new corporate villain (a company called Apex) and a slate of human characters. These include Ilene Hall (a scientist sympathetic to Kong), Jia (a deaf girl—the last of Skull Island's indigenous population—who has a special bond with Kong), Madison Russell (a high schooler sympathetic to Godzilla), and Nathan Lind (an expert in Hollow Earth theory). These characters hold varying attitudes about the giant Titan monsters, essentially making Godzilla and Kong avatars for various human points of view.

The action is straightforward. As the film opens, Kong remains under Monarch's watchful eye in a secret biodome, where Jia, a deaf girl from Skull Island, has formed a special bond with him. The creature lives there peacefully until the decision is made to transport the great ape to another location for clandestine research.

Meanwhile, after disappearing at the end of the previous movie, Godzilla abruptly reemerges in the Gulf of Mexico. It then attacks an Apex facility in Florida, where the organization conducts mysterious research. Madison Russell, who attends school nearby, hears news of the incident and sets off to find "the truth" about a conspiracy that seems to involve Apex and Godzilla. Not long after, Godzilla resurfaces far away, near the ship transporting Kong to the secret project. In a warm-up to the main event, the two giant monsters briefly battle before Godzilla disappears beneath the surface. Meanwhile, Madison and a few allies infiltrate the Apex facility and figure out the company has menacing plans.

Monarch airlifts Kong to a Hollow Earth Launch Station in Antarctica, one of many secret portals to a vast network of tunnels connecting to a primordial subterranean world. Kong enters the tunnel, followed by Nathan Lind, Ilene Hall, and others who fly through the passageways in futuristic vehicles. When they arrive at the ancient subterranean world, many terrifying monsters are ready to attack.

In Florida, Madison and her friends accidentally stumble across a similar specialized vehicle, which automatically whisks them to an Apex base in Hong Kong. There they discover the organization is building a gigantic robotic kaiju called Mechagodzilla. Around the same time, Godzilla and Kong emerge from Hollow Earth as they continue their fight in Hong Kong. As much of the city is destroyed, Kong is severely injured just as Apex activates Mechagodzilla.

When Apex's mechanical giant bursts from the secret facility, it nearly kills Godzilla. By then, however, Jia and Ilene Hall have arrived on the scene. Jia encourages Kong and tells the great ape that Godzilla is an ally. With new motivation, Kong rises to fight alongside Godzilla. After one final and spectacular battle, the kaiju destroy Mechagodzilla.

In the aftermath, Kong and Godzilla roar with admiration for each other. Then, as has happened countless times before, the colossal reptile returns to the sea. The film concludes as Kong is taken to live freely in a remote paradise as Jia, Ilene Hall, and Nathan Lind look on.

As this synopsis suggests, Wingard delivered a movie that builds on some of the ideas presented in previous Monsterverse entries, most notably by fleshing out more of the Hollow Earth story. The film also introduces Apex, a sinister new counter organization to Monarch. Yet, in most respects, this movie deals with familiar elements that do not veer very far in substance from what appeared in kaiju films that predate the Monsterverse. Considering the muted response to *King of the Monsters,* that may have been a wise decision on Wingard's part.

Following a trend that began in previous Monsterverse movies featuring Godzilla, the film continues down the path of cultural internationalization. As part of that process, it further reduces most references to Japan. The only significant Japanese character, the adult son of scientist Serizawa in earlier movies, appears in a few scenes, most notably when he remotely pilots Mechagodzilla late in the film.

Interestingly, the filmmakers had gone to the trouble of lining up a very prominent Japanese actor, Oguri Shun, to play that role. Therefore, before the premiere, many people presumed Oguri's character would be a substantial part of the story. However, the actor appears only briefly and sporadically in the final version, making a scant impression. The minimal attention to the Serizawa character is perhaps inadvertently symbolic of the film overall. As with each of the previous U.S. productions featuring the monster under license from Toho, *Godzilla vs. Kong* provides scarcely a hint of having any significant Japanese roots whatsoever. The creature is an internationalized and generic giant monster with a narrative without a meaningful connection to Japanese storytelling. Whether that is a positive development is up to viewers to decide. However, the result arguably gives the film a cultural blandness that, for some, may make it more one-dimensional than it might otherwise have been.

Indeed, the movie seems engineered to appeal to those mainly looking for entertainment that fits within the universe of a bombastic international blockbuster. As most people probably expected—and many seemingly wanted—the film expends most of its energy in providing exciting visual effects and spectacle-oriented battle scenes. To do that, it draws from a wide range of cinematic sources. *New Yorker* critic Richard Brody identified elements reminiscent of *Star Wars,* the Marvel Cinematic Universe, and DC comics movies.[20] *Vanity Fair's* Richard Lawson suggests that *Pacific Rim* and its sequel are among its "closest inspirations."[21]

The film has a large cast of gifted actors. However, they do not have much to do throughout most of the proceedings. The human storylines mainly provide respite from the kaiju action in familiar ways. These include a delusional antagonist who does irrational things, a vague conspiracy that is up to no good, some "Disneyfied" (according to Richard Brody) teenagers sleuthing, and some heart-warming moments with a deaf indigenous girl. That said, little about the human characters registered much with most critics or audiences. But since Wingard uses the human stories primarily as a backdrop, that may not matter. The director offers much of what many viewers probably wanted by keeping things simple, focusing on kaiju, and avoiding any urge to make grand statements or aim for serious drama.

Many people seem to have enjoyed this film precisely because it did not try to be a "great movie" in the classic sense and primarily stayed true to expectations. It earned numerous positive reviews, even if some, such as Richard Lawson's in *Vanity Fair,* may seem to be faint praise at best. (Lawson's piece was published with the title "*Godzilla vs. Kong* Is Just the Right Kind of Dumb."[22]) Still, the movie is a more serious effort than the somewhat campy 1962 Toho production, *King Kong vs. Godzilla,* from which it derives some inspiration. However, it does not take itself too seriously and backs away from the overarching darkness of 2019's *Godzilla: King of the Monsters.*

Considering the challenging circumstances under which it was released, the movie did well. As a result, in 2022, the studios announced a sequel, again to be directed by Adam Wingard. Interestingly, the director mentioned one specific aim for the next movie: reducing the role of humans in the story to place an even greater focus on the kaiju. According to one source, the director planned for a "full-on monster film … [that would be roughly ] 30 percent humans, the rest monsters, basically flipping the formula of what a lot of these movies generally are."[23]

A few months after news of Legendary's planned *Godzilla vs. Kong* sequel, Toho Studio announced that it, too, would proceed with a new Godzilla film. After releasing *Shin Godzilla* in 2016, the Japanese studio stayed out of the way while its American licensees continued filling out their Monsterverse using Godzilla as an essential building block. But now, Toho was ready to move forward with its franchise. The announcement's timing may have surprised some, but many had expected it sooner or later, given *Shin Godzilla*'s stellar performance, particularly in Japan.

Neither film has been completed at this time, so it remains to be seen if things will turn out as planned. However, one thing is already evident. By the late 2010s and early 2020s, the directorial approach to Godzilla movies had split, at least temporarily, along two different but parallel paths. Legendary's Monsterverse strategy increasingly aimed to attract audiences by emphasizing thrills, loud and raucous kaiju battles, and state-of-the-art special effects. The films relegate the human angle to secondary status. By contrast, Toho's *Shin Godzilla* devoted significant attention to the human stories suggested by a kaiju attack.

These differences can be seen in the two starkly contrasting ways the films treat human victims. In *Godzilla vs. Kong,* the numerous kaiju battles imply human casualties on a colossal scale, but that is hardly acknowledged. In *Shin Godzilla,* human suffering is explicitly treated as a significant part of the story. Whether this type of split approach will continue remains to be seen.

As of the early 2020s, the future of Godzilla movies has yet to be determined. However, it is clear that after the long slumber that began after Toho's 2004 *Godzilla Final Wars,* the great kaiju's return to theaters a decade later was more than incidental. After Legendary's 2014 resurrection of the beast, Godzilla appeared on screen often and was the subject of much publicity. Indeed, as the 75th anniversary of *Gojira* approached, the monster remained firmly ensconced in international popular culture, which is a remarkable feat.

# Conclusion

A series of crises swept the world in the first two decades of the 21st century. From terrorist attacks to an economic meltdown, natural disasters, and an unprecedented global pandemic, worrying calamities came fast and furious. It is no wonder that year after year of upheaval took a psychological toll on people in far-flung places. In those circumstances, perhaps it was inevitable that many would turn to make-believe tales of horror and devastation. Visiting fictionalized worlds at the movie theater could provide refuge from the troubled world people knew all too well. And stories of fights against imaginary monsters may have been cathartic in some ways. Watching movie characters battle fictional monsters may have indirectly helped people process the fraught realities experienced or heard about in the media almost every day.

There is more to the story of the era's kaiju cinema than that, of course. But when broken down into a basic schema, the common storyline in many giant monster movies has more in common with recent real-world troubles than may be evident at first glance. Just as in the era's real-life crises, the usual timeline in these films often begins with the abrupt and unexpected arrival of an unknown or forgotten problem (in the movies, a giant monster) that severely damages and disrupts ordinary life. That is followed by a period of chaos in which officials make frantic efforts to understand and conquer the problem. Things generally become increasingly dire along the way until, at some point, there is a resolution. If all goes well at that stage, the problem is put to rest. But in kaiju movies, as in the real world, there remains a lingering fear that the menace will somehow return in the future.

This same flow of events roughly coincides with the actual timelines of many large-scale emergencies, from the 2001 terror incidents to the Covid pandemic. Many films in the kaiju genre take this rudimentary schema mainly as is, perhaps adding only a few plot variations. Those extra elements often reflect versions of behaviors and reactions familiar in the real world. *Pacific Rim*, for example, sets up its action by showing that

## Conclusion    175

the higher-ups have poorly assessed humanity's situation and have hampered efforts to fight the kaiju threat by closing an effective program. *The Host* and *Shin Godzilla* portray the ineptness of governments in dealing with crises. *The Mist* showcases people's poor coping skills under duress. *Kong: Skull Island* reveals how things can go wrong when people blindly shoot first (here, literally) before assessing the situation. In these and other examples, the shape of the overall plots in many giant monster movies essentially mirrors the flow of real-world crises in an abstract way.

Some giant monster movies deviate from that schema more than others. Of the films discussed in previous chapters, *Colossal* is somewhat an outlier, though it does not entirely abandon the formula. The behemoths in Nacho Vigalondo's movie—depicted unambiguously as psychological extensions of the two main human characters—unleash death and destruction not in their own space but on a faraway continent. The devastation in Seoul cannot be solved by people living in the area because it has nothing to do with them. According to the story's internal logic, resolution can only come if the conflict between the two American characters, thousands of miles away for most of the movie, is resolved. Interestingly, if one were to abstract and generalize the situation presented in *Colossal*, it would look like a schematic description of a real-world proxy war, a type of military conflict the world knows all too well.

Nearly every giant monster movie is subject to various interpretations, of course. To some extent, that is true of the film medium overall. Movies often function as de facto Rorschach ink blots. People project many different and sometimes surprising meanings onto them depending upon their own experiences and points of view. Cinematic monsters (of all kinds) provide an almost ideal opportunity for multiple interpretations in that way.

Still, people who buy movie tickets are not usually undertaking a quest for meaning. Meanings in films, intended or not, can be found by those looking for them. But most movie-goers, particularly those flocking to blockbuster-style movies, are looking more for entertainment than enlightenment about the human condition. Although those who attend screenings of serious-minded productions may be important exceptions to that general observation, most movie-goers are not usually seeking a life-altering experience. On the contrary, most typically prefer movies that do not challenge their worldviews or ask them to spend too much time probing into life's profound questions.

The upshot of this is that when the directors of kaiju movies choose to pour most of their attention into creating believable giant monsters and exciting action scenes, many people think they have gotten the genre right. And indeed, many of these movies can fit into the mold of pure—or nearly pure—entertainment, particularly when directors do not push other messaging in the films beyond what audiences can choose to ignore.

The choice to make a movie focusing more on action and excitement than deeper meaning may seem like the easy way out. However, it is no simple task in a crowded marketplace flooded with many such films. Developing something new to meet or exceed audience expectations is particularly challenging in the giant monster genre. And such an undertaking is almost always massively expensive. Modern blockbuster audiences have been groomed to expect every special effects–oriented motion picture to be bigger and better than anything before. But the cost of producing eye-popping special effects that will wow viewers can be astronomical.

Barring unforeseen advances in computer technologies and methods that radically reduce costs, it seems unlikely that the makers of these movies will be able to meet these spiraling audience expectations without spending even more than in the past. And if production budgets continue to skyrocket, the pressures to generate income to offset those expenses will increase, too. Under such circumstances, can filmmakers create motion pictures generating enough revenue to justify the mounting costs indefinitely? Or, at some point, will it become too expensive to continue on the present course? At the moment, these are unanswered questions, not only for kaiju movies but also for spectacle-oriented films more generally.

Another potentially more profound issue is looming for giant monster movies and for much of the film world: changing consumer habits. The main question at issue is the long-term viability of theatrical films in an era where it is not certain that mass audiences still value the experience of seeing a film in that setting as much as they once did. Although the Covid pandemic created an apparent rupture in how people chose to see movies, especially in the United States, viewing habits had started to change long before that.

In the modern blockbuster era, now decades old, a steady stream of big-budget movies has slowly crowded other types of films out of theaters. Over time, that phenomenon seems to have accelerated to the point where so-called mid-budget and small-budget movies appear far less often on theater schedules than in the past.

Yet, although their role in theaters seems to have declined, modestly budgeted productions did not so much disappear as change venues. They may have become less important in theaters. However, that void was filled by other screen options, mainly video streaming services that rose to prominence throughout the century's first decades. Indeed, competition from other theatrical releases is now far from a given movie's only rival. Instead, new films must lure people to theaters who might otherwise be content to watch a top-quality production on HBO, Netflix, or another cable or streaming service at home.

Since the dampening effect of television on theatrical movies was first widely felt in the middle of the 20th century, studios have always looked for ways to respond. One method, now well established, is to offer viewers a theatrical movie experience that cannot be easily matched at home. Of significance when considering giant monster movies of the era, one way to differentiate the theatrical experience from the home viewing experience is to double down on special effects. In the blockbuster era, one allure of that category of motion pictures has been the ability of movies in theaters to overwhelm the senses. Traditionally, the home experience often paled compared to what theaters could offer in that regard. That remained true for as long as home viewing could not compete with the more immersive experience possible in theaters. However, that presumed advantage has been shrinking rapidly in recent years due to considerable advances in home video technology.

In the U.S. market many years ago, kaiju movies often appeared on home screens. That phenomenon dates to the early decades of television when old movies and imports featuring giant monsters provided inexpensive options for television program directors. (For example, most people in the United States who have seen Toho kaiju movies have seen them via television.)

Added to that phenomenon, by the late 20th century, some studios were already making giant monster productions intended to be released directly to video formats. For a long time, many thought these were sub-par and lacked the type of production values of a top-quality theatrical release. However, by the 2010s, that was less likely to be true. Advances in computerized special effects and increases in the money available to make video-oriented productions led to new efforts to bring quality kaiju productions to home screen platforms. The rising popularity of large, high-definition televisions and advanced home audio systems fueled that trend. Many of the perceived advantages of seeing a movie on the big screen at the local theater were eroding.

There is another complication for theatrical-oriented giant monster movies, too. The long-form storytelling possibilities of video offer something that theatrical movies cannot easily duplicate. For those aiming to push the genre beyond a desire merely to overwhelm audience senses, the case to create a production in long-form video format, rather than for the movie theater, could be compelling. That could help send the more conceptually and thematically adventurous kaiju screen productions straight to non-theatrical distribution. And that would leave mainly spectacle-oriented blockbusters for theatrical release. Such a development would be a change, but there is no reason to believe that there would not be room for both tracks.

As the world emerges from the pandemic crisis that began in 2020 and audiences start to attend movie theaters in large numbers once again, the lure of film franchises remains robust. Indeed, it may be stronger than ever. In the kaiju movie world, Legendary remains committed to its Godzilla-Kong-centered Monsterverse.

Beyond that, there have been efforts to create new giant monster franchises, but it has been challenging. For example, in response to the original *Cloverfield,* two sequels were produced: *10 Cloverfield Lane* (2016) and *The Cloverfield Paradox* (2018). (The latter was picked up by Netflix and bypassed theaters.) Elsewhere, *Pacific Rim Uprising*, a sequel to Guillermo del Toro's original film, was released in 2018. (By then, del Toro, had moved on to other projects, and he had little to do with the sequel.) All these sequels had fans but also critics. So far, it has proven challenging to transform the original properties into bona fide franchises. It is too soon to determine the final word.

It is worth noting that creating kaiju movies with blockbuster aspirations comes with varying costs that extend beyond finances. One of those costs is cultural. Although *King Kong*—in many ways a classic Hollywood film—may have launched the genre, much of the giant monster tradition, as it exists today, stems from the legacy of Japanese kaiju movies. In the U.S. market, traditional perceptions of those movies as "foreign" were probably built into how they were consumed from the beginning. Unfortunately, those perceptions were undoubtedly accompanied by racist assumptions unacknowledged by the predominantly white audiences of those films in the United States.

Years later, when U.S.-based studios eventually licensed Godzilla and other Toho kaiju intellectual properties to make Hollywood movies, it may have been inevitable that the resulting works would be repurposed for those studios' intended audiences. Indeed, the Americanization of kaiju worlds created in other cultural settings has led to not only homogenizing those other worlds by removing some things that made them distinctive. The process, to date, has also resulted in adding U.S.-centric concerns, attitudes, and values in their place. As a result, distinct cultural voices present in the original productions have been lost.

That change may not be widely noticed in the United States and elsewhere. After all, to many average viewers in Western nations, the word blockbuster is nearly synonymous with a big, bold production that comes out of Hollywood. So, for many viewers, it may not seem unusual for Hollywood movies inspired by other traditions to have erased most evidence of those different traditions and Americanized the content. In other words, that is primarily what people have expected from a Hollywood movie, at least in the past.

Indeed, material imported from other nations is typically heavily processed when Hollywood acquires and uses it. Partly for business reasons, studios aim to make the intellectual property they import palatable to what the U.S. industry imagines as average viewers—those whose values, interests, and expectations conform to the presumptions of an American viewpoint. Whether that is seen as a problem may depend on who is watching. However, there can be little doubt that such changes typically occur in the adaptation process.

Ultimately, one challenge that the kaiju genre faces in the international market is how to invigorate and maintain the voices of other cultures that have been so instrumental in creating the genre in the first place. Studios beyond the United States usually cannot compete with the massive capital available to make blockbuster movies in America, which often dominate global screens. Yet, there is no reason that productions from Japan or any other country must be made in the Hollywood mold. Indeed, the opposite is more likely true.

The giant monster genre in cinema was nurtured elsewhere across the decades because the films were made by studios and appealed to audiences beyond American shores. Despite Hollywood's relatively recent interest in making these movies, it had little to do with the rising popularity of kaiju movies until very recently. But now that the genre has attracted the attention of U.S. studios, Hollywood's support of cultural diversity—and diversity of all kinds—in kaiju storytelling will be critical.

There is something alluring and perhaps satisfying in seeing visual representations of humongous monsters—creatures that could not credibly be regarded as something ever to appear in real life. Whether we interpret the colossal beasts as representations of hidden fears, allegories for unsettling conditions, heroic avatars, or manifestations of the fears and demons lurking in our minds and under our beds, they can serve as the basis of engaging films. As Barry Keith Grant has written about monster movies more generally, kaiju films are "modern society's equivalent of cultural myths."[1]

Although it is still too soon to predict the fate of the kaiju movie genre, there is no reason to think it will disappear anytime soon. For centuries, humans have been drawn to stories about dragons, giants, and other colossal beasts. Giant monsters of the cinema are only one of their latest incarnations. As long as the cinema's menacing behemoths continue to strike a chord in popular culture, the genre seems likely to continue in one form or another.

# Chapter Notes

## Preface

1. Jenny Hamilton, "Monsters and Posttraumatic Stress: An Experiential-Processing Model of Monster Imagery in Psychological Therapy, Film and Television," *Humanities and Social Science Communications* 7, no. 142 (2020). https://doi.org/10.1057/s41599-020-00628-2.

## Introduction

1. The word *genre* is used in the everyday sense, not as a technical term of film or literary studies, throughout this book.
2. Susan Sontag, "The Imagination of Disaster," *Commentary* (October 1965): 42–48.
3. *Ibid.*
4. *Ibid.*
5. Courtney Crowder, "Head-On Train Crashes, Buying an Elephant and Other Crazy Stunts the Iowa State Fair Once Pulled," *The Des Moines Register*, August 16, 2019.
6. Certain films and subcategories are not included for various reasons. For example, the *Jurassic World* series, which has been highly successful, is not covered simply since, being based on dinosaurs, it is taken to fall somewhat outside the usual scope of the genre. Similarly excluded are movies primarily featuring humanoid giants, trolls, and huge mechanical monsters.
7. Bosley Crowther, "Screen: Horror Import; 'Godzilla' a Japanese Film, Is at State," *New York Times*, April 28, 1956.

## Chapter 1

1. "On Screen: Godzilla Goes Hi-Tech," *Tampa Bay Times*, December 20, 1992.
2. Brett Homenick, "On Directing Godzilla and Gamera," *Vantage Point Interviews*, June 13, 2018, https://vantagepointinterviews.com/2018/06/13/on-directing-godzilla-and-gamera-shusuke-kaneko-on-filmmaking-the-kaiju-way/.
3. Motoori Norinaga (1697–1769) cited in John J. Keane, *Cultural and Theological Reflections on the Japanese Quest for Divinity* (Leiden: Brill, 2016), 10.
4. "Yokai," in Jeffrey B. Webb, *American Myths, Legends, and Tall Tales: An Encyclopedia of American Folklore* (Santa Barbara: ABC-CLIO, 2016), 1086.
5. Michael Dylan Foster, *The Book of Yokai: Mysterious Creatures of Japanese Folklore* (Berkeley: University of California Press, 2015), 19.
6. Michael Dylan Foster, "The Current State of Japanese *Yokai* Studies in North America," *Japanese Studies Around the World* (2014), 149.
7. Michael Dylan Foster, *The Book of Yokai*, 23.
8. Yuki Tanaka, "Godzilla and the Bravo Shot: Who Killed the Monster?" in *Filling the Hole in the Nuclear Future: Art and Popular Culture Respond to the Bomb*, ed. Robert Jacobs (Lanham, MD: Lexington Books, 2010), 161.
9. It is worth noting that the film bypassed a U.S. theatrical run. It was released to television and home video instead.
10. "Japanese Box Office for 2001," Box Office Mojo, [n.d.], https://www.

boxofficemojo.com/year/2001/?area=JP&grossesOption=totalGrosses

11. *Ibid.*

## Chapter 2

1. This should not be confused with two similarly titled Toho movies, known in the United States as *Godzilla vs. Mechagodzilla* (1974) and *Godzilla vs. Mechagodzilla* II (1993).
2. All of these numbers are derived from "Japanese Box Office for 2002," Box Office Mojo, [n.d.], https://www.boxofficemojo.com/year/2002/?area=JP&ref_=bo_yl_table_20.
3. "Japanese Box Office for 2003," Box Office Mojo, [n.d.], https://www.boxofficemojo.com/year/2003/?area=JP&ref_=bo_yl_table_19.
4. "Japan Movie Index [Top-Grossing Movies]," The Numbers, [n.d.], https://www.the-numbers.com/Japan/movies#tab=year.
5. "Movies Produced by Japan and Released in 2001," The Numbers, [n.d.], https://www.the-numbers.com/Japan/movies/year/2001.
6. "Movies Produced by Japan and Released in 2002," The Numbers, [n.d.], https://www.the-numbers.com/Japan/movies/year/2002.
7. Hjorth Larissa and Dean Chan, *Gaming Cultures and Place in Asia-Pacific* (New York: Routledge, 2009), 278.
8. Jason Bainbridge, "'Gotta Catch 'Em All!' Pokémon, Cultural Practice and Object Networks," *IAFOR Journal of Asian Studies* 1, no. 1 (2014), https://doi.org/10.22492/ijas.1.1.04.
9. Kenji Hall, "After 50 Years, Godzilla Is Taking a Break," *The Victoria Advocate*, March 11, 2004.
10. *Ibid.*
11. *Ibid.*
12. Manohla Dargis, "'Azumi' Offers Sharp Sword, Short Skirt and Blood," *New York Times*, July 21, 2006.
13. Brett Homenick, "Godzilla's Final Cut: Director Ryuhei Kitamura on Crafting Godzilla's 50th Anniversary Film, 'Godzilla: Final Wars,'" *Vantage Point Interviews*, January 2, 2002, https://vantagepointinterviews.com/2019/01/02/godzillas-final-cut-director-ryuhei-kitamura-on-crafting-godzillas-50th-anniversary-film-godzilla-final-wars/.
14. *Ibid.*
15. *Ibid.*
16. *Ibid.*
17. "Godzilla," *Daily Sentinel*, December 12, 2004.
18. *Ibid.*
19. Brett Homenick, "Godzilla's Final Cut."
20. Ty Burr, "Godzilla Goes Out in a Blaze of Overkill," *Boston Globe*, August 5, 2005.
21. Kevin L. Lee, "Revisiting Godzilla and His Foes," *Film Inquiry*, May 30, 2019, https://www.filminquiry.com/revisiting-godzilla/.
22. "Japanese Box Office for December 2004," Box Office Mojo, [n.d.], https://www.boxofficemojo.com/month/december/2004/?area=JP&grossesOption=totalGrosses&sort=releaseDate&ref_=bo_md__resort.
23. *Ibid.*
24. "Godzilla Receives Star on Walk of Fame," *Today*, November 29, 2004, https://www.today.com/popculture/godzilla-receives-star-walk-fame-wbna6614532.
25. "Giant Monsters of Japan Film Series, *Godzilla: Final Wars*," Center for East Asian Studies, [n.d.], https://ceas.sas.upenn.edu/events/giant-monsters-japan-film-series-godzilla-final-wars.
26. Brett Homenick, "Godzilla's Final Cut."

## Chapter 3

1. Mordaunt Hall, "A Fantastic Film in Which a Monstrous Ape Uses Automobiles for Missiles and Climbs a Skyscraper," *New York Times*, March 3, 1933.
2. An unusual, animated musical, *The Mighty Kong*, was released in 1998. Skipping theatrical distribution and heading instead straight to the home video market, it had little cultural impact.
3. Stone Phillips, "Peter Jackson's Labor of Love," NBC News, December 2, 2005, https://www.nbcnews.com/id/wbna10299834.
4. Ray Morton, *King Kong: The History of a Movie Icon from Fay Wray to Peter Jackson* (New York: Applause Theatre & Cinema Books, 2005), 321.

5. *Ibid.*

6. "20 Facts You Might Not Know About Peter Jackson's *King Kong*," YB Entertainment, January 10, 2023, https://www.yardbarker.com/entertainment/articles/20_facts_you_might_not_know_about_peter_jacksons_king_kong/s1__37702963#slide_4/.

7. Gary Susman, "Peter Jackson Will Direct *King Kong* Remake," *Entertainment Weekly*, August 12, 2003, https://ew.com/article/2003/08/12/peter-jackson-will-direct-king-kong-remake/.

8. Stone Phillips, "Peter Jackson's Labor of Love."

9. Emine Saner, "Andy Serkis: 'King Kong was the epiphany. It was like: you can now do anything,'" *The Guardian*, October 12, 2017, https://www.theguardian.com/film/2017/oct/12/andy-serkis-king-kong-was-the-epiphany-it-was-like-you-can-now-do-anything/.

10. Quoted in Daniel Kilkelly, "Watts Chooses King Kong for Jackson," *Digital Spy*, March 27, 2005, https://www.digitalspy.com/movies/a20255/watts-chooses-king-kong-for-jackson/.

11. Horton, 326.

12. "*King Kong* Goes $32m Over Budget," BBC News, October 28, 2005, http://news.bbc.co.uk/2/hi/entertainment/4384458.stm.

13. *Ibid.*

14. Kwame McKenzie, "Big, black and bad stereotyping," *The Times* [UK], December 13, 2005.

15. This difference was noted almost immediately by some viewers. See Roger Ebert, "The Heart of a Big Gorilla," RogerEbert.com, December 12, 2005, https://www.rogerebert.com/reviews/king-kong-2005.

16. *Merriam-Webster.com Dictionary*, s.v. "monster," [accessed December 29, 2021], https://www.merriam-webster.com/dictionary/monster.

17. Stone Phillips, "Peter Jackson's Labor of Love."

18. Alan Rice, *Radical Narratives of the Black Atlantic* (New York: Continuum, 2003), 190.

19. Cynthia Erb, *Tracking Kong: A Hollywood Icon in World Culture* (Detroit: Wayne State University Press), 210.

20. *Ibid.*, 239–240.

21. *Ibid.*

22. A.O. Scott, "'You Beast,' She Said, and Meant It," *New York Times*, December 13, 2005.

23. "King Kong (2005)," The Numbers, [n.d.], https://www.the-numbers.com/movie/King-Kong-(2005)#tab=summary.

24. "King Kong (2005), Home Market Performance," The Numbers, [n.d.], https://www.the-numbers.com/movie/King-Kong-(2005)#tab=summary.

25. A.O. Scott, "'You Beast,' She Said, and Meant It."

## Chapter 4

1. Mark Schilling, "Kadokawa Announces Daiei 70th Anniversary Projects," *Variety*, June 22, 2012.

2. Sean Rhodes and Brooke McCorckle, *Japan's Green Monsters: Environmental Commentary in Kaiju Cinema* (Jefferson, NC: McFarland, 2018), 128.

3. Roger Ebert, "Gamera: Guardian of the Universe," RogerEbert.com, August 29, 1997, https://www.rogerebert.com/reviews/gamera-guardian-of-the-universe-1997.

4. Jasper Sharp, *Historical Dictionary of Japanese Cinema* (Lanham, MD: Scarecrow Press, 2011), 49.

5. Mark Schilling, "Toei's Kamen Rider Accelerates Toward International Markets," *Variety*, July 1, 2021, https://variety.com/2021/film/global/toei-kamen-rider-1235009716/.

6. Sophia Staite, "Kamen Rider: A Monstrous Hero," *M/C Journal* 24, no. 5 (2021), doi: https://10.5204/mcj.2834.

7. *Ibid.*

8. Ono Shuntaro, *Gamera no seishinshi: Shōwa kara Heisei e* [The spiritual history of Gamera from Showa to Heisei] (Tokyo: Takanashi Shobo, 2018), 210.

9. Some viewers may have been reminded of a similar scene in a film four decades earlier. In that movie, a young boy named Toshio also runs against a crowd trying to reach Gamera.

10. Ono Shuntaro, *Gamera no seishinshi: Shōwa kara Heisei e*, 211–212.

11. *Ibid.*, 213.

12. *Ibid.*, 214–215.

13. "Japanese Box Office for 2006," Box Office Mojo, [n.d.], https://www.boxofficemojo.com/year/2006/?area=JP.

## Chapter 5

1. Derek Elley, "The Host," *Variety*, May 22, 2006.
2. Ibid.
3. Park Chan-kyong, "Horror Wins the Day," *The Nation*, September 5, 2006, 15.
4. Ibid.
5. Ibid.
6. "Bulgasari," *Chosun Ilbo*, December 7, 1962.
7. Nick Romano, "How Kim Jong Il Kidnapped a Director, Made a Godzilla Knockoff, and Created a Cult Hit," *Vanity Fair*, April 6, 2015, https://www.vanityfair.com/hollywood/2015/04/pulgasari-north-korea-cult-hit.
8. Numerous sources report this incident as the source for the film, including "Korean Monster Goes on the Rampage at Midnight," *The Register-Guard*, April 6, 2007.
9. Derek Elley, "The Host," *Variety*, May 22, 2006.
10. Kevin B. Lee, "The Han River Horror Show: Interview with Bog Joon-ho," *Cineaste* 32, no. 2 (2007), https://www.cineaste.com/spring2007/interview-with-bong-joon-ho.
11. Ibid.
12. Edward Douglas, "Exclusive: *The Host*'s Bong Joon-ho," ComingSoon.net, March 6, 2007, https://www.comingsoon.net/movies/features/19126-exclusive-the-host-s-bong-joon-ho.
13. Alain Bielik, "'The Host': Creepie Korean Creatures," *AWN* [Animation World Network], August 3, 2006, https://www.awn.com/vfxworld/host-creepie-korean-creatures.
14. Kevin B. Lee, "The Han River Horror Show: Interview with Bog Joon-ho."
15. Ibid.
16. Ju-Won Kim, *Relocating the Alliance: The U.S.-South Korea Military Alliance in Cultural Representations*, diss. Emory University, 2011.
17. Mark Weisbrot, "IMF Blunders Through Asia, Leaving Disaster in Its Wake," *Los Angeles Times*, May 29, 1998.
18. Ibid.
19. J.W. Kwon, H. Chun, and Si Cho, "A Closer Look at the Increase in Suicide Rates in South Korea from 1986–2005," *BMC Public Health* 9, no. 72 (2009), https://doi.org/10.1186/1471-2458-9-72.
20. Nam Lee, *The Films of Bong Joon Ho* (New Brunswick: Rutgers University Press, 2020), 89.
21. Ibid., 79.
22. Kevin B. Lee, "The Han River Horror Show: Interview with Bong Joon-ho."
23. Ibid.
24. Ibid.
25. Jim Emerson, "Attack of the Giant Amphibian," RogerEbert.com, March 8, 2007, https://www.rogerebert.com/scanners/attack-of-the-giant-amphibian.
26. Steven Borowiec, "Korea's Smash Summer Hit Is a Zombie Movie That Strikes a Deep Chord," *Chicago Tribune*, August 14, 2016.
27. "The Host," Box Office Mojo, [n.d.], https://www.boxofficemojo.com/release/rl525895169/.

## Chapter 6

1. Scott Von Doviak, *Stephen King Films FAQ* (Milwaukee: Applause Theatre & Cinema Books, 2014), 185.
2. Ibid.
3. Ibid., 186.
4. Ibid.
5. Ibid.
6. Terence McSweeny, "'Daddy, I'm Scared. Can We Go Home?' Fear and Allegory in Frank Darabont's *The Mist* (2007)," in *American Cinema in the Shadow of 9/11*, ed. Terence McSweeney, et al., pp. 227–247 (Edinburgh: Edinburgh University Press, 2016), p. 244.
7. Aviva Briefel, "Shop 'Til You Drop: Consumer and Horror," in *Horror After 9/11: World of Fear, Cinema of Terror*, ed. Aviva Briefel and Sam J. Miller, pp. 142–164 (Austin: University of Texas, 2011), p. 156.
8. Ibid.
9. "Bush Tells Americans to "Get on Board," *The Spokesman-Review*, September 28, 2001.
10. "President Bush's News Conference," *New York Times*, December 20, 2006.
11. Aviva Briefel, "Ship 'Til You Drop," 142–143.
12. Stephen King, "The Mist," *Skeleton Crew*, pp. 21–134 (New York: Putnam's, 1985), p. 132.
13. Roger Ebert, "Attention Shoppers!

Get Eaten During Our Loading Dock Sale!" RogerEbert.com, November 20, 2007, https://www.rogerebert.com/reviews/the-mist-2007.
14. *Ibid.*
15. Justin Change, "The Mist," *Variety*, November 12, 2007, https://variety.com/2007/film/markets-festivals/the-mist-1200554625/.
16. "The Mist (2007)," The Numbers, [n.d.], https://www.the-numbers.com/movie/Mist-The#tab=summary.
17. *Ibid.*

## Chapter 7

1. "Rumsfeld: Military Is Battle Hardened, Not Stretched Too Thin," *Today's News-Herald*, January 26, 2006.
2. Thomas Riegler, "Through the Lenses of Hollywood: Depictions of Terrorism in American Movies," *Perspectives on Terrorism* 4, no. 2 (May 2010): 40.
3. Theresa Shea, *Godzilla* (New York: Rosen, 2016), 32.
4. Abrams is quoted in Andrew Housman, "Cloverfield Is Hollywood's Best Godzilla Movie," *Screen Rant*, November 6, 2020, https://screenrant.com/cloverfield-godzilla-movie-best-similarities/.
5. Sharon Knolle, "21 Things You Never Knew About J.J. Abrams' 'Cloverfield,'" *Moviefone*, January 16, 2018, https://www.moviefone.com/news/cloverfield-jj-abrams-matt-reeves-movie-facts/.
6. Lucio Reis-Filho, "Cloverfield," in *Aliens in Popular Culture*, ed. Farah Mendelsohn and Michael M. Levy (Santa Barbara: Greenwood, 2019), 87.
7. Stephen Galloway, "What Is the Most Profitable Movie Ever?" *The Hollywood Reporter*, January 18, 2020, https://www.hollywoodreporter.com/movies/movie-news/what-is-profitable-movie-ever-1269879/.
8. "The Blair Witch Project (1999)," Box Office Mojo, [n.d.], https://www.boxofficemojo.com/release/rl2269611521/.
9. "Cloverfield (2008)," Box Office Mojo, [n.d.], https://www.boxofficemojo.com/title/tt1060277/?ref_=bo_se_r_1.
10. Donato Totaro, "*Cloverfield*: An Intimate Apocalypse," *Off|Screen* 12, no.

2 (February 2008), https://offscreen.com/view/cloverfield_apocalypse.
11. Homay King, "*The Host* vs. *Cloverfield*," in *Horror After 9/11: World of Fear, Cinema of Terror*, ed. Avia Breifel and Sam J. Miller (Austin: University of Texas Press, 2011), 128.
12. Andrew Housman, "*Cloverfield* Is Hollywood's Best Godzilla Movie," *Screen Rant*, November 6, 2020, https://screenrant.com/cloverfield-godzilla-movie-best-similarities/.
13. *Ibid.*
14. These details can be found in Angus Finney, *The International Film Business: A Market Guide Beyond Hollywood*, 2nd ed. (New York: Francis & Taylor, 2014), 171.
15. *Ibid.*

## Chapter 8

1. Gareth Edwards quoted in David Whiteley, *The Galaxy Britain Built: The British Talent Behind Star Wars* (Albany, GA: Bear Manor Media, 2019), [unpaginated digital edition].
2. "Classic Feature: The Making of Gareth Edwards' *Monsters*," *Empire*, November 2010, https://www.empireonline.com/movies/features/gareth-edwards-monsters/.
3. *Ibid.*
4. "Low Budget but High Quality in *Monsters*," *Daily Emerald*, January 19, 2011, https://www.dailyemerald.com/ethos/archives/low-budget-but-high-quality-in-monsters/article_19b9f685-1c06-5210-aa11-0adfe6939817.html.
5. *Ibid.*
6. *Ibid.*
7. Steve Rose, "*Monsters*: The Bedroom Blockbuster That's Anti-*Avatar*," *The Guardian*, November 2, 2010.
8. *Ibid.*
9. John Carter, "Border Fence: The Job Needs Finishing," *Victoria Advocate*, July 28, 2009.
10. Ryan Lambie, "Gareth Edwards Interview: On Making *Monsters*, Meeting Quentin Tarantino and More," *Den of Geek*, November 29, 2010, https://www.denofgeek.com/movies/gareth-edwards-interview-on-making-monsters-meeting-quentin-tarantino-and-more/.
11. Roger Ebert, "Monsters Should Be

Heard and Not Seen," RogerEbert.com, November 17, 2020, https:www.rogerebert.com/reviews/monsters-2010.
  12. Brian Eggert, *"Monsters," Deep Focus Review*, October 29, 2010, https:/deepfocusreview.com/reviews/monsters
  13. *Ibid.*
  14. See, for example, Peter Bradshaw, *"Monsters*—Review," *The Guardian*, December 2, 2010.
  15. Ryan Lambie, "Gareth Edwards Interview: On Making *Monsters*."
  16. Beth Accomando, "Review: *Monsters*," *KBS Morning Edition*, November 5, 2010, ://www.kpbs.org/news/arts-culture/2010/11/05/review-monsters.
  17. Jack Giroux, "Gareth Edwards on *Monsters*," DVD Talk, [n.d.], htpps://dvdtalk.com/interviews/gareth-edwards.html.
  18. Brian Eggert, *"Monsters."*
  19. *"Monsters* (2010)," The Numbers, [n.d.], https://www.the-numbers.com/movie/Monsters#tab=box-office.

## Chapter 9

  1. The international box office was somewhat different. *Iron Man* edged out *Indiana Jones and the Kingdom of the Crystal Skull* in U.S. theaters, but the film managed to reach only eighth place on international box-office list.
  2. These details are recounted in multiple sources, including Ian Nathan, *Guillermo del Toro: The Iconic Filmmaker and His Work* (London: White Lion, 2021), 114–115.
  3. *Ibid.*, 115–166.
  4. Angela Watercutter, "Inside *Pacific Rim*—The Movie That Saved Guillermo del Toro's Life," *Wired*, June 18, 2013, https://www.wired.com/2013/06/pacific-rim-guillermo-del-toro-feature/.
  5. Nathan, *Guillermo del Toro*, 119–120.
  6. David Fear, "Time Out with *Pacific Rim*'s Guillermo del Toro," *Time Out*, November 21, 2016, https://www.timeout.com/film/time-out-with-pacific-rims-guillermo-del-toro
  7. Angela Watercutter, "Inside *Pacific Rim*."
  8. Ian Nathan, *Guillermo del Toro*, 128.
  9. David Fear, "Time Out with *Pacific Rim*'s Guillermo del Toro."
  10. *Ibid.*
  11. *Ibid.*
  12. "Charlie Hunnam Strikes Up Creative Partnership with Guillermo del Toro," *Young Hollywood*, July 6, 2013, https://younghollywood.com/news/charlie-hunnam-strikes-up-creative-partnership-with-guillermo-del-toro.html.
  13. Justin Chang, "Film Review: *Pacific Rim*," *Variety*, July 7, 2013, https://variety.com/2013/film/reviews/film-review-pacific-rim-1200535260/.
  14. Matt Zoller Seitz, *"Pacific Rim,"* Rogerebert.com, July 12, 2013, https://www.rogerebert.com/reviews/pacific-rim-2013.
  15. *Ibid.*
  16. Justin Chang, "Film Review: *Pacific Rim*."
  17. Brooke Jaffe, *"Pacific Rim* Is Not Your Average Action Juggernaut," *The Mary Sue*, August 16, 2013, https://www.themarysue.com/pacific-rim-gender-tropes/.
  18. Ian Nathan, *Guillermo del Toro*, 122.
  19. Justin Chang, "Film Review: *Pacific Rim*."
  20. Brooke Jaffe, *"Pacific Rim* Is Not Your Average Action Juggernaut."
  21. *Ibid.*
  22. *Ibid.*
  23. Jason Barr, *The Kaiju Film: A Critical Study of Cinema's Biggest Monsters* (Jefferson, NC: McFarland, 2016), 158.
  24. Brooke Jaffe, *"Pacific Rim* Is Not Your Average Action Juggernaut."
  25. *Ibid.*
  26. Jason Barr, *The Kaiju Film*, 33.
  27. *Ibid.*, 51.
  28. Asawin Suebsaeng "'Pacific Rim': The Most Exciting, Monster-Filled Anti-Pollution PSA Ever," *Mother Jones*, June 12, 2013, https://www.motherjones.com/politics/2013/07/film-review-pacific-rim-pollution/.
  29. Jason Barr, *The Kaiju Film*, 55.
  30. *Ibid.*
  31. Nicholas Bollinger, "Archetypes in War: Kaiju as Cult Icons in *Pacific Rim*," in *Giant Creatures in Our World: Essays on Kaiju and American Popular Culture*, ed. Camille D.G. Mustachio and Jason Barr, pp. 77–91 (Jefferson, NC: McFarland, 2017), 78.
  32. *Ibid.*, 78.

33. "*Pacific Rim* (2013)," The Numbers, [n.d.], https://www.the-numbers.com/movie/Pacific-Rim#tab=summary.

## Chapter 10

1. In the interim, there was talk of a short IMAX film that would resurrect the creature, but nothing came of those efforts.
2. Bill Graham, "Legendary Pictures Nabs Godzilla Rights; Sets Sights for a Destructive 2012," *Collider*, March 29, 2010, https://collider.com/legendary-pictures-nabs-godzilla-rights-sets-sights-for-a-destructive-2012/.
3. Legendary Pictures Press release, quoted in "Legendary Pictures to Take Another Stab at American *Godzilla*," *Geeks of Doom*, March 29, 2019, https://geeksofdoom.com/2010/03/29/legendary-pictures-to-take-another-stab-at-american-godzilla.
4. Ibid.
5. Quoted in *Ibid*.
6. Mark Cotta Vaz, *Godzilla: The Art of Destruction* (San Rafael, CA: Insight Editions, 2014).
7. Mark Cotta Vaz, *Godzilla: The Art of Destruction* (San Rafael, CA: Insight Editions, 2014), 11.
8. Ibid.
9. Karen Butler, "*Godzilla* Director Praises Top-Notch Cast," United Press International, May 26, 2014, https://www.upi.com/Entertainment_News/Movies/2014/05/26/Godzilla-director-praises-top-notch-cast/1321401116547/.
10. Ibid.
11. Ibid.
12. Kirsten Acuna, "12 Gorgeous Early Concepts Designs for Godzilla," *Business Insider*, May 17, 2014, https://www.businessinsider.com/godzilla-early-concept-art-2014-5.
13. Ryan Lambie, "*Godzilla*: 10 things we learned from Gareth Edwards," *Den of Geek*, March 4, 2014, https://www.denofgeek.com/movies/10-things-we-learned-about-godzilla-from-gareth-edwards/.
14. Willmore, "Behind the Groundbreaking Special Effects in *Godzilla*," *BuzzFeed*, May 13, 2014, https://www.buzzfeed.com/alisonwillmore/behind-the-groundbreaking-special-effects-in-godzilla.
15. "*Godzilla* 2014: How VFX Pioneer Jim Rygiel Remade Japan's Most Famous Monster," *Take Two*, May 15, 2014, https://www.kpcc.org/show/take-two/2014-05-15/godzilla-2014-how-vfx-pioneer-jim-rygiel-remade-japans-most-famous-monster.
16. Jason Barr, *The Kaiju Film*, 144.
17. Michael O'Sullivan, "'*Godzilla* Movie Review: The Monsters Are More Interesting Than the Men," *Washington Post*, May 15, 2014.
18. Ibid.
19. Leonard Maltin, "*Godzilla*," Leonard Maltin, May 15, 2014, https://leonardmaltin.com/godzilla/.
20. Jason Barr, *The Kaiju Film*, 33.
21. Beth Hanna, "New Restoration of Uncut 'Godzilla: The Japanese Original' to Premiere at TCM Film Fest, Followed by Rialto Release," *Indie Wire*, February 18, 2014, https://www.indiewire.com/2014/02/new-restoration-of-uncut-godzilla-the-japanese-original-to-premiere-at-tcm-film-fest-followed-by-rialto-release-193576/.
22. Peter Debruge, "Film Review: 'Godzilla,'" *Variety*, May 10, 2014, https://variety.com/2014/film/reviews/film-review-godzilla-1201174616/.
23. "*Godzilla* (2014)," *The Numbers*, https://www.the-numbers.com/movie/Godzilla-(2014)#tab=summary.
24. These figures are reported in "*Godzilla* (2014)," The Numbers, [n.d.], https://www.the-numbers.com/movie/Godzilla-(2014)#tab=summary.
25. "Domestic Box Office for 2014," Box Office Mojo, [n.d.], https://www.boxofficemojo.com/year/2014/.

## Chapter 11

1. "2014 Worldwide Box Office," Box Office Mojo, [n.d.], https://www.boxofficemojo.com/year/world/2014//.
2. "Gojira 12 nenburi ni Nipponban shinsaku eiga seisaku kettei! Tōhō Hariuddo ni mo makenai" ["A new Japanese version of "Godzilla" will be produced after 12 years! Toho: "We won't lose to Hollywood!"], *Cinema Cafe*, December 8, 2014, https://www.

cinemacafe.net/article/2014/12/08/27888.html.
3. Ibid.
4. "2016 nen shinsaku Gojira kyakuhon sō kantoku an no Hideaki shiando kantoku Higuchi Shin kara Messe" ["Message from 2016 new work 'Godzilla' Screenplay/General Director: Hideaki Anno & Director: Shinji Higuch"], *Oricon News*, April 1, 2015, https://www.oricon.co.jp/special/47834/.
5. Ibid.
6. "Upcoming Godzilla Movie to Feature Largest Cast in Japanese Film History," *Japan Today*, April 16, 2016).
7. Meagan Damore, "Look: 'Godzilla: Resurgence' Art Book Reveals Early Concept Work of the Film's Title Character," CBR.com, June 13, 2016, https://www.cbr.com/look-godzilla-resurgence-art-book-reveals-early-concept-work-of-the-films-title-character/.
8. Simon Abrams, "*Shin Ultraman*: Director Shinji Higuchi on His Optimistic Approach to Kaiju Movies," *Vulture*, July 23, 2022, https://www.vulture.com/2022/07/an-interview-with-shin-ultraman-director-shinji-higuchi.html.
9. Yoichi Funabashi and Kay Kitazawa, "Fukushima in Review: A Complex Disaster, a Disastrous Response," *Bulletin of the Atomic Scientists* 68, no. 2 (2012): 13.
10. Ibid., 15.
11. Ibid.
12. Ibid., 16.
13. Ibid., 17.
14. Michishita Narushige, "Myths and Realities of Japan's Security Policy," Wilson Center, February 18, 2020, https://www.wilsoncenter.org/blog-post/myths-and-realities-japans-security-policy.
15. Kenji Ando, "Shin Gojira no hitto wa 'Jieitai e no shiji' Abe shushō ga kataru" ["Shin Godzilla's hit is 'support for the Self-Defense Forces' Prime Minister Abe says], *Huffington Post* [Japan edition], September 12, 2016, https://www.huffingtonpost.jp/2016/09/12/godzilla-abe_n_11985200.html.
16. Luke Y. Thompson, "Review: In *Shin Godzilla* the Real Bad Guy Is Big Government," *Forbes*, October 11, 2016, https://www.forbes.com/sites/lukethompson/2016/10/11/review-in-shin-godzilla-the-real-bad-guy-is-big-government/.

## Chapter 12

1. Jordan Zakarin, "The Monster Heart of the Best American Kaiju Film in Years," *Inverse*, April 3, 2017, https://www.inverse.com/article/29822-kaiju-monsters-colossal-mazinger-z-pulgasari-godzilla-anne-hathaway.
2. Ibid.
3. Shelagh Rowan-Legg, *The Spanish Fantastic: Contemporary Filmmaking in Horror, Fantasy and Sci-Fi* (London: I.B. Tauris, 2016), 153.
4. Andrew Pulver, "*Truecrimes*" [film review], February 5, 2009, https://www.theguardian.com/film/2009/feb/05/timecrimes-cronocrimenes-film-review.
5. Ibid.
6. Ibid.
7. Ibid.
8. Ibid.
9. Kristy Puchko, "How Monsters & Rom-Coms Come Together for *Colossal*," *Screen Rant*, April 7, 2017, https://screenrant.com/colossal-movie-interview-nacho-vigalondo/.
10. Ibid.
11. Kate Erbland, "*Colossal* Is the Monster Movie No Studio Would Ever Make, and It's Teaching Hollywood a Lesson," *Indie Wire*, April 5, 2015, https://www.yahoo.com/entertainment/colossal-monster-movie-no-studio-152727780.html.
12. Ibid.
13. Ibid.
14. Geoffrey McNab, "How New U.S. Distribution Outfit Neon Is Chasing Younger Audiences," *Screen Daily*, October 1, 2017, https://www.screendaily.com/news/-how-new-us-distribution-outfit-neon-is-chasing-younger-audiences/5122827.
15. Jeannette Catsoulis, "Strangers, with Aliens Above," *New York Times*, June 12, 2012.
16. Richard Whittaker, "Nacho Average Thriller," *Austin Chronicle*, March 7, 2014.
17. Ben Child, "Battle of the giant lizards: Toho sues over Anne Hathaway's rival 'Godzilla' movie," *The Guardian*, May 20, 2015.
18. Ibid.
19. Eriq Gardner, "Anne Hathaway Monster Movie Settles Lawsuit from Godzilla Rights Holders," *The Hollywood*

*Reporter*, October 30, 2015, https://www.hollywoodreporter.com/business/business-news/anne-hathaway-monster-movie-settles-835733/.

20. Yvonne Sherratt, *Adorno's Positive Dialectic* (Cambridge: Cambridge University Press, 2002), 104.

21. Tasha Robinson, "*Colossal* Movie Director Nacho Vigalondo on Making a 'Smaller and More Humble' Giant-Monster Movie," *The Verge*, April 7, 2017, https://www.theverge.com/2017/4/7/15218450/nacho-vigalondo-interview-colossal-anne-hathaway-jason-sudeikis-monster-movie.

22. Ibid.

23. N. Megan Kelley, *Projections of Passing: Cold War Anxieties and Hollywood Films 1947–1960* (Jackson: University of Mississippi Press, 2016).

24. Alissa Wilkinson, "*Colossal* Is a Surprisingly Mature Film About Addiction, Toxic Friends, and Big Ol' Monsters," *Vox*, April 11, 2017, https://www.vox.com/culture/2017/4/6/15167690/colossal-review-kaiju-anne-hathaway.

25. Tasha Robinson, "*Colossal* Movie Director Nacho Vigalondo."

26. "*Colossal* (2017), The Numbers, [n.d.], https://www.the-numbers.com/movie/Colossal-(Canada)#tab=summary.

27. Ibid.

28. Justin Gunterman, "The Ten Biggest Box Office Flops of 2017," *Taste of Cinema*, January 17, 2018, http://www.tasteofcinema.com/2018/the-10-biggest-box-office-flops-of-2017/.

## Chapter 13

1. Ibid.

2. Peter Sciretta, "Legendary Wants Joe Cornish to Direct Kin Kong Preque 'Skull Island' Movie," *Film*, July 28, 2014, https://www.slashfilm.com/533021/skull-island-movie/.

3. Ibid.

4. Mike Fleming, Jr., "'Skull Island': Tom Hiddleston Stars in King Kong Origin Tale," *Deadline*, September 16, 2014, https://deadline.com/2014/09/skull-island-tom-hiddleston-king-kong-835067/.

5. Mike Fleming, Jr., "King Kong on Move to Warner Bros, Presaging Godzilla Monster Matchup," *Deadline*, September 10, 2015, https://deadline.com/2015/09/king-kong-godzilla-legendary-monster-movie-warner-bros-1201521004/.

6. Ibid.

7. Ibid.

8. Borys Kit, "*Jurassic World* Writer Heads to *Kong: Skull Island*," *Hollywood Reporter*, August 18, 2015, https://www.hollywoodreporter.com/movies/movie-news/jurassic-world-writer-heads-kong-816144/.

9. Ibid.

10. Christopher McKittrick, "Monstrous Undertaking: Screenwriter Max Borenstein Says His *Kong: Skull Island* Script 'Is Its Own Beast,'" *MovieMaker*, March 10, 2017, https://www.moviemaker.com/max-borenstein-kong-skull-island/.

11. Ibid.

12. Ibid.

13. Ibid.

14. Kathryn Schroeder, "King Kong and the Evolution of Special Effects," *Film Fracture*, October 10, 2018, https://www.filmfracture.com/king-kong-and-the-evolution-of-special-effects/.

15. Bryan Bishop, "How Industrial Light & Magic Built a Better Kong for *Skull Island*," *The Verge*, March 24, 2017, https://www.theverge.com/2017/3/24/15051178/kong-skull-island-lucasfilm-ilm-visual-effects-interview.

16. Ibid.

17. See, for example, Hayleigh Foutch, "King Kong and Godzilla to Throw Down for Legendary and Warner Bros.," *Collider*, September 10, 2015, https://collider.com/king-kong-godzilla-throw-down-for-legendary-warner-bros/.

18. Matthew J. Theriault, "*Kong: Skull Island* Is *Apocalypse Now* Meets *Moby Dick*," *Hub City Review*, March 11, 2017, https://hubcityreview.com/2017/03/11/kong-skull-island-is-apocalypse-now-meets-moby-dick/.

19. Ibid.

20. Ibid.

21. Ibid.

22. Wendy idea, "Kong: Skull Island Review—Unsubtle Adventure," *The Guardian*, March 12, 2017, https://www.theguardian.com/film/2017/mar/12/kong-skull-island-review-tom-hiddleston-unsubtle-adventure.

23. Owen Gleiberman, "Film Review:

*Kong: Skull Island*," *Variety*, March 2, 2017, https://variety.com/2017/film/reviews/kong-skull-island-review-1202000823/.

24. Stephanie Zacharek, "Review: Kong: Skull Island Is Grand, Nutty and Visually Splendid," *Time*, March 9, 2017, https://time.com/4696420/kong-skull-island-review/.

25. Ryan Faughnder, "'Rampage' Is Poised for Top Box-Office Spot as Dwayne Johnson Fights Video Game Movie Curse," *Los Angeles Times*, April 11, 2018, https://www.latimes.com/entertainment/la-fi-ct-movie-projector-rampage-20180411-htmlstory.html.

26. "Kong: Skull Island," Box Office Mojo, [n.d.], https://www.boxofficemojo.com/release/rl710837761/.

27. Anthony D'Alessandro and Nancy Tartaglione, "'Kong: Skull Island' Hopes To Leave Huge Footprint at Global B.O. in Face of 'Logan's Wrath,'" *Deadline*, March 8, 2017, https://deadline.com/2017/03/kong-skull-island-box-office-opening-worldwide-logan-1202039270/.

## Chapter 14

1. Scott Collura, *Godzilla: King of the Monsters* Review," *IGN.com*, May 20, 2019 (updated Aril 21, 2020), https://www.ign.com/articles/2019/05/30/godzilla-king-of-the-monsters-review.

2. Simran Hans, "*Godzilla: King of the Monsters* Review: Beastly in All the Wrong Ways," *The Guardian*, June 2, 2019, https://www.theguardian.com/film/2019/jun/02/godzilla-king-of-the-monsters-review.

3. Adam Holmes, "*Godzilla vs. Kong* Has Been Delayed," *Variety*, November 25, 2019, https://www.cinemablend.com/news/2485616/godzilla-vs-kong-has-been-delayed.

4. Ibid.
5. Ibid.
6. Ibid.

7. Borys Kit, "*Godzilla vs. Kong* Film Sets Writers Room," *The Hollywood Reporter*, March 10, 2017, https://www.hollywoodreporter.com/movies/movie-news/kong-skull-island-sequel-plans-godzilla-kong-sets-writers-room-984992/.

8. Borys Kit, "*Godzilla vs. Kong* Finds Its Director with Adam Wingard," *The Hollywood Reporter*, May 30, 2017, https://www.hollywoodreporter.com/movies/movie-news/godzilla-kong-finds-director-adam-wingard-1008773/.

9. Kate Walsh, "Review: 'Godzilla: King of the Monsters' Has Too Much Human Drama, Too Little Kaiju Action," *Los Angeles Times*, May 30, 2019, https://www.latimes.com/entertainment/movies/la-et-mn-godzilla-king-of-the-monsters-review-20190530-story.html.

10. "Warner Bros. Pictures' and Legendary Entertainment's Monsterverse Shifts into Overdrive as Cameras Roll on the Next Big-Screen Adventure *Godzilla Vs. Kong*," *Business Wire*, November 12, 2018, https://www.businesswire.com/news/home/20181112005664/en/Warner-Bros.-Pictures%E2%80%99-Legendary-Entertainment%E2%80%99s-Monsterverse-Shifts.

11. Clark Collis, "*Godzilla vs. Kong* Wraps Shooting," *Entertainment Weekly*, April 20, 2019, https://ew.com/movies/2019/04/20/godzilla-vs-kong/.

12. Adam White, "Godzilla vs Kong Delayed by Eight Months Following King of the Monsters Flop," *The Independent*, November 26, 2019.

13. Ibid.
14. Ibid.

15. Adam Holmes, "*Godzilla vs. Kong* Has Been Delayed," *Cinema Blend*, November 25, 2019.

16. Allie Gemmill, "*Godzilla vs. Kong* Release Date Delayed to 2021 in Wave of Warner Bros. Schedule, Shifts," *Collider*, June 13, 2020, https://collider.com/godzilla-vs-kong-release-date-2021/.

17. Rebecca Rubin and Brent Lang, "*Dune* Producer Legendary May Sue Warner Bros. Over HBO Max Deal," *Variety*, December 7, 2020, https://variety.com/2020/film/news/legendary-entertainment-warner-bros-hbo-max-deal-dune-godzilla-1234847605/.

18. Kim Masters and Borys Kit, "Warner Bros., Legendary Nearly Deal to Resolve Clash Over *Godzilla vs. Kong*," *The Hollywood Reporter*, January 8, 2021, https://www.hollywoodreporter.com/movies/movie-news/warner-bros-legendary-nearing-deal-to-resolve-clash-over-godzilla-vs-kong-exclusive-4113497/.

19. Ibid.

20. Richard Brody, "*Godzilla vs. Kong* Reviewed: A Monster Mash of Two

Venerable Franchises," *The New Yorker*, April 2, 2021, https://www.newyorker.com/culture/the-front-row/godzilla-vs-kong-reviewed-a-monster-mush-of-two-venerable-franchises.

21. Richard Lawson, "*Godzilla vs. Kong* Is Just the Right Kind of Dumb," *Vanity Fair*, March 30, 2021, https://www.vanityfair.com/hollywood/2021/03/review-godzilla-vs-kong-is-just-the-right-kind-of-dumb.

22. *Ibid.*

23. Quoted in "*Godzilla vs. Kong* Sequel Announced," *Comicbook.com*, June 30, 2022, https://comicbook.com/movies/news/godzilla-vs-kong-sequel-release-date-march-2024/.

## Conclusion

1. Barry Keith Grant, *Monster Cinema* (New Brunswick: Rutgers University Press, 2018), 8.

# Bibliography

Abrams, Simon. "*Shin Ultraman*: Director Shinji Higuchi on His Optimistic Approach to Kaiju Movies." *Vulture*. July 23, 2022. https://www.vulture.com/2022/07/an-interview-with-shin-ultraman-director-shinji-higuchi.html.
Ando, Kenji. "Shin Gojira no hitto wa 'Jieitai e no shiji' Abe shushō ga kataru." ["*Shin Godzilla* Hit is 'Support for the Self-Defense Forces,' Prime Minister Abe Says."] *Huffington Post* [Japan edition]. September 12, 2016. https://www.huffingtonpost.jp/2016/09/12/godzilla-abe_n_11985200.html.
Bainbridge, Jason. "'Gotta Catch 'Em All!' Pokémon, Cultural Practice and Object Networks." *IAFOR Journal of Asian Studie*, 1, no. 1 (2014): 63–78. https://doi.org/10.22492/ijas.1.1.04.
Barr, Jason. *The Kaiju Film: A Critical Study of Cinema's Biggest Monsters*. Jefferson, NC: McFarland, 2016.
Bielik, Alain. "'*The Host*': Creepie Korean Creatures." *AWN* [Animation World Network]. August 3, 2006. https://www.awn.com/vfxworld/host-creepie-korean-creatures.
Bishop, Bryan. "How Industrial Light & Magic Built a Better Kong for *Skull Island*." *The Verge*. March 24, 2017. https://www.theverge.com/2017/3/24/15051178/kong-skull-island-lucasfilm-ilm-visual-effects-interview.
Bollinger, Nicholas. "Archetypes in War: Kaiju as Cult Icons in *Pacific Rim*." In *Giant Creatures in Our World: Essays on Kaiju and American Popular Culture*, edited by Camille D.G. Mustachio and Jason Barr, 77–91. Jefferson, NC: McFarland, 2017.
Briefel, Aviva. "Shop 'Til You Drop: Consumer and Horror." In *Horror After 9/11: World of Fear, Cinema of Terror*, edited by Aviva Briefel and Sam J. Miller, 142–164. Austin: University of Texas, 2011.
Brody, Richard. "*Godzilla vs. Kong* Reviewed: A Monster Mash of Two Venerable Franchises." *The New Yorker*. April 2, 2021. https://www.newyorker.com/culture/the-front-row/godzilla-vs-kong-reviewed-a-monster-mush-of-two-venerable-franchises.
Damore, Meagan. "Look: 'Godzilla: Resurgence' Art Book Reveals Early Concept Work of the Film's Title Character." CBR.com. June 13, 2016. https://www.cbr.com/look-godzilla-resurgence-art-book-reveals-early-concept-work-of-the-films-title-character/.
Eggert, Brian. "*Monsters*." *Deep Focus Review*. October 29, 2010. https:/deepfocusreview.com/reviews/monsters.
Erb, Cynthia. *Tracking Kong: A Hollywood Icon in World Culture*. Detroit: Wayne State University Press, 2009.
Finney, Angus. *The International Film Business: A Market Guide Beyond Hollywood*, 2nd ed. New York: Francis & Taylor, 2014.
Foster, Michael Dylan. *The Book of Yokai: Mysterious Creatures of Japanese Folklore*. Berkeley: University of California Press, 2015.
Foster, Michael Dylan. "The Current State of Japanese *Yokai* Studies in North America." *Japanese Studies Around the World* (2014). https://core.ac.uk/download/pdf/198405698.pdf.
Foutch, Hayleigh. "King Kong and Godzilla to Throw Down for Legendary and Warner Bros."

*Collider.* September 10, 2015. https://collider.com/king-kong-godzilla-throw-down-for-legendary-warner-bros/.
Funabashi, Yoichi, and Kay Kitazawa. "Fukushima in Review: A Complex Disaster, a Disastrous Response." *Bulletin of the Atomic Scientists* 68, no. 2 (2012): 9–21.
Homenick, Brett. "Godzilla's Final Cut: Director Ryuhei Kitamura on Crafting Godzilla's 50th Anniversary Film, 'Godzilla: Final Wars.'" *Vantage Point Interviews.* January 2, 2002. https://vantagepointinterviews.com/2019/01/02/godzillas-final-cut-director-ryuhei-kitamura-on-crafting-godzillas-50th-anniversary-film-godzilla-final-wars/.
Homenick, Brett. "On Directing Godzilla and Gamera." *Vantage Point Interviews.* June 13, 2018. https://vantagepointinterviews.com/2018/06/13/on-directing-godzilla-and-gamera-shusuke-kaneko-on-filmmaking-the-kaiju-way/.
Housman, Andrew. "*Cloverfield* Is Hollywood's Best Godzilla Movie." *Screen Rant.* November 6, 2020. https://screenrant.com/cloverfield-godzilla-movie-best-similarities/.
Jaffe, Brooke. "*Pacific Rim* Is Not Your Average Action Juggernaut." *The Mary Sue.* August 16, 2013. https://www.themarysue.com/pacific-rim-gender-tropes/.
Keane, John J. *Cultural and Theological Reflections on the Japanese Quest for Divinity.* Leiden: Brill, 2016.
Keith Grant, Barry. *Monster Cinema.* New Brunswick: Rutgers University Press, 2018.
Kelley, N. Megan. *Projections of Passing: Cold War Anxieties and Hollywood Films 1947–1960.* Jackson: University of Mississippi Press, 2016.
Kim, Ju-Won Kim. *Relocating the Alliance: The U.S.–South Korea Military Alliance in Cultural Representations.* Diss. Emory University, 2011.
King, Homay. "*The Host* vs. *Cloverfield.*" In *Horror After 9/11: World of Fear, Cinema of Terror,* edited by Avia Briefel and Sam J. Miller, 124–141. Austin: University of Texas Press, 2011.
Kwon, J.W., H. Chun, and Si Cho. "A Closer Look at the Increase in Suicide Rates in South Korea from 1986–2005." *BMC Public Health* 9, no. 72 (2009). https://doi.org/10.1186/1471-2458-9-72.
Lambie, Ryan. "Gareth Edwards Interview: On Making *Monsters,* Meeting Quentin Tarantino, and More." *Den of Geek.* November 29, 2010. https://www.denofgeek.com/movies/gareth-edwards-interview-on-making-monsters-meeting-quentin-tarantino-and-more/.
Lee, Kevin. "The Han River Horror Show: Interview with Bong Joon-ho." *Cineaste* 32, no. 2 (2007). https://www.cineaste.com/spring2007/interview-with-bong-joon-ho.
Lee, Kevin L. "Revisiting Godzilla and His Foes." *Film Inquiry.* May 30, 2019. https://www.filminquiry.com/revisiting-godzilla/.
Lee, Nam. *The Films of Bong Joon Ho.* New Brunswick: Rutgers University Press, 2020.
McKittrick, Christopher. "Monstrous Undertaking: Screenwriter Max Borenstein Says His *Kong: Skull Island* Script 'Is Its Own Beast.'" *MovieMaker.* March 10, 2017. https://www.moviemaker.com/max-borenstein-kong-skull-island/.
McSweeny, Terence. "'Daddy, I'm Scared. Can We go Home?' Fear and Allegory in Frank Darabont's *The Mist* (2007)." In *American Cinema in the Shadow of 9/11,* edited by Terence McSweeny, et al., 227–247. Edinburgh: Edinburgh University Press, 2016.
Michishita, Narushige. "Myths and Realities of Japan's Security Policy." Wilson Center. February 18, 2020. https://www.wilsoncenter.org/blog-post/myths-and-realities-japans-security-policy.
Morton, Ray. *King Kong: The History of a Movie Icon from Fay Wray to Peter Jackson.* New York: Applause Theatre & Cinema Books, 2005.
Nathan, Ian. *Guillermo del Toro: The Iconic Filmmaker and His Work.* London: White Lion, 2021.
Ono, Shuntaro. *Gamera no seishinshi: Shōwa kara Heisei e* [The spiritual history of Gamera from Showa to Heisei]. Tokyo: Takanashi Shobo, 2018.
Phillips, Stone. "Peter Jackson's Labor of Love" NBC News [transcript]. December 2, 2005, https://www.nbcnews.com/id/wbna10299834.
Puchko, Kristy. "How Monsters & Rom-Coms Come Together for *Colossal.*" *Screen Rant.* April 7, 2017. https://screenrant.com/colossal-movie-interview-nacho-vigalondo/.

Reis-Filho, Lucio. "Cloverfield." In *Aliens in Popular Culture*, edited by Michael M. Levy and Farah Mendelsohn, 86–87. Santa Barbara: Greenwood, 2019.
Rhodes, Sean, and Brooke McCorckle. *Japan's Green Monsters: Environmental Commentary in Kaiju Cinema*. Jefferson, NC: McFarland, 2018.
Rice, Alan. *Radical Narratives of the Black Atlantic*. New York: Continuum, 2003.
Riegler, Thomas. "Through the Lenses of Hollywood: Depictions of Terrorism in American Movies." *Perspectives on Terrorism* 4, no. 2 (May 2010): 35–45. https://www.jstor.org/stable/26298447.
Robinson, Tasha. "*Colossal* Movie Director Nacho Vigalondo on Making a 'Smaller and More Humble Giant-Monster Movie." *The Verge*. April 7, 2017. https://www.theverge.com/2017/4/7/15218450/nacho-vigalondo-interview-colossal-anne-hathaway-jason-sudeikis-monster-movie.
Romano, Nick. "How Kim Jong Il Kidnapped a Director, Made a Godzilla Knockoff, and Created a Cult Hit." *Vanity Fair*. April 6, 2015. https://www.vanityfair.com/hollywood/2015/04/pulgasari-north-korea-cult-hit.
Rowan-Legg, Shelag. *The Spanish Fantastic: Contemporary Filmmaking in Horror, Fantasy and Sci-fi*. London: I.B. Tauris, 2016.
Schroeder, Kathryn. "King Kong and the Evolution of Special Effects." *Film Fracture*. October 10, 2018. https://www.filmfracture.com/king-kong-and-the-evolution-of-special-effects/.
Sharp, Jasper. *Historical Dictionary of Japanese Cinema*. Lanham, MD: Scarecrow Press, 2011.
Shea, Theresa. *Godzilla*. New York: Rosen, 2016.
Sherratt, Yvonne. *Adorno's Positive Dialectic*. Cambridge: Cambridge University Press, 2002.
Sontag, Susan. "The Imagination of Disaster." *Commentary* (October 1965): 42–48.
Staite, Sophia. "Kamen Rider: A Monstrous Hero.'" *M/C Journal*, 24, no. 5 (2021). doi: https://10.5204/mcj.2834.
Suebsaeng, Asawin. "'Pacific Rim': The Most Exciting, Monster-Filled Anti-Pollution PSA Ever." *Mother Jones*. June 12, 2013. https://www.motherjones.com/politics/2013/07/film-review-pacific-rim-pollution/.
Susman, Gary. "Peter Jackson Will Direct *King Kong* Remake." *Entertainment Weekly*. August 12, 2003. https://ew.com/article/2003/08/12/peter-jackson-will-direct-king-kong-remake/.
Tanaka, Yuki. "Godzilla and the Bravo Shot: Who Killed the Monster?" In *Filling the Hole in the Nuclear Future: Art and Popular Culture Respond to the Bomb*, edited by Robert Jacobs, 159–170. Lanham, MD: Lexington Books, 2010.
Theriault, Matthew. "*Kong: Skull Island* Is *Apocaplyse Now* Meets *Moby Dick*." *Hub City Review*. March 11, 2017. https://hubcityreview.com/2017/03/11/kong-skull-island-is-apocolypse-now-meets-moby-dick/.
Thompson, Luke Y. "Review: In *Shin Godzilla* the Real Bad Guy Is Big Government." *Forbes*. October 11, 2016. https://www.forbes.com/sites/lukethompson/2016/10/11/review-in-shin-go.
Totaro, Donato. "*Cloverfield*: An Intimate Apocalypse." *Off|Screen* 12, no. 2 (February 2008). https://offscreen.com/view/cloverfield_apocalypse.
Vaz, Mark Cotta. *Godzilla: The Art of Destruction*. San Rafael, CA: Insight Editions, 2014.
Von Doviak, Scott. *Stephen King Films FAQ*. Milwaukee: Applause Theatre & Cinema Books, 2014.
Watercutter, Angela. "Inside *Pacific Rim*—The Movie That Saved Guillermo del Toro's Life." *Wired*. June 18, 2013. https://www.wired.com/2013/06/pacific-rim-guillermo-del-toro-feature/.
Webb, Jeffrey B. *American Myths, Legends, and Tall Tales: An Encyclopedia of American Folklore*. Santa Barbara: ABC-CLIO, 2016.
Whiteley, David. *The Galaxy Britain Built: The British Talent Behind Star Wars*. Albany, GA: Bear Manor Media, 2019.
Wilkinson, Alissa. "*Colossal* Is a Surprisingly Mature Film About Addiction, Toxic

Friends, and Big Ol' Monsters." *Vox*. April 11, 2017. https://www.vox.com/culture/2017/4/6/15167690/colossal-review-kaiju-anne-hathaway.

Zacharek, Stephanie. "Review: Kong: Skull Island Is Grand, Nutty and Visually Splendid." *Time*. March 9, 2017. https://time.com/4696420/kong-skull-island-review/.

Zakarin, Jordan. "The Monster Heart of the Best American Kaiju Film in Years." *Inverse*. April 3, 2017. https://www.inverse.com/article/29822-kaiju-monsters-colossal-mazinger-z-pulgasari-godzilla-anne-hathaway.

# Index

Able, Whitney  96, 97, 99, 101
Abrams, J.J.  83, 85–86
Afghanistan War  72, 78–79, 83
*Aguirre, the Wrath of God*  104
*Aliens*  104
Ammato, Hideyo  21
Anno, Hideaki  131–132, 139, 140
*Apocalypse Now*  99, 100, 104, 152, 156, 158
Article 9 (Japan Constitution)  139
*At the Mountains of Madness*  108
Atomic Age  15
*Attack on Titan*  132
Azaria, Hank  19
*Azumi*  30

*Babel* (2006)  110
Bae, Doona  64
*Barking Dogs Never Bite*  61–62, 64
Barr, Jason  115, 124
Bay, Michael  109
Beacham, Travis  108–109
Beer, Lindsey  167
Binoche, Juliette  120
Black, Jack  43, 44
*Blade II*  107
*Blair Witch Project*  87
*The Blob* (1988)  73
Bollinger, Nicholas  116
Bong, Joon-ho  6, 12, 61–64, 67–68, 69–71, 72, 92
Borenstein, Max  119, 152, 153–154, 167
Braugher, Andre  75, 76
*Breaking Bad*  121
Briefel, Aviva  79
Brightlight Pictures  144
Broderick, Matthew  19
Brody, Adrian  43, 44
Brown, Millie Bobby  165, 167
*Bulgasari*  62
Burr, Raymond  125
Burr, Ty  32, 34
Bush, George W.  37, 73, 79, 84

Cafe FX  76
Callaham, David  119

Cannes Film Festival  61, 63, 71
Caplan, Lizzy  86, 88
Carter, John  102
Chandler, Kyle  165, 167
Chang, Justin  113
Choi, Yog-bae  63
Chungeorahm Films  63
Clooney, George  43
*Cloverfield*  12, 83–83, 101, 124
*Colossal*  12, 141–151, 161, 175
Columbia Pictures  18
Connolly, Derek  154
Connolly, Joseph S.  8
Conrad, Joseph  99, 158
Cooper, Merian C.  39
Coppola, Francis Ford  99, 104, 152, 158
Cornish, Joe  152
Covid-19 pandemic  168–169, 174
Cranston, Bryan  120, 123
*Cronos*  110
Crowther, Bosley  13

Daiei Film Company (Japan)  12, 51, 52, 53
Darabont, Frank  72, 73, 74, 75, 76, 80–81, 119
Day, Charlie  110
Dead Can Dance  77
del Toro, Guillermo  6, 12 107–109, 111–116, 123, 152
De Niro, Robert  43
*District 9*  104
Doerksen, Heather  115
Dougherty, Michael  164–165, 167
*Dreamcatcher*  75

Ebert, Roger  53, 81
Edwards, Gareth  94–97, 100–105, 109, 119–121, 123–130
Elba, Idris  110
Emmerich, Roland  18, 19, 31, 118, 128
Emoto, Akira  132
Erb, Cynthia  47
*E.T.: The Extra-Terrestrial*  50
*Extraterrestre* (*Extraterrestrial*)  142, 144

197

# Index

*Factory Farmed* 95
Farmiga, Vera 165
*The Floating Castle* 131
*Forbidden Planet* 149
Foster, Michael Dylan 23
Fox, Michael J. 40
*Frankenstein* 107
Freud, Sigmund 147, 148–149
*The Frighteners* 41
Frye, Don 32, 37
Fukushima disaster 134–137

Game Boy 28–29
*Gamera* 19
*Gamera 2: Attack of Legion* 53
*Gamera 3: Revenge of Iris* 53, 55
*Gamera: Guardian of the Universe* 53
*Gamera, Super Monster* 53
*Gamera the Brave* 12, 50–60, 61–71, 91, 124
*Gamera, the Monster* 52
*Gamera vs. Barugon* 52
*Gamera vs. Guiron* 52
*Gamera vs. Jiger* 52
*Gamera vs. Viras* 52
*Gamera vs. Zigra* 52
Gatins, John 153
Gentle Giant Studios 65
Gilroy, Dan 153
Go, Ah-sung 64
*Godzilla* (1998) 5, 20, 27, 32, 63
*Godzilla* (2014) 11, 118–129, 130, 139
*Godzilla: Final Wars* 11, 27–38, 49, 64, 124, 134, 173
*Godzilla, King of the Monsters* (1956) 13, 16, 92, 125
*Godzilla, King of the Monsters* (2019) 11, 164–168, 172
*Godzilla, Mothra, and King Ghidorah* 11, 15–26, 27, 51, 127
*Godzilla 2000* 19, 28
*Godzilla vs. Destoroyah* 17
*Godzilla vs. Kong* (2021) 11, 166–173
*Godzilla vs. Mechagodzilla* 30
*Gojira* 13, 17, 22, 85, 92, 119, 120, 125, 126, 133, 135, 173
Goodman, John 153
Goyer, David S. 119
*Great Monster Yongary* 62
*The Green Mile* 73, 76
Greengrass, Paul 84
Guillermin, John 39
Gwangju Uprising 69

Hall, Mordaunt 39
Hall, Rebecca 167
Hamilton, Jenny 3
Harden, Marcia Gay 75
Hasegawa, Hiroki 132
Hathaway, Anne 143, 145
Hawkins, Corey 153

Hawkins, Sally 120, 165
*Heart of Darkness* 99, 158
*Hellboy* 107
*Hellboy 2: The Golden Army* 107
Herzog, Werner 104
*hibakusha* 24
Hiddleston, Tom 153, 156
Higuchi, Shinji 131–132, 140
Hironobu, Kanagawa 120
*The Hobbit* 108
Holden, Laurie 75, 76
Honda, Ishiro 16
Horton, Ray 43
*The Host* 12, 61–71, 72, 91, 92, 161, 175
"Host of Seraphim" 77
Hunnam, Charlie 110, 111, 114

"Imagination of Disaster" 7
*In Search of a Midnight Kiss* 96
Iñárritu, Alejandro González 110
*The Incredibles* 35, 38
*Independence Day* 18, 32
Industrial Light & Magic 109
International Monetary Fund Crisis 68
Iraq War 37, 72, 73–79, 83, 90
Ishihara, Satomi 132

Jackson, Peter 6, 40, 41, 46–47, 50, 63, 123, 157, 159
Jackson, Samuel L. 153, 156
Jaffe, Brooke 113
Jane, Thomas 75, 76
*Japan Sinks* 131
*Jaws* 103
Johnson, Dwayne 162
Jones, Richard T. 120
Jones, Toby 75
*Jurassic Park* 104
*Jurassic World* 154

Kadokawa Daiei Motion Picture Company 53
Kaho 55
*Kamen Rider* series 54–55
*kami* 23–24
Kaneko, Shusuke 15, 16, 19, 20, 21, 22, 24, 25, 26, 53, 59, 127
*kawaii* 29
Kebbell, Tony 153
Kelly, N. Megan 148
Kikuchi, Rinko 110, 111, 114
Kikukawa, Rei 32
King, Homay 90
King, Stephen 12, 72–74, 80, 81, 120
*King Kong* (1933) 39–40, 44
*King Kong* (1976) 39
*King Kong* (1986) 142
*King Kong* (2005) 11, 39–49, 50, 63, 65, 157, 159
*King Kong Escapes* 21, 39, 157

# Index

King Kong Lives  39
Kinimura, Jun  132
Kit, Borys  154
Kitamura, Ryuhei  30, 34
*Kong: Skull Island*  11, 152–162, 164, 175
*Kong vs. Godzilla* (1963)  39, 157, 164

Lambert, Christopher  32
Larson, Brie  153, 156
Legendary Pictures  11, 105, 108–110, 116–119, 123–124, 130, 152–153, 155, 162–168, 170, 173, 178
Legion M  144
Lerner, Michael  19
*Little Heroes: Gamera*  55; see also *Gamera the Brave*
*Lord of the Rings* (film trilogy)  40, 42, 108, 121
Lovecraft, H.P.  108
Lucas, George  95

Maeda, Ai  55
Maeda, Mahiro  132
Magnet Releasing  105
Magnolia Pictures  71, 105
Maltin, Leonard  124
*The Matrix*  32
Matsuoka, Masahiro  32
McFarland Incident (South Korea)  65, 70
McKay, Patrick  167
McKellan, Ian  43
McLuhan, Marshall  137
McNairy, Scoot  96, 97, 99, 101
McSweeney, Terence  79
Melville, Herman  158
*Memories of Murder*  61, 64
*Mighty Joe Young* (1949)  39
*Mighty Joe Young* (1988)  41
"Millennium Series" (Godzilla films)  19, 26
Miller, T.J.  86, 88
*The Mist*  12, 72–82, 83, 88, 91, 101, 115, 120, 124, 161
Miyazaki, Hayao  53
*Moby Dick*  158
*Monsters* (film)  94–105, 115, 119, 124, 126
Moore, Michael  71
*Mystery Science Theater 3000*  52

*Nausicaä of the Valley of the Wind*  53
Nelson, Tim Blake  144, 145
Neon (production company)  144
Nicotero, Greg  76
Niiyama, Chiharu  21
Nowlin, T.S.  167

Odette Annable  86
Oguri, Shun  167, 171
Olsen, Elizabeth  120, 124
*oni*  23–24
*Open Windows*  142, 145

Orphanage (studio)  65
Oswin, Verity  97

*Pacific Rim*  12, 106–117, 118
*Pacific Rim Uprising*  116, 174
Page, Neville  86
*Pan's Labyrinth*  107
*Parasite*  64, 71
Pearce, Drew  119
*Perfect Disasters*  95
Perlman, Ron  110
*Platoon*  85
Pokémon  28
*Pokémon Forever*  28
*Pokémon Heroes*  28
*Pokémon 2000*  28
projection, psychology of  147–149, 175
*Pulgasari*  62, 144, 145

*Rampage*  162
Reeves, Matt  86
Reilly, John C.  153
Reno, Jean  19, 32
*Return of Godzilla*  131
Rice, Alan  46
Richardson, James  96, 97
Riegler, Thomas  83
*Rogue One: A Star Wars Story*  124, 129`
Rossio, Terry  167
Route One Entertainment  144
"rubber suit" special effects  35, 64
Rygiel, Jim  121

Sayaka Productions  144
Scott, A.O.  48, 49
Seitz, Zoller  113
September 11 attacks  5, 26, 48, 50, 72–73, 79, 83–85, 94
Serkis, Andy  42
*The Shape of Water*  107
*Shawshank Redemption*  73
Shearer, Harry  19
Sherratt, Yvonne  147
Shields, Zac  167
Shin, Sang-ok  62–63
*Shin Godzilla*  130–140, 144, 150, 151, 164–165, 173, 175
Shinto beliefs  23–24
Shyamalan, M. Night  103
*Silence of the Lambs*  46
*Sinking of Japan*  131
Skarsgård, Alexander  167
*Snowpiercer*  64
*Son of Kong*  39
Song, Kang-ho  64
Sontag, Susan  7
Sony Corporation  18, 27, 38, 41, 92, 118
*Space Monster Wangmagwi*  62
Spielberg, Steven  16, 50, 95, 103, 104
*Spirited Away*  26, 28, 53

Stahl-David, Michael  86, 88
Staite, Sophia  54
*Star Wars*  32, 95
Stevens, Dan  144
Stone, Oliver  84–85
Stowell, Austin  144, 145
Strathairn, David  120
Studio Ghibli  53
Sudeikis, Jason  144, 145

Taguchi, Tomorowo  55
Takuma Shoten  52, 53
Tanaka, Yuki  23
Tarantino, Quentin  95
*Tarantula*  7, 71
Tasaki, Ryuta  50, 51, 54–55, 56
Tatsui, Yukari  55
Taylor-Johnson, Aaron  120, 124
*The Tempest*  148
Tepco (Japanese company)  135
Terajima, Susumu  55
*Them!*  7, 39, 71
Theriault, Matthew J.  159
Tippett Studio  87
Toho Studio  15, 17–18, 20, 25, 27–30, 34, 36–37, 52, 82, 86, 92, 101, 108, 118, 126–127, 130, 132, 134, 145, 172
Tohoku Earthquake  135–137
Tomioka, Ryo  55
Toronto International Film Festival  144, 150
Toy Fight  144
*Transformers*  109
TriStar Pictures  5, 18–20, 26–27, 31–32, 38, 41, 63, 92, 118

*Truecrimes*  142
Tsuda, Kanjii  55
Tull, Thomas  152

*United 93*  84
Universal Studios  40, 41, 43, 84, 108, 154
Uzaki, Ryudo  21, 22

Vasko, Cat  167
Vertigo Films  96
Vietnam War  78, 153, 152–153, 158–159
Vigalondo, Nacho  141–144, 148–151, 175
Vogel, Mike  86
Vogt-Roberts, Jordan  152–161
Voltage Pictures  143

*War of the Gargantuas*  108
*War of the Worlds*  104
War on Terror  40, 73, 78–79, 91, 94
Warner Bros.  105, 108, 116, 118–119, 123, 152–153, 162–163, 166, 168–170
Watanabe, Ken  120, 121, 124, 163
Watts, Naomi  43, 44
Weinstein, Bob  74
Wells, H.G.  104
Weta (special effects company)  42, 65, 154
*World Trade Center*  84
Wrightson, Bernie  76

*yokai*  23–24

Zhang, Ziyi  120
Zilla  31; see also *Godzilla* (1998)

www.ingramcontent.com/pod-product-compliance
Lightning Source LLC
Chambersburg PA
CBHW032044300426
44117CB00009B/1187